Criminal Responsibility

L.S.E. research monographs 8

This series is published jointly with the London School of Economics and Political Science. It aims to make available research of originality and quality from the whole range of the social sciences, including all the fields and disciplines which are studied at the School. The intention is to provide a continuing outlet for serious scholarly work, and relatively quick publication. The books will be of interest to specialists in the various fields, irrespective of whether they are in universities, government departments, industries or elsewhere, as well as to libraries throughout the world.

Each monograph will be introduced with a foreword by a distinguished authority on the subject, whose aim will be to set the particular research into the wider framework of the appropriate discipline. The following monographs have already been published:

Changes in Subject Choice at School and University
Celia M. Phillips

The Criminal Liability of Corporations in English Law
L.H. Leigh

The Politics of Decontrol of Industry: Britain and the United States
Susan Armitage

Industrial Demand for Water: A study of South East England
Judith Rees

Students in Conflict: L.S.E. in 1967
Tessa Blackstone, Kathleen Gales, Roger Hadley, Wyn Lewis

The Administrative Functions of the French Conseil d'Etat
Margherita Rendel

The Theory of Customs Unions: A General Equilibrium Analysis
Richard G. Lipsey

Criminal responsibility

Francis G. Jacobs

With a Preface by H.L.A. Hart

London School of Economics and Political Science

Weidenfeld and Nicolson
5 Winsley Street London W1

SBN   297   00324   0

Printed in Great Britain by
Lewis Reprints Limited
Port Talbot, Glamorgan

Contents

Preface

The main concern of this book is to determine the extent to which the conception of the criminal responsibility of the individual, reflected in the legal doctrine of *mens rea*, has been displaced or modified by certain features of contemporary English law. Some of these, such as the introduction into the law of murder of the idea of 'diminished responsibility' by section 2 of the Homicide Act 1957, are relatively simple and self-contained; others, such as the scope and incidence of strict liability, the change made by the Mental Health Act 1959 and by the legislation relating to the criminal responsibility of children and young persons, and the cultural and civil functions of the Juvenile Courts, are complex and wide-ranging, and can be understood only by reference to previous history and the actual working of institutions. The assessment of their effect on criminal responsibility is not a simple task, but it is discharged by Dr Jacobs here with admirable lucidity and balance.

It has been said, most notably and clearly by Lady Wootton, that these features of modern law point in the direction of the elimination of criminal responsibility or at least to its 'withering away'. This has been hailed as a step towards a more rational legal system in which Courts are relieved of an impossible task, thrust upon them by now outmoded theories of punishment, of determining an issue which cannot be 'scientifically' determined: the issue whether an offender at the time of the offence had the capacity to do otherwise than he did. Hence the discussion of the law in its bearing upon the elimination of responsibility and the survey of the arguments for and against its retention as part of the system of criminal law calls for Dr Jacobs' rare combination of legal scholarship and philosophical acumen. For not only is the notion of responsibility itself in need of clarification but the sense in which it may be said to be 'eliminated' is different in regard to different changes in the law and requires different kinds of evidence in its support. The argument which has been urged that findings of responsibility are necessarily 'circular', or undecidable because they involve the impossible feat of getting inside another man's skin, plainly raise philosophical issues. These are expertly handled by Dr Jacobs, as are the less overtly philosophical bases of Holmes' doctrine of 'objective' liability on which the House of Lords fathered one of its most controversial decisions on criminal law. Dr Jacobs writes in the conviction that the doctrine of *mens rea* is not vulnerable to these philosophical criticisms, and, though findings of responsibility may often involve difficult decisions, there are strong reasons for retaining the doctrine and the conception of responsibility which it reflects. The true issue, too infrequently considered, concerns the benefits and social costs of retaining it. Arguments about criminal responsibility have, as he shows, too often been befogged by the invocation of what are thought to be clear dichotomies such as that between 'punishment' and treatment or between penal and remedial methods. Perhaps like every dog, every dichotomy must have its day, but Dr Jacobs' patient and illuminating study of the facts suggests that the day of this one is over, and yet that there is still a place for criminal responsibility. His book will instruct not only the lawyer but the philosopher and social scientist as well.

H.L.A. Hart

Introduction

The object of this book is to examine the concept of responsibility in the light of the modern development of the criminal law. The opening chapter discusses some basic distinctions between the civil and criminal law in terms of their respective functions. Different theories as to their functions are compared and it is suggested that they cannot be adequately explained by a single theory. A brief historical survey illustrates the argument that no consistent pattern can be traced in the antinomy between a principle of absolute liability and a principle of liability dependent on fault; and that the extent to which one principle or the other prevails at a given stage of legal development may depend upon a variety of apparently unrelated factors. In English criminal law some of the chief instances of liability independent of fault, traces of which can still be found in the modern law, are shown to have special features which would not justify a wider application of the principle. Recent developments, however, are said to have more fundamental implications for the concept of responsibility, and the more important of these are examined in turn in the succeeding chapters.

Chapter 2 considers some problems raised by the mentally abnormal offender. Recent innovations in this area of the law have been said to raise the question whether it is possible to draw any rational distinction between those who are and those who are not responsible for their actions. These innovations are examined in their historical context and an attempt is made to assess their significance for the concept of responsibility.

Chapter 3 is concerned with the young offender. Here too it has been argued that recent developments have at least blurred the edges of the concept of responsibility. While historically young offenders were treated by the law in the same way as adults, recent reforms have largely removed the differences between the criminal and the civil jurisdiction of the juvenile courts. The measures available to the courts are often the same in both cases, and always have a remedial object. Treatment rather than punishment is regarded as the solution to juvenile delinquency, and this attitude is reflected by the increasing tendency to deprive the courts of the tasks of selecting the appropriate institution for training and of determining the period of training; it is reflected also by recent legislation extending provision for after-care and liability to recall. Proposals to abolish the juvenile courts, or to curtail their criminal jurisdiction, would carry the tendency further. But there are practical difficulties and objections of principle to the more extreme proposals. A survey of the measures available to the juvenile courts shows that there is no simple antithesis between treatment and punishment. Present arrangements embody a compromise in which, while the principle of equal responsibility with adults has been abandoned, the concept of criminal responsibility has to some extent been preserved. No development of policy can be shown to have justified its complete elimination.

In Chapter 4 an attempt is made to assess the effects of the doctrine of strict liability. Apart from the social and economic factors which explain the origin and development of the doctrine in response to the changing functions of the law, the extent of the doctrine depends largely on the policy of the courts and on their view of the law's purposes. There has been a perceptible change of attitudes among the judges in recent years, and it is suggested that the common assumption that strict liability is increasing rests upon a number of fallacious arguments. A brief survey illustrates the tendencies of the common law to place greater restrictions on the operation of the doctrine. The wider implications for the concept of responsibility are examined, and it is shown that strict liability cannot on any view be equated with the complete elimination of responsibility.

The notion of objective liability is analysed in Chapter 5. It is shown that this doctrine may take different forms, and that the test of the 'reasonable man' applied in the modern law differs at a number of points from the theory of O.W. Holmes. When allowance is made for these differences Holmes's theory can be treated as characteristic but can be shown to be objectionable on several grounds. The modern law seems again increasingly reluctant to apply the doctrine. Apart from objections of principle, the principal criticisms are that the arguments in its favour are confused and rest ultimately on an unacceptable social philosophy.

More general philosophical arguments are examined in greater detail in the concluding chapter. It is argued that the controversy over *mens rea* has been largely conducted on false premises. At times it has been based upon dubious philosophical theories, such as a form of Cartesian dualism or a general scepticism about the possibility of knowledge of other minds; at other times upon a false antithesis, such as that between treatment or punishment as the function of the criminal law. When these fallacious arguments are discounted, the genuine issue can be seen to be whether, granted the value of the doctrine of *mens rea,* its social cost is too high for a modern industrialised society to be able to afford. Finally it is argued that though the social cost of retaining *mens rea* must be recognised, the social cost of abolishing it would also be considerable; and that although traditional arguments for retaining *mens rea* may no longer be valid in the light of the changing functions of the criminal law, it can still be justified on different grounds, both in terms of principle and of social policy.

Publication of this monograph has been delayed to take account of the enactment of the Children and Young Persons Act 1969.

Chapter 1

The Basis of Responsibility

In the modern law, if A injures B, the legal consequences will depend on A's state of mind at the time. If it was A's intention to injure B, he may be liable to criminal prosecution and punishment. The criminal law has evolved various gradations of offence; the offence is more or less serious, the penalty more or less severe, depending on whether A intended to wound, or to inflict grievous bodily harm, or to murder. Generally, if A had no intention to injure B (recklessness being equated for this purpose with intention), he will not be criminally liable, but B may succeed in a civil action against A if he can show that A was negligent, that is that A failed to exercise, when driving his car for example, the degree of care which a reasonably careful driver would have exercised, and that B has suffered injury as a result. This form of civil liability is based on an objective test, in the sense that it does not involve any inquiry into A's actual state of mind at the time when he injured B. It is sufficient for the purposes of civil liability that his conduct did not conform to the standards of the hypothetical reasonable man; that he failed to take the degree of care which was reasonable in the circumstances; and it does not matter for these purposes whether his failure was deliberate, so that his conduct might be described as reckless, or whether it was merely accidental. All these terms of course require, and have received, detailed analysis; but it is enough for the present to say that the basis of civil liability is negligence as defined above.

In the criminal law, again subject to many qualifications and exceptions, the general rule is that liability requires *mens rea*, lawyers' Latin for a 'guilty mind'. This requirement is usually interpreted in such a way that it does involve a subjective inquiry into the actual state of mind of the accused at the time of the offence charged. If A admits that he hit B, but says that he did so by accident, or by mistake, or in self-defence, the prosecutor must prove *mens rea*, or A will be acquitted.

Apart from the conditions of liability, there are many other differences between civil and criminal law, especially in the processes of trial and judgement. A heavier burden of proof is placed on the prosecutor at a criminal trial than is placed on the plaintiff in civil proceedings: in a criminal trial the prosecutor must prove guilt beyond reasonable doubt, while the plaintiff in a civil action needs only to satisfy the court on the balance of probabilities. The heavier onus in criminal proceedings is justified by the fact that the enforcement of the criminal law necessarily involves a serious infringement of the liberty of the individual. Similarly, while the jury has gradually disappeared from the civil courts in England, its retention on more serious criminal charges is still defended on the same ground. Again, the Criminal Division of the Court of Appeal, like its predecessor, the Court of Criminal Appeal, considers itself less rigidly bound by judicial precedent than its civil counterpart, in cases where the liberty of the individual is affected.

The same justification has been advanced for the requirement of *mens rea*. A characteristic illustration is a case in which Lord Goddard CJ said: [1]

'It is of the utmost importance for the protection of the liberty of the subject that the court should always bear in mind that, unless a statute either clearly or by necessary implication rules out *mens rea* as a constituent part of a crime, the court should not find a man guilty of an offence against the criminal law unless he has a guilty mind.'

The justification of the requirement of *mens rea* in terms of the liberty of the individual is particularly interesting because on the traditional view of the distinction between civil and criminal law, no such justification was necessary. On the traditional view, at least one of the objects of the civil law was to compensate a person who has been harmed for the loss he had suffered. The law of torts, or 'civil wrongs', was therefore less concerned with A's state of mind than with B's injury. B had suffered harm, whether A's act was intentional or not. Nor was it clear, on this view, that the law of torts should require even negligence, if it was concerned to compensate B rather than to penalise A; and in some cases the law of torts imposed what was later termed 'strict' liability, independent of any fault on A's part. The criminal law, however, was on the traditional view concerned with punishing the offender, and punishment was clearly inappropriate in the absence of a guilty mind. *Actus non facit reum nisi mens sit rea*, 'the act does not make a man guilty unless his mind be guilty', seemed to be as far as the lawyers needed to go in justifying the requirement of *mens rea* as a condition of criminal liability.

The difference was succinctly stated in an early case.[2]

'In all civil acts the law doth not so much regard the intent of the actor, as the loss and damage of the party suffering. If a man shoots at butts and hurt a man unawares an action lies ... if a man assaults me and I lift up my staff to defend myself and in lifting it up hit another, an action lies by that person, and yet I did a lawful thing. And the reason is because he that is damaged ought to be recompensed. But otherwise is it in criminal cases, for there *actus non facit reum nisi mens sit rea.'*

Civil liability

This was simple; but unfortunately inadequate, at least so far as concerns civil liability. For one thing, notions of justice had to be taken into account in deciding whether the defendant in a civil action could fairly be made to pay for the harm he had inadvertently caused. Some lawyers were prepared to argue that civil liability, like criminal liability, should always be based upon fault. Some even adopted what might be termed a penal theory of tort; on this theory, compensating the injured person was a subsidiary function of the law, and indeed the distinction between civil and criminal law is minimal. The theory is a natural corollary of Austin's definition of law as commands of the sovereign enforced by sanctions, and was a conclusion drawn from it most explicitly by Stephen who argued that all laws are in one sense criminal: [3]

'A law is a command enjoining a course of conduct. A command is an intimation from a stronger to a weaker rational being that if the weaker does or forbears to do some specified thing the stronger will injure or harm him. A crime is an act of disobedience to a law forbidden under pain of punishment. It follows from these definitions that all laws are in one sense criminal, for by the definitions they must be commands and any command may be disobeyed _ ... the notions of law and crime are thus in reality, correlative and co-extensive.'

The theory was accepted also by Salmond who went so far as to apply the doctrine of *mens rea*, today associated only with the criminal law, to the law of tort and in his classic treatment of the subject most clearly exemplified the penal theory of tort. Writing on the conditions of civil liability, he said that there must first be damage suffered by the plaintiff from the act of the defendant. He continued,[4]

'The second condition usually demanded by the law for liability in an action of tort is the existence of either wrongful intention or culpable negligence on the part of the defendant. These two different mental attitudes of the defendant towards his act and its consequences may be classed together under the name of *mens rea* – a guilty mind – and a fundamental principle of delictual liability is expressed in the maxim, *Actus non facit reum nisi mens sit rea,* the act itself creates no guilt in the absence of a guilty mind. The reason for this rule is that the ultimate purpose of the law in imposing liability on those who do harm to others is to prevent such harm by punishing the doer of it. He is punished by being compelled to make pecuniary compensation to the person injured. It is clear, however, that it is useless to punish any person, either civilly or criminally, unless he acted with a guilty mind in the sense already explained. No one can be deterred by a threat of punishment from doing harm which he did not intend and which he did his best to avoid. All that the law can hope to effect by way of penal discipline is to make sure that men will not either wilfully or carelessly break the law and inflict injuries upon others.

Pecuniary compensation is not itself the ultimate object or a sufficient justification of legal liability. It is simply the instrument by which the law fulfils its purpose of penal coercion. When one man does harm to another without intent to do so and without any negligence, there is in general no reason why he should be compelled to make compensation. The damage done is not thereby in any degree diminished. It has been done, and cannot be undone. By compelling compensation the loss is merely shifted from the shoulders of one man to those of another, but it remains equally heavy. Reason demands that a loss shall lie where it falls, unless some good purpose is to be served by changing its incidence; and in general the only purpose so served is that of punishment for wrongful intent or negligence. There is no more reason why I should insure other persons against the harmful results of my own activities, in the absence of any *mens rea* on my part, then why I should insure them against the inevitable accidents which result to them from the forces of nature independent of human actions altogether.'

It is clear what principles of liability are associated with the penal theory of tort. It was easy to draw the conclusion that the defendant was liable only where the loss was caused by his fault. In the nineteenth century the principle of no liability without fault had achieved the status of a political slogan, appropriate to the individualist philosophy and to the *laissez-faire* economics of the age. Holmes in the United States, starting from somewhat different premises from Salmond, had produced a similar justification of the doctrine.[5] There was no social benefit in shifting the loss between individuals for its own sake. Any benefit to one was offset by the loss to the other. The economic assets of the community were not increased and expense was incurred in the re-allocation, so there must be some special factor before the defendant could be required to bear the loss. Underlying this view there was clearly the desire to avoid discouraging enterprise.

Many objections could be raised against the penal theory of tort. To take first a comparatively minor point, it must be observed that the defendant is entitled, and in some cases obliged, to insure against liability. Any deterrent property is thereby considerably reduced, but it is in any case very doubtful whether the law of tort has much deterrent effect and is therefore of much value as an instrument of social control.

Further, insofar as it can be so used, what is required under modern conditions is to discourage the unintentional infliction of harm. At any rate in a modern social and economic context, most serious harm is caused by events in which the intention to injure characteristically plays little part, as the statistics of road accidents and industrial accidents amply demonstrate. What is necessary under these conditions is to encourage higher standards of care, and once more it is doubtful how far the law of tort is appropriate as a means to this end.

A further objection to the penal theory of tort is that it rests on a social philosophy when even in Salmond's own time was outdated, and which today would be wholly unacceptable. But some qualifications are necessary in formulating this objection. It may still be true to say that there is no reason why *I* should insure others against the harmful results of my actions, in the absence of fault on my part; but there is every reason why society should insure them, particularly if society benefits from activities in factories and on the roads at the expense of the victims which such activities necessarily produce. This argument leads therefore not to the development of strict liability in the law of tort but to the replacement of the common law action for damages for personal injuries by a comprehensive and adequate system of social insurance.

To the extent that the introduction of such a system reduces the effectiveness of the law as a means of social control, the solution must be found in an extension of the criminal law, which is any case better suited for this purpose. On the penal theory of tort, the penalty for the wrongdoer is determined by the harm suffered by his victim, a factor which in an industrialised society is quite arbitrary. The grossest negligence on the road may lead to multiple deaths or to the slightest injury to the driver himself; a moment's inadvertence in the stress of factory conditions may cripple a young workman for life. The criminal law can attempt, however crudely, to relate the penalty to the circumstances of the case, whether by consideration of deterrence, or of the fault of the offender, or of a combination of these and other factors.

These objections to the penal theory of tort militate equally against the theory which goes to the opposite extreme, and which might be termed the compensatory theory. The objection to penalising a person in the absence of fault applies equally to obliging him to compensate another, and the fact that another benefits from the injustice hardly meets the objection. And again, even where there is fault, the amount of harm, and thus the damages payable, though not conceived as a penalty, may be totally disproportionate to the degree of fault.

Corresponding to these two different theories as to the function of

B

the law, there can be seen a difference in methods of analysing it. On the one hand, given the formalism of early law, there is a tendency to classify the law in accordance with specific nominate delicts comparable to the specific offences of the criminal law. It is on this pattern that the Roman law was based and it can also be seen in the early English law of tort. Salmond said: 'Just as the criminal law consists of a body of rules establishing specific offences, so the law of torts consists of a body of rules establishing specific injuries. Neither in the one case nor in the other is there any general principle of liability.' But gradually developing alongside this, there is to be found an alternative analysis where the law is phrased in terms of a general obligation to take reasonable care in defined categories of situation to avoid causing harm to others. Such formulations of a general obligation are to be found in the modern civil law systems and it can be suggested that English law has gradually progressed from the first to the second type of analysis.

Winfield went so far as to attempt to reduce the entire law of torts to a single unifying principle, that the infliction of all harm is tortious unless it can be 'justified'. Whereas Salmond's work is entitled *Law of Torts*, Winfield preferred to speak of the law of tort.

An alternative classification of the law which reflects the compensatory theory is based not on the wrong of the defendant but on the injury to the victim. Here the law is classified according to the interest which the law is intended to protect. This classification recognises more explicitly that what is sought is not simply compensation for wrongdoing, but compensation for the infringement of an interest of the plaintiff, whether the infringement was intentional or not. A classification of interests replaces the classification of wrongs. The law may be further classified according to whether the interest is protected only if it is intentionally infringed or only in the event of negligence or regardless of the presence of any degree of fault.

No doubt if we were to try to trace the actual development of the principles of civil liability no consistent pattern would emerge. It was suggested somewhat paradoxically by Holmes [6] that there had been a development from a system of fault liability to a system of strict liability, but the reverse was accepted by most Anglo-American legal historians, including Holdsworth,[7] Wigmore[8] and Ames.[9] This view was judicially approved by Lord Macmillan in the case of *Read* v. *Lyons*,[10] a case of some significance for the development of the principles of civil liability in that the courts refused to supplement the rule in *Rylands* v. *Fletcher* [11] by establishing a general doctrine of strict liability for ultra-hazardous activities. Lord Macmillan said, [12]

'The action is one of damages for personal injuries. Whatever may have been the law of England in early times, I am of opinion that as the law now stands an allegation of negligence is in general essential to the relevancy of an action of reparation for personal injuries. The gradual development of the law in the matter of civil liability is discussed and traced by the late Sir William Holdsworth in his *History of English Law,* Volume VIII, p.446 ff. and need not here be rehearsed. Suffice it to say that the process of evolution has been from the principle that every man acts at his peril and is liable for all the consequences of his acts to the principle that a man's freedom of action is subject only to the obligation not to infringe any duty of care which he owes to others. The emphasis formerly was on the injury sustained and the question was whether the case fell within one of the accepted classes of common law actions. The emphasis now is on the conduct of the person whose act has occasioned the injury and the question is whether it can be characterised as negligent.'

More recent historians, however, notably Winfield [13] and Fifoot [14] have shown that no uniform movement can be discerned. At most, generalisations can be ventured about a particular period. It is true, for example that in the nineteenth century it was generally assumed by the courts that, apart from trespass and related areas, liability in tort was almost universally based on fault. Those cases where it was not, such as *Rylands* v. *Fletcher,* and cases of vicarious liability, were treated as narrow exceptions to the rule and no attempt was made to establish the existence of any unifying principles behind the exceptions. [15] In the light of the historians' findings, it is tempting to say that there has been neither a simple progress from fault liability to strict liability nor a simple movement in the other direction, but rather a cyclical development with now one principle, now another, prevailing. But this too must be regarded as an over-simplification since at all times, as in the criminal law, there have been varying elements of both forms of liability and the predominance of one or the other has depended on a variety of factors. These factors should be considered to include, for example, the degree of formalism in the legal system, as reflected especially in rules of evidence and procedure, and current standards of social morality, apart from the social and economic conditions of the day. It is clear too that here, as elsewhere, legal forms may continue, even while the law's function is constantly changing. An example of this can be seen in the law of tort today. The modern law of tort is still based on the premise of no liability without fault. Indeed, this principle has gained even greater recognition in cases such as *Read* v. *Lyons,* already referred to. Another significant decision, in *Fowler* v. *Lanning,* [16] held that an allegation simply that 'the defendant shot the plaintiff,' without any allegation that the shooting was intentional or negligent, disclosed no cause of action even in trespass. This has come at a time when it is increasingly recognised that the function of the law of tort is not penal nor even primarily one of social control, when this principle of no liability without fault would make sense, but rather one of compensation where it seems to be of less relevance.

The explanation of this discrepancy seems to be that the framework of fault has been retained but that, within this formal framework, the law in response to its changing functions has used a number of different techniques to circumvent its rigidity. Increasingly, the plaintiff's capacity to recover in cases of negligence has been enlarged by, for example, the introduction of the doctrine of contributory negligence,[17] by restricting the scope of defences such as common employment[18] and *volenti*,[19] by extending the area of vicarious liability,[20] by raising the standard of care in some types of case so that negligence can no longer be equated with ordinary conceptions of fault, by lessening the difficulties of proof with the doctrine of *res ipsa loquitur*, and by adjustment of the rules relating to causation and remoteness of damage.[21] In all these ways the principles of liability have been gradually developed to reflect changes in the law's function without departing from its basic form.

Criminal liability

It is natural to ask whether a similar relationship can be found between the principles of liability in criminal law and its social function. It is tempting to think that changes in the criminal law have taken place parallel to changes in the civil law. To some extent, the analogy does hold. Here again, there have been two principal views about the function of punishment. On one view punishment is regarded as an end in itself, as a right which in some sense balances out the wrong which has been done. On this view punishment may be said to be required by justice. The offender may be said to deserve his punishment. It is even said by some writers that he has a right to be punished. This view is associated with Kant[22] and may be described as the retributive theory of punishment. This term is also used to refer to the theory that the measure of punishment should be related to the crime, and in the case of Kant the two views were connected. He maintained that the punishment must be exactly proportioned to the degree of guilt on the part of the offender. The retributive theory is here considered, however solely as a theory of the purpose of punishment, as the view that punishment is intrinsically right and just. This view of punishment is also connected with particular religious beliefs and many of its ideas were developed in the context of a belief in divine retribution. But it has also been regarded as the ideal of human justice.

The principal objection to this theory can be simply stated. It is that punishment is not something intrinsically right, but, on the contrary, since it involves the deliberate infliction of harm, is *prima facie* wrong, and can only be justified if it is likely to lead to some further good. The mere fact that harm has been done by one man does not itself justify the doing of harm to him. Some further social end must be aimed at in order to justify the punishment. This view was perhaps first clearly formulated by Plato[23] around 400 BC but, although it has been current among writers on penal theory since the eighteenth century[24], it has only recently been accepted in practice as the aim of the penal system. It is associated particularly in England with the utilitarian philosophy of Jeremy Bentham[25] and may be called the utilitarian theory of punishment.

The social ends at which it aims may be diverse. They include deterrence, whether of the individual or of society at large ('general deterrence'), other methods of crime prevention, and perhaps also reform, though it has been questioned whether this last aim is compatible with a system described as punishment.

The fundamental objection to the utilitarian theory of punishment derives from the fact that it treats an individual as instrumental, as a means to the achievement of social ends. In Kantian terms, a man should never be used as a means but should always be treated as an end in himself. This has been described[26] as 'a stupidly inaccurate version of the Kantian position', but it does seem to represent the view which he took at any rate in respect of punishment: 'Judicial punishment . . . can never serve merely as a means to further *another* good, whether for the offender himself or of society, but must always be inflicted on him for the sole reason that *he has committed a crime*. . . . The law of punishment is a categorical imperative, and woe to him who crawls through the serpentine windings of the happiness theory, seeking to discover something which in virtue of the benefit it promises will release him from the duty of punishment or even from a fraction of its full severity.'[27]

The philosophical controversy was reflected in legal writings in the nineteenth century. The Kantian argument was advanced in a treatise of 1880 on criminal law by the American writer Francis Wharton, who described utilitarian theories of punishment as 'terrorism'. He said that such penalties 'undertake to punish the offender, not merely for what he has actually done in the past, but for what others may possibly do in the future. Terrorism, also, treats the offender not as a *person* but a *thing;* not as a responsible, self-determining being with rights common to all members of the same community, to whom justice is to be distinctively meted out as a matter between him and the State, but as a creature without any rights, on whom punishment is imposed so that others should be deterred from acts requiring punishment. The theory . . . violates the fundamental principle of all free communities, that the members of such communities have equal rights to life, liberty and personal security.'[28] The fundamental assumptions underlying these views were expressly rejected by Holmes, writing at the same time. 'At the bottom of all private relations,' he said, 'however tempered by sympathy and social feelings, is a justifiable self-preference,'[29] and he noted with approval that 'public policy sacrifices the individual to the general good.'[30]

On either theory of punishment there is an important connexion between the institution of punishment and the concept of responsibility. The concept of responsibility, however, is a complex one and a preliminary analysis may be useful at this point.[31]

The concept of responsibility

In what may be described, if only for etymological reasons, as the primary sense of the word, a person is responsible for something if he can be called upon to answer questions about it. In such cases he is responsible *to* someone if it is their questions he must answer. Thus under the conventions of the British constitution a minister is said to be responsible to Parliament for the conduct of his department; indeed these conventions provide the main form by which the accountability of the executive is secured. It is significant that in this case too responsibility is dependent on the existence of a rule, although the rule is not a legal rule in that no legal sanction is prescribed for failure to comply with it. It is in virtue of this rule that we can say that a minister 'must' or 'is required' to answer, even in the absence of a prescribed sanction. It may be doubted, however, whether we could use this language, or the language of responsibility, if there existed no sanction of any kind; in this case, the sanctions might be the effects on the minister's political career; in other cases, they might take less precise forms such as the effects of unorganised public opinion, or other forms of undefined social pressure. To this extent responsibility outside the law may be regarded as related to, though distinct from, the notion of liability to some form of extra-legal sanction.

A minister may be held responsible, in this primary sense, for the conduct of his department even though he might be said, in another sense, not to be responsible because in the particular circumstances of the case he did not know and had no direct control over what was being done by a junior official. In this secondary sense, which is clearly in point when we are thinking in the context of moral responsibility, knowledge or control of some kind seems to be required as a necessary condition of ordinary conceptions of responsibility. It might even be argued that it would be contradictory to say that a person was morally responsible for something over which he had no control whatever. The argument would then be that the requirement of some form of control as a condition of moral responsibility was not merely to be regarded as the reflection of a particular moral viewpoint, but was part of the very meaning of morality.

In a moral context, therefore, it may be difficult to separate two questions: the question whether a person had any control over a particular action or event, and the question whether he is liable to moral criticism (a term that may be used to include both praise and blame, though moralists no less than lawyers seem more concerned with responsibility for harm). The questions of control and of liability to moral criticism are so closely related that no difficulty arises from the use of the concept of responsibility to link them; it does not ordinarily matter, in a moral context, whether 'responsible' is used to refer to control, or to liability to moral criticism.

Much confusion, however, as will shortly be apparent, may arise in legal thinking if no distinction is drawn between control and liability to legal sanctions, and if the concept of responsibility is applied indifferently to both. Such confusion is quite unnecessary, since the term 'liability' is a convenient and accepted alternative to denote liability to the sanctions of both the criminal law and the law of tort. Much discussion of criminal responsibility, in particular, serves only to obscure the crucial issue, which is how far criminal liability is or should be dependent upon some form of control. For this reason the expressions 'strict liability', 'vicarious liability', etc., are used in the present discussion in preference to the terms 'strict responsibility', 'vicarious responsibility', etc. It is also proposed to speak of legal 'liability' for an act, or for the consequences of an act, although one would ordinarily be said to be 'responsible' for an act or its consequences.

It would at first sight seem clear that there is no necessary connexion between the concept of control and liability to legal sanctions, of the kind that does seem to exist in a moral context. While it might be regarded as immoral to hold someone legally liable for an act over which he had no control, it could not *ex hypothesi* be described as illegal to do so. The case of *Larsonneur*[32] provides a striking example of the imposition of legal sanctions without any requirement of control. The defendant in that case was convicted under the Aliens Order 1920 in that she, 'being an alien to whom leave to land in the United Kingdom has been refused was found in the United Kingdom'. She had in fact been brought into the United Kingdom in the custody of the police, but the court held that this was 'perfectly immaterial'.

It may be argued, however, that although in a particular case, and indeed over a whole range of offences where proof of *mens rea* is not required, legal liability may exist in the absence of control, these cases must nevertheless always be regarded as exceptions to the general rule. It may be argued that to abandon the whole concept of control as a condition of legal liability would not be possible; or, if it were possible, would amount to a transformation of the legal system into something totally different. It might be said, therefore, that although in a particular case legal liability is not dependent on control, nevertheless our conception of law requires some relationship which precludes the total abandonment of control.

This argument is considered further in the concluding chapter, when the implications of recent developments in the law can be more fully assessed, but it is possible to see at this stage why the concept of responsibility is so deeply embedded in our social institutions. The clearest case is presented by the doctrine of ministerial responsibility. The constitutional function of this doctrine is, as has been said, to secure the accountability of the executive to Parliament. Such accountability, to operate at all, requires not only that some person should be answerable to Parliament for the activities of a government department, but also that he should in fact have some control over those activities. At a further stage, the members of the House of Commons are ultimately answerable to the electorate, and the institution of responsible government in this sense depends for its significance on the extent to which the Commons can in fact control the executive. The language of ministerial responsibility and of responsible government would lose its point if it were not generally believed that by means of political institutions it was possible to influence the future activities of the executive. Responsibility in this context presupposes some form of control precisely because it is an instrument of political control.

Equally, responsibility both in law and in morals may be regarded as an instrument of social control. On this view, although of course in a particular case a person might be held responsible without any intention of influencing the future actions either of himself or of others, it may be said that ultimately the practice of ascribing responsibility would cease to serve a useful social purpose.

Responsibility and punishment
Neither the retributive theory of punishment nor the utilitarian theory entails as such any specific principles of criminal liability. So far as the retributive theory is concerned, the question that arises is whether it

seeks to pay back the individual for the harm he has done, for the consequences of his conduct, or whether it seeks in some way to redress his moral guilt, where this is conceived as something independent of the outward consequences of his actions. On the utilitarian theory, Bentham attempted to justify the defences traditionally recognised by the criminal law under the doctrine of *mens rea* by the argument that in these cases (accident, insanity, infancy, duress, etc.) punishment must be inefficacious;[33] but his arguments were so obviously fallacious that they have led later critics either to reject utilitarianism altogether or to argue that *mens rea* should be abolished. Both reactions, it will be suggested, are unjustified.

The law, as so often, has rested on a compromise. Certainly before Bentham, there was no clear theory to which liability could be reduced. The general acceptance of *mens rea* has never been unqualified and the law has always retained traces of its primitive origins; and more recent 'preventive' theories and ideas of 'social defence' seem to herald a return to an earlier system of liability without fault.

Early law knew no distinction between civil and criminal wrongs. In the absence of a legal remedy, the person injured, or his kin, might avenge the wrong; and the act of vengeance might itself in turn be avenged. The law's main function was to preserve the peace by providing an alternative to self-help and private vengeance. To this end, it reserved to itself the right of avenging wrongs.

No distinction was necessary, at this stage, between compensation and punishment. It is generally said that most wrongs were treated by early law primarily as matters for compensation. But to say this may be read into the law more refined notions of justice than were then current. The distinction between compensation as the principal object of the civil law and punishment as the object of the criminal law is a product of a system which attaches some importance to fault. But fault, at any rate as now understood, was immaterial if the wrong which had been done was likely to be avenged whether it had been done intentionally or unintentionally. In a society with rougher notions of justice than our own, the danger to the peace was the same whether the wrong was deliberate or accidental.

If fault was disregarded, there was no reason for the law to make any distinction between compensation and punishment. To make the wrongdoer 'pay for' his wrong was simultaneously, as the ambiguity of the expression still suggests, to compensate the injured and to punish the wrongdoer. The measure of guilt was identical with the amount of harm done.

Implicit in this doctrine is a conception of man as an instrument of harm, rather than as a moral agent. Accordingly, some systems of primitive law punished not only the man who inflicted harm, but also the weapon with which he did it; and a beast, as well as a man, might be executed for homicide.

Slowly these attitudes are replaced with a different conception of man, a view of man as a moral agent, possessed of reason and free will, capable of understanding the social norms to which he is subject, and of choosing whether to conform to them. It would be difficult to say when this conception of man, which survived almost unquestioned until the twentieth century, first became current in England; but its effect on the criminal law was first apparent in the writings of Bracton in the thirteenth century.

Before Bracton, attempts seem to have been made, especially by the clergy, to mitigate the rigours of the laws of the Saxon kings by attaching importance to the actor's intention; but the absence of a voluntary or intentional act was regarded as a mitigating circumstance rather than as exempting him from liability. The doctrine of *mens rea* makes its first recorded appearance in the laws of Henry I, compiled about the year 1118. Bracton committed himself to perhaps the first generalisation on the subject:[34] 'for a crime is not committed unless the will to harm be present;' and for five centuries, from Bracton to Blackstone, the general theory of *mens rea* was little further developed. But the law of course was not consistent.

Alongside the references to *mens rea,* we find more than once in the laws of Henry I, the ominous phrase *Qui inscienter peccat, scienter emendat,* 'He who does wrong unknowingly, must pay knowingly'.[35] There runs through the whole of legal history, from the earliest times to the present day, this dichotomy between the principle of *mens rea* and the principle of absolute liability, or liability independent of fault.

It therefore seems that two extreme hypotheses must both be rejected. It cannot be said that absolute liability was a universal feature of early law, nor that *mens rea* was everywhere required. Instead, it may be suggested that insofar as any generalisation can approximate to the truth, criminal liability in early law was in general based on intention, or foresight of consequences; but that at any rate on charges of a serious crime there were categories of offence where liability was independent of foresight.

The first and most important category is the type of case where the unforeseen consequences are very serious in their nature, for instance if an assault upon a person results in his unintended death. The importance of this category is demonstrated by two converse features of ancient legal systems: on the other hand, very many cases where death results were in fact cases of absolute liability; while, on the other hand, even where there was no general principle of absolute liability for acts resulting in death, many of the specific applications of absolute liability, for instance under the rule *versanti in re illicita imputantur omnia* (to be discussed below), actually operated in cases resulting in death. Further, it is significant that in such cases the rules of law are frequently formulated in such a way as to emphasise that no distinction is to be drawn between, say, deliberate murder and an entirely accidental killing. 'If someone in the sport of archery or other form of exercise kill another with a missile or by some such accident, let him repay; for the law is, that he who does wrong unknowingly must pay knowingly.' [36] Germanic law can be quoted to the same effect: [37] 'Whoever shall have killed a man, whether he committed the homicide voluntarily or not *(volens aut nolens)* . . . let him be handed over to the *potestas* of the parents or next-of-kin of the deceased'. Such attitudes to accidental killing seem to be a common if not universal feature of ancient law.

Not only was death by misadventure equated with deliberate murder; even killing in self-defence, which later systems not merely excused but sometimes encouraged, was treated by early law in the same way.[38] Indeed it has been said that in early times, with the sole exception of killing under the king's warrant or in the pursuit of justice, the killer seems to have been held liable for every death which he caused, whether intentionally or by chance. [39]

The imposition of severe penalties regardless of fault is not even by later standards of morality entirely inexplicable. It derives partly, no doubt, from a *lex talionis* equating guilt with harm done rather than with the intention of the person causing harm; but it may also be said to reflect, in these cases, an overriding regard, commendable also by later standards, for the sanctity of human life. Further, this category of cases shows, it is arguable, an obscure appreciation of two further principles, which still form part of accepted morality. The first of these principles recognises that the gravity of a crime is a function of two factors: not only of the offender's intention to cause harm, but also of the actual harmfulness of his conduct. Normally this principle will be applied only in the sentencing policy of the courts; but occasionally it is reflected in the classification of offences: thus the element of intention alone distinguishes the offence of wounding with intent to cause grievous bodily harm from the offence of simple wounding. Conversely the consequences alone may make the offence a more serious one. An example in the modern law is that while the maximum penalty for the offence of dangerous driving is two years, the maximum penalty for causing death by dangerous driving is five years imprisonment.[40] The second principle, endorsed perhaps by every morality, requires, where the chances of harm are greater, higher standards of care, so that the more serious the harm done the less readily is failure to take care acceptable as an excuse. As J.L. Austin said, 'We may plead that we trod on the snail inadvertently: but not on a baby.' [41]

None of these considerations, of course, is sufficient to justify absolute liability, even in cases where death results. A concern for human life does not justify requiring it as a penalty whenever another life is taken. The fallacy is quite plain in Blackstone: [42] 'for the law sets so high a value upon the life of a man, that it always intends some misbehaviour in the person who takes it away, unless by the command or express permission of the law. In the case of misadventure it presumes . . . at least a want of sufficient caution in him who was so unfortunate as to commit it; who therefore is not altogether faultless. And as to the necessity which excuses a man who kills another *se defendendo* . . . the law intends that the quarrel or assault arose from some unknown wrong or provocation either in word or deed.' Secondly, the recognition that intention is not, in the law, the sole index to culpability does not justify a total disregard of it. And it is one thing to say that an actual intention is not required because negligence may be a sufficient basis of liability in cases where serious harm is probable; it is quite another thing to say that intention is unnecessary because simple causation is an adequate ground of liability, regardless of any state of mind, where serious harm actually results. It is the latter principle which early law seems to accept in cases where the result is death; the former principle represents a second category of exception to the requirement of an actual intention to produce the proscribed consequences as a general condition of liability for those consequences.

The second category of exception, the imposition of liability for some degree of negligence, is also of great antiquity. Although the basic categorial distinction drawn by early law is the distinction between intentional and unintentional, or between voluntary and involuntary actions, it was recognised that even where there is in general no liability for unintended or unwanted consequences, there may nevertheless exist a form of liability for them if they arise from a lack of what was termed due diligence. This concept is employed notably by Bracton, under the combined influence of civil lawyers and canon lawyers. [43]

The creation of liability for negligence, although it does not fit neatly into the schema of those moralists who would make liability dependent entirely upon intention, is nevertheless an acknowledgement of a moral rule requiring the exercise of due care in social relations, and, as there is no doubt that a failure to take due care may be morally culpable, this feature of the law does not necessarily entail a departure from the accepted criteria of moral responsibility. On what theory of punishment liability for negligence is justified may be a separate question, and may involve the recognition of two distinct varieties of negligence, the deliberate and the thoughtless failure to take the required precautions. But it can clearly be maintained that it has constituted, and still does constitute, at any rate in some cases a justifiable exception from the rule requiring intention as a condition of liability.

The justification of a third category of exception is less obvious. The doctrine was long received that if a person was engaged in some activity which was itself illegal, his criminal responsibility for the consequences of that activity was absolute. The principle underlying this particular extension of liability is expressed in the maxim *Versanti in re illicita imputantur omnia quae sequuntur ex delicto:* 'A person engaged on an illegal activity is answerable for all its consequences'. This maxim was borrowed from Bernardus Papiensis by Bracton, who introduced it into English law.[44] It was given the specious justification that he who wills the means necessarily wills the ends, and thus reconciled with the requirement of *mens rea,* but, although greater justification could be advanced in some instances, its indiscriminate application to cases of all kinds led inevitably to injustices which, as will be seen, became increasingly glaring with the passage of time.

If we compare this schematic account of early law with the structure of the modern law, we find that there have survived distinct traces of the three categories of exceptions to the general principle that a person is not responsible for such consequences of his actions as he did not foresee. Thus there have survived until recent times cases where, if a person's actions resulted in the death of another, he could be convicted of murder although he had not intended, or indeed foreseen, fatal consequences. These cases may be given a historical explanation in terms of the continuity of the ancient rules; but they may also be regarded as reflecting a continuing application of the principles which those rules embodied, only partially modified by later conceptions of justice.

Thus the first exception, which might in an extreme application result in the equation of accidental killing with murder, is now reflected in the limited form that a lesser degree of *mens rea* is required for murder than for other offences against the person. English law has never required an actual intention to kill as a condition of liability for murder. In early times, as we have seen, the act of killing was itself sufficient. But even with the recognition that liability should depend on the individual's state of mind, this requirement was qualified in two ways. In the first place, it is sufficient that a person should have intended to cause grievous bodily harm; if death results, this intention, although less than an intention to kill, may nevertheless be sufficient *mens rea* for murder.

A further and most important qualification of the principle of *mens rea* in cases of this type was illustrated by a decision of the House of Lords in 1960. The case of *D.P.P.* v. *Smith* [45] will be examined in detail at a later stage of the argument. For the present it is sufficient to note that, according to the ruling of the House of Lords in this case, it would be enough to render a person guilty of murder if he aimed at the deceased a voluntary, unlawful act which a reasonable man in the circumstances would realise to be likely to cause death or grievous bodily harm. Before this case, there was some controversy over the state of the law; some had argued that the question was whether the accused himself had realised the possible consequences of his actions, and that the question whether a reasonable man would have foreseen them was designed only to assist the jury in deciding whether they were actually foreseen by the accused. This view was indeed accepted by the Court of Criminal Appeal in the case; but the House of Lords repudiated this view, stating that the only question was whether a reasonable man in the circumstances would have known that the act was likely to cause death or grievous bodily harm. A full consideration of the implications of this decision, and of its modification by the Criminal Justice Act 1967, must await an analysis of the whole doctrine of 'objective liability'; but one effect of the ruling appears to be the application to the criminal law of canons of negligence different from those of the civil law, yet departing also from the normal standards of criminal liability. There are, however, three types of case particularly noteworthy in this connexion, where criminal liability for negligence has been justified.

Liability for negligence

Three characteristic cases, apart from murder, where negligence has been justified as an adequate basis of criminal liability are, first, where great harm results, under the law of manslaughter; second, where great danger is likely, as in the case of certain motoring offences, and third, where special responsibilities are imposed on persons having special roles in society, for example on parents in the upbringing of their children, on the management of factories, and on distributors of food and drugs. Parents, employers, shopkeepers having a greater social responsibility are expected to attain standards higher than those set for the rest of the community. This basis of liability is discussed in Chapter 5 and need not be considered further here.

Versanti in re illicita

The final category of cases mentioned above comprised those in which serious consequences followed from some activity which was itself illegal; a person might be liable, under the doctrine *versanti in re illicita imputantur omnia,* for consequences which he had neither intended nor foreseen. This doctrine exercised a powerful influence over the development of English criminal law which has not yet been entirely extinguished. Subsequent applications of the doctrine, whose origin has already been traced, were founded on the dictum of Sir Edward Coke to the effect that if a man shoots at a tame fowl in order to steal it, and accidentally kills a person, he is guilty of murder.[46] In 1697 Chief Justice Holt attempted to circumscribe the operation of the rule.[47] He laid down as a condition of its application that 'There must be a design of mischief to the person, or to commit a felony, or great riot'. This limitation, it is true, was not of great practical import at first, since at that time most crimes belonged to the category of felony. Until recently felonies included, for example, damaging mohair or alpaca. On the other hand, since almost all felonies, with the exception of petty larceny, were in any case punished with death, the application of the doctrine of *versanti in re illicita* did not aggravate the penalty. In the nineteenth century with the progressive reduction in the incidence of the death penalty, the doctrine came under increasing criticism. It was attacked in 1839 in the Fourth Report of the Commissioners on the Criminal Law, in 1866 in the Report of the Royal Commission on Capital Punishment, and in 1883 by Stephen in his *History of the Criminal Law;* and in a succession of cases the courts showed an increasing tendency to limit its application and to exclude from its scope cases where, although death was caused in the commission of a felony, it was purely accidental or was a consequence which could not reasonably have been foreseen by the offender. [48] Subsequently the rule was evolved by the courts that the 'felony-murder' doctrine applied only where the felony was one of violence; this was (until 1957) the modern law, as laid down in the case of *Jarmain.*[49] Thus, if a person killed another in the course of a violent felony, such as robbery or rape, he was guilty of murder even though he did not intend or foresee any harm to the deceased. This doctrine of 'constructive malice' was abolished by the Homicide Act of 1957; but the principle still survives in the law of manslaughter.

From Foster's time there existed, alongside the felony-murder rule, a parallel doctrine of constructive manslaughter. If a person caused death in the course of committing an unlawful act other than a felony, he was guilty of manslaughter. The doctrine has survived almost unchanged in the modern law, and even today most convictions for manslaughter arise out of accidental killing. Those that are not cases of murder reduced to manslaughter, by the doctrines of provocation and diminished responsibility, generally arise from an unlawful act which has accidentally resulted in death. Some qualification has been placed on the doctrine in recent decisions of the Court of Criminal Appeal, which held in Creamer's case [50] that the unlawful act must be 'one likely to do harm to the person', and in Church's case [51] that it must be 'such as all sober and reasonable people would inevitably recognise must subject the other person to, at least, the risk of some harm resulting therefrom, albeit not serious harm'. But although these decisions suggest that some degree of negligence is the basis of liability, manslaughter still remains a 'constructive crime'. This was expressly recognised in Creamer's case. The accused had arranged for a girl to have an abortion but was not present when it was performed. The girl died and the woman who performed the abortion was convicted of manslaughter. The accused was clearly an accessory before the fact to the abortion, but the question for the Court of Criminal Appeal was whether he was also an accessory before the fact to manslaughter, an offence which, though subject to the same maximum penalty as abortion, is commonly regarded as more serious. The Court held that he was properly convicted of this offence.

'A man is guilty of involuntary manslaughter when he intends an unlawful act and one likely to do harm to the person and death results which was neither foreseen nor intended. It is the accident of death resulting which makes him guilty of manslaughter as opposed to some lesser offence such as assault or, in the present case, abortion. This can no doubt be said to be illogical since the culpability is the same, but nevertheless it is an illogicality which runs throughout the whole of our law, both the Common Law and the Statute Law. A comparatively recent example is clearly that of dangerous driving and causing death by dangerous driving. Bearing that in mind it is quite consistent that a man who has counselled and procured such an illegal and dangerous act from which death results should be guilty of being an accessory before the fact to manslaughter.'

If the basis which might justify departures from the requirement of *mens rea* was never fully worked out, the justification of *mens rea* itself was postulated rather than genuinely understood. Lawyers often related individual defences to the maxim *'actus non facit reum nisi mens sit rea'*, but rarely went beyond. It was treated as an ultimate principle, not itself in need of any further justification. And it is an ultimate principle on one hypothesis of the function of the criminal law. For it can be taken as axiomatic that in this period the presence of a 'guilty mind' was a necessary condition of moral guilt. Ultimately however the concept of *mens rea* served to prejudice rather than to assist the systematic development of principles of criminal liability. For as penal statutes gradually became more specific about the state of mind required for particular offences, and as the criminal courts began to take these statutes at their face value, rather than read into them general common law doctrines, the old equation of *mens rea* with moral guilt was tacitly dropped, and it came to be used instead to refer to whatever state of mind the law required for a particular offence. This varied, of course, with the passage of time, as well as from one offence to another. Sometimes an actual intention, or even fraud, might be required; sometimes a constructive intention sufficed; sometimes recklessness, or certain forms of negligence, might be the basis of liability; sometimes as in manslaughter the subjective requirement almost totally disappeared. In consequence the maxim *actus non facit reum nisi mens sit rea* was a specious justification of particular defences. It could not logically justify any principle of liability for it denoted no more than that particular defences were accepted in particular cases. The attempt to justify these defences by reference to *mens rea* could only be based on a confusion which the term might seem to have been designed to create: a confusion between the requirement of moral guilt as a general condition of liability and the requirement of a particular state of mind in the definition of a particular offence. As Stephen J said in Tolson's case:[52]

'. . . the mental elements of different crimes differ widely. *'Mens rea'* means in the case of murder, malice aforethought; in the case of theft, an intention to steal; in the case of rape, an intention to have forcible connection with a woman without her consent; and in the case of receiving stolen goods, knowledge that the goods were stolen. In some cases it denotes mere inattention. For instance, in the case of manslaughter by negligence it may mean forgetting to notice a signal. It appears confusing to call so many dissimilar states of mind by one name. It seems contradictory indeed to describe a mere absence of mind as a *mens rea*, or guilty mind. The expression again is likely to and often does mislead. To an unlegal mind it suggests that by the law of England no act is a crime which is done from laudable motives in other words, that immorality is essential to crime. . . '

The sole remaining value of *mens rea* might have been to exclude liability based on the *actus reus* alone; but even this value is denied it by the absurd argument sometimes adopted in strict liability cases that the doing of the act 'supplied' the *mens rea.*

The elimination of *mens rea* ?
In recent years the elimination of *mens rea* has been predicted or

c

advocated by some critics,[53] and they have interpreted recent developments in the law as symptoms of this drastic reform. The implications
of these developments for the concept of criminal responsibility therefore require careful analysis.

The evidence adduced is of two kinds. In the first place, the classes
of persons exempt from liability are being extended, and new categories
of exemption are being created. It is said that the raising of the age of
criminal responsibility, and the introduction of new provisions for the
welfare of children and young persons, have almost completed a radical
transformation in the attitude to juvenile offenders from an era when
they were credited with an adult's responsibility for their crimes. The
juvenile courts, it is argued, are, or are becoming, in all but name not
courts but rather administrative agencies whose primary concern is
with questions of social welfare; and to this function, it is said, the
concept of criminal responsibility is dangerously irrelevant. Similar
transformations have been taking place so far as the mentally abnormal
are still liable to be brought before the courts. The introduction of the
doctrine of diminished responsibility into the law of homicide in 1957,
although it does not entirely exempt from liability, may be said to have
considerably widened the scope of mental abnormality as a defence to
a charge of murder, and to have brought a new range of psychiatric
problems before the courts. And some of the more far-reaching provisions of the Criminal Justice Act 1948, and of the Mental Health
Act 1959, it is claimed, have absolved the courts from determining
questions of responsibility in cases where before this legislation they
would have been required to do so. Only in the case of the supposedly
sane adult, who is neither child nor lunatic, are questions of responsibility still asked; and it may be said further than even here the concept
is of doubtful validity. Once we extend the categories of the exempt,
where are we to draw the line? How valid is any criterion for distinguishing the irrational from the supposedly rational?

Secondly, quite apart from questions of infancy, mental abnormality,
and other forms of incapacity, there is another category of arguments
which might be used to show that the courts are already less concerned
with questions of responsibility. There is increasing evidence, it might
be said, of a development of principles of liability which, even in the
case of an adult of full mental capacity, to a greater or lesser degree
disregard the state of mind of the accused. These principles of liability
to which the accused's intention is simply irrelevant clearly include both
strict liability, which excludes at least the defences of ignorance and
mistake, and what may conveniently be called 'objective liability',
according to which the state of mind is judged by the standard of the

notional 'reasonable man'. Thus, one question which must be considered is the extent to which these principles operate in the law, the arguments which justify them, and whether these arguments would justify the extension of the principles and perhaps ultimately the total disappearance of *mens rea*. It is with these problems that the second part of this argument is concerned.

It is necessary for a number of reasons to keep separate the two categories of evidence for the proposition that responsibility is already being eliminated. For it will be apparent that, in these two categories, the proposition embodies very different assertions. In fact it will be suggested that, within each category, the proposition has a different meaning: that its practical effects are quite distinct; and that its theoretical justification must be correspondingly different. There is in the first place a difference in the meaning of the proposition, reflecting an ambiguity in the concept of responsibility. This is clear from the most cursory examination of the arguments advanced in support of the proposition. Thus, in the case of the mentally abnormal it is argued that we now have no psychological or other scientific criteria to enable us reliably to distinguish persons who are responsible for their actions from those who are not. But no such implication is, of course, involved in the doctrine of strict liability. What this doctrine does is not to cast doubt on the existence of that distinction, but to exclude certain questions as to the state of mind of a person in deciding whether he should be liable for a particular offence.

Two quite different proposals are therefore involved in the 'elimination of responsibility'. In the first case it is either a refusal to recognise the category of mental abnormality or to discriminate, for the purposes of conviction, between the mentally normal and the mentally abnormal. (If the distinction is preserved, the strongest argument for refusing to distinguish at the stage of conviction is the growing similarity of forms of treatment between supposedly normal and supposedly abnormal offenders.) In the second case it is a rejection of the requirement of *mens rea*.

There is consequently a difference in the effects of the two developments on the administration of the criminal law. The effect of the first development has been in some (but by no means all) cases to exempt from penal treatment persons suffering from certain forms of mental abnormality who would otherwise have been liable to it, and to substitute other types of treatment; whereas the effect of the second development has been in some respects the reverse. The effect of the doctrine of strict liability has been to increase the number of people liable to penal treatment. Strict liability extends the class of persons who may be held liable for an offence to include all those who did the prohibited act, however involuntarily or inadvertently, within the limits defined by the doctrine. The defences of ignorance and mistake, at least, are excluded, and the ambit of the criminal law correspondingly widened.

Finally, any attempt to justify these two developments, themselves very different in their nature and consequences, must rely on different arguments. Both developments certainly affect the traditional doctrine of *mens rea,* but the effects are of different kinds. In the first category, the case for re-drawing the boundaries of irresponsibility must presumably rest on changing views about the procedures appropriate for the young and the mentally abnormal; whereas in the second category the strongest, at any rate, of the arguments against the doctrine of *mens rea* are based on a theory of liability which can be traced back for centuries but may be described today as a form of social control.

For a variety of reasons, therefore, it is necessary to weigh the evidence and evaluate the arguments in each category separately before a decision can be reached whether responsibility is being, or whether it should be, eliminated. In examining the concept of responsibility in the modern law we will consider first the increasing exemption from liability of the young and of the mentally abnormal offender, and, secondly, the adoption of principles of liability not dependent on the offender's state of mind.

Chapter 2

The Mentally Abnormal Offender

The law relating to the criminal responsibility of the mentally abnormal is of central importance to the subject. For it raises the critical question whether it is possible in principle or in practice to provide any rational criteria for distinguishing on grounds of supposed abnormality between those who are and those who are not responsible for their actions. It may be thought that the confused state of the law in this area, made more complex by recent elaborations and refinements, is a symptom of an underlying insecurity in the theory and practice of existing arrangements for dealing with such cases, and this in turn has cast doubt on the validity of the concept of responsibility itself.

Insanity before M'Naghten[1]
Very little is known about the treatment of the insane in the earlier history of the English criminal law. The earliest discussion of the subject is to be found in Bracton. Writing in the mid-thirteenth century he grouped together cases of accident, infancy, and insanity, but it is not clear that they were similarly treated. In the context of a discussion of accidental homicide he observes that a crime is not committed unless the will to harm be present. He continues:[2]

'And then there is what can be said about the child and the madman *(furiosus)*, for the one is protected by his innocence of design, the other is excused by the misfortune of his deed. In misdeeds we look to the will and not to the outcome ...'

This account of why the madman is not responsible is hardly intelligible and it seems best to accept an emendation of the text. The passage in Modestinus[3] which Bracton was following refers not to 'the misfortune of his deed' *(infelicitas facti)*, but to 'the misfortune of his fate' *(infelicitas fati)*; for Modestinus was simply recalling one of the reasons given by Roman law for treating the insane offender with leniency, that he was sufficiently punished by his madness itself: *Satis furore ipso punitur.*[4]

The main advantage of this theory is that it does not rely on the alternative justification at which Bracton hints in the passage quoted above, the argument that the madman does not intend or 'will' the prohibited act. This second argument, although it is consonant with the traditional theory of *mens rea* which requires intention or knowledge as a condition of liability, seems satisfactory in relatively few cases of madness. It is much more plausible, for example, in cases of insane delusion than in other cases where the madman may realise and fully intend the consequences of his actions. The disadvantage of the Roman theory, on the other hand, is that while it may be applicable to all cases of madness, it serves only to explain why the madman, if convicted, should be treated more leniently than the sane offender. It fails to explain why he should be regarded as not responsible for his actions and not liable to any form of punishment. Indeed the argument that he is sufficiently punished by his madness is logically incompatible with this view of the madman as not responsible.

By a very considerable modification of this theory, however, it may be possible to present it in a more acceptable form. It could be said, perhaps, that to punish a madman for an act which was caused by his insanity would be in effect to punish him *for* his misfortune. He would be punished, not for a crime, but for his madness. It is this, it could be said, which makes punishment in such cases morally unacceptable; for the crime could then hardly be described as his own act: 'Hamlet does it not . . . . Who does it then? His madness.'

After Bracton, progress in succeeding centuries was slow. Sir Edward Coke (1552-1634) had little to say on the subject; he was content to argue that a madman does not know what he is doing and is lacking in mind and reason 'and therefore he cannot have a felonious intent.'[5] Coke repeats the argument that the madman is sufficiently punished by his madness, but adds nothing that is not to be found in Bracton.

A more valuable source is the *History of the Pleas of the Crown* by Sir Matthew Hale, published in 1736 sixty years after his death, which remained for a century the most influential work on the English criminal law. Chapter IV of this work contains the first authoritative and systematic treatment of 'the defects of ideocy, madness and lunacy in reference to criminal offences and punishments.' Perhaps the most important contribution of the author to this subject was the distinction which he drew between total insanity and partial insanity; the latter in his view would not exempt from criminal liability:[6]

'The best measure that I can think of is this; such a person as labouring under melancholy tempers hath yet ordinarily as great an understanding, as ordinarily of fourteen hath, is such a person as may be guilty of treason or felony ...'

Again the criterion is formulated in cognitive terms; the emphasis is on the understanding of the accused, and comparison is made with a child. Similarly Hale advances the justification for exempting the insane that 'they have not the use of understanding, and act not as reasonable creatures, but their actions are in effect in the condition of brutes.'[7]

Meanwhile the test of insanity finally formulated in the M'Naghten Rules was slowly evolving through a series of celebrated cases. The summing-up in Arnold's case in 1724[8] was remarkable both for the variety of criteria of insanity offered to the jury and for the reason given for exempting the insane. The reason was plainly utilitarian: 'punishment is intended for example, and to deter other persons from wicked designs; but the punishment of a madman, a person that hath no design, can have no example.' The argument is unconvincing, but this was of no direct concern to the jury. Two crucial passages in the summing-up contain the direction on the issue of insanity; in the first, the question for the jury was said to be:

'... whether this man hath the use of his reason and senses. If he was under the visitation of God, and could not distinguish between good and evil, and did not know what he did, though he committed the greatest offence yet he could not be guilty of any offence against any law whatsoever; for guilt arises from the mind, and the wicked will and intention of the man. If a man be deprived of his reason, and consequently of his intention, he cannot be guilty ...'

and again in rather different language:

'When a man is guilty of a great offence it must be very plain and clear before a man is allowed such an exemption; therefore it is not every kind of frantic humour, or something unaccountable in a man's actions, that points him out to be such a madman as is to be exempted from punishment: it must be a man that is totally deprived of his understanding and memory, and doth not know what he is doing, no more than an infant, than a brute or a wild beast, such a one is never the object of punishment; therefore I must leave it to your consideration, whether the condition this man was in, as it is represented to you on one side or the other, doth shew a man, who knew what he was doing, and was able to distinguish whether he was doing good or evil, and understood what he did:. . .'

What is most significant in this summing-up is the emphasis on the capacity to distinguish good and evil, together with the comparison with children. Coke had described the feeble-minded *(stultus)*, but not the madman, as unable to tell good from evil, but it may have

been Hawkins, whose *Treatise of Pleas of the Crown* was published
a few years before Arnold's case, who first adopted this test to
explain the exemption accorded to both infancy and insanity:[9]
Those who are under a natural disability of distinguishing between
good and evil, as infants under the age of discretion, ideots and
lunaticks, are not punishable by any criminal prosecution whatever.'

This alternative test, the incapacity to distinguish good and evil, was
of little practical importance in Arnold's case; indeed, the judge did not
make it clear that it was an alternative test. But it was of considerable
theoretical signifcance and had important practical consequences. For
when developed in later cases as an independent criterion of insanity,
it enabled juries to return a special verdict on those who knew, at
least in some sense, what they were doing, but did not know that it was
wrong. Arnold's case was thus a significant stage in the forumlation of
the M'Naghten Rules.

When Lord Ferrers was tried before the House of Lords in 1760 the
M'Naghten formula was almost fully developed. There was no summing-
up, but the law was clearly stated in the closing speech for the
prosecution: [10]

'If there be a total permanent want of reason, it will acquit the prisoner. If there
be a total temporary want of it, when the offence was committed, it will acquit
the prisoner : but if there be only a partial degree of insanity, mixed with a
partial degree of reason; not a full and complete use of reason but (as Lord Hale
carefully and emphatically expresses himself) a competent use of it, sufficient to
have restrained those passions, which produced the crime, if there be thought and
design; a faculty to distinguish the nature of actions; to discern the differences
between moral good and evil, then upon the fact of the offence proved, the judgement of the law must take place.'

The most remarkable of all the cases prior to M'Naghten was the
trial of James Hadfield in 1800 for shooting George III. [11] Hadfield
suffered from a delusion that he was called on to sacrifice his life for
the salvation of the world and, not wishing to be guilty of suicide, chose
to commit his crime for the sole purpose of being executed for it.
Erskine in a famous speech in Hadfield's defence succeeded in utterly
discrediting the traditional test and anticipated modern criticism of
the narrow formulation of the legal definition of insanity. On Coke's
view that 'there must be a total deprivation of memory and understanding' Erskine argued that no one but a helpless idiot would satisfy
the test. Indeed, a test would hardly be necessary to meet such cases,
which would not present any problem to either physicians or judges.
The true problem arose in cases where 'reason is not driven from her

seat' but is overcome by delusion. In such cases 'delusion, ... where there is no frenzy or raving madness, is the true character of insanity', and a person suffering from such a delusion was not responsible even though reason was not wholly dethroned.

But the underlying logic of Erskine's argument was incompatible with the law as it then stood. Partial insanity was of itself no defence; for this proposition there was the authority of Hale. It was impossible to argue on the facts of the case that Hadfield did not appreciate what he was doing, or that it was wrong. He could argue only that the understanding was 'incapable of resistance because unconscious of attack'. Hadfield's acquittal was due rather to the brilliance of his counsel's oratory than to the logic of his defence.

The line of argument which had succeeded in Hadfield's case was tried again in M'Naghten's case [12] itself in 1843. Once more the charge arose out of an attempt at assassination, in this case of the Prime Minister, Sir Robert Peel. M'Naghten shot and killed his private secretary, Drummond, apparently mistaking him for Peel. Cockburn's argument on behalf of M'Naghten, like Erskine's, had to rely essentially not on any defect of knowledge or judgment, but on lack of control. Partial insanity of itself was no defence, but :

'it can lead to a partial or total aberration of moral senses and affections, which may render the wretched patient incapable of resisting the delusion, and lead him to commit crimes for which morally he cannot be held responsible.'

The jury, presented with a varied assortment of tests of insanity by the lawyers, largely unanimous evidence by the medical witnesses, and the briefest of summings-up by the judge, had no hesitation in acquitting.

The public reaction to the outcome of M'Naghten's case affords valuable evidence of social attitudes at this time to the relationship of insanity and criminal responsibility. The general mood of scepticism was captured by *The Times :* [13]

'still we would, not captiously nor querulously, but in a spirit of humble and honest earnestness, of hesitating and admiring uncertainty, and of almost painful dubitation, ask those learned and philosophic gentlemen to define, for the edification of commonplace people like ourselves, where sanity ends and madness begins, and what are the outward and palpable signs of the one or the other ...'

In the House of Commons, one Member sought leave to introduce a Bill to abolish the plea of insanity in cases of murder or attempted murder, except where it could be proved that the accused was publicly known as a maniac and not afflicted by partial insanity. In the House of

Lords, the Lord Chancellor initiated a debate on the subject. [14] He himself had no doubt about the law ; it was clear, distinct, and defined, and 'it will be quite impossible beneficially to alter the law, or to render it better adjusted than it is'; but if their Lordships were in doubt they could summon the judges before them to give their opinion. The suggestion was accepted, and in due course the judges gave their considered answers to five questions put to them;[15] the answers to the second and third questions, which were taken together, embody the M'Naghten test :

The M'Naghten test

'... the jurors ought to be told in all cases that every man is to be presumed to be sane, and to possess a sufficient degree of reason to be responsible for his crimes, until the contrary be proved to their satisfaction ; and that to establish a defence on the ground of insanity, it must be clearly proved that, at the time of the committing of the act, the party accused was labouring under such a defect of reason, from disease of the mind, as not to know the nature and quality of the act he was doing ; or, if he did know it, that he did not know he was doing what was wrong.'

It must remain a matter for speculation how far the public alarm manifested at the acquittal of M'Naghten influenced the judges in refusing to recognise the development in the law to which Hadfield's case and M'Naghten's case itself might have pointed the way ; a failure which was only partly remedied by the Homicide Act of 1957. However that may be, the M'Naghten Rules satisfied the peers ; their authority was never seriously questioned; and they still provide the test of insanity in the modern law.

Their main interest, for our purposes, lies in the conception of responsibility which they embody ; a peculiar conception, in several respects. In the first place, the test adopts a strictly cognitive approach ; it is framed exclusively in terms of knowledge. For the accused to fall within the Rules, it must be proved that he did not *know* what he was doing, or he did not *know* he was doing wrong. If he knew what he was doing and knew that it was wrong, it could not be argued in his defence that he could not help doing it. No defect in his powers of control could avail ; only a lack of knowledge. Indeed, the effect of the Rules was almost to assimilate the defence of insanity to the pleas of ignorance or mistake which afforded a defence under the ordinary doctrine of *mens rea* as it applied to the sane ; the only difference was that under the M'Naghten Rules the ignorance or mistake had to be the result of a defect of reason due to disease of the mind. This is very clearly illustrated by the law relating to insane delusions, which represent the *reductio ad absurdum* of the cognitive approach to insanity. If a person is under an insane delusion, he will be acquitted if he would not have been guilty on the facts as he imagines them to be. The case is governed by the same principles as ordinary cases of mistake of fact. The judges said after M'Naghten's case :

' ... we think he must be considered in the same situation as to responsibility as if the facts with respect to which the delusion exists were real. For example, if under the influence of his delusion he supposes another man to be in the act of attempting to take away his life, and he kills that man, as he supposes, in self-defence, he would be exempt from punishment. If his delusion was that the deceased had inflicted a serious injury to his character and fortune, and he killed him in revenge for such supposed injury, he would be liable to punishment.'

Subsequent cases, in which the Court of Criminal Appeal reaffirmed the validity of the M'Naghten Rules, have in effect placed still greater emphasis on the cognitive aspect of the test. In the case of *Codere* [16] it held that the words 'the nature and quality of the act' refer only to the physical character of the act in question and are not meant to distinguish between its physical and moral aspects. In this case, and again in the case of *Windle*, [17] it held that 'wrong' does not mean 'morally wrong', but, in effect, 'punishable by law'.

The requirement that the ignorance must have been the result of a defect of reason due to disease of the mind also reflects what might be described as the traditional conception of responsibility. The critical time is the time of the offence ; subsequent insanity may result in the accused being found unfit to plead, or insane on arraignment, but cannot logically affect his responsibility for his past acts. Further, the traditional conception of responsibility requires not merely that the insanity should have existed at the time of the act, but that the act should be directly attributable to the insanity. In this respect the formula adopted in the M'Naghten Rules may be contrasted with the 1846 Report of the Second Criminal Law Commissioners [18] which proposed *inter alia* the simple test : 'No person shall be criminally responsible for any act or omission who, at the time of such act or omission, is in a state of idiocy.' It may be constrasted also with the French law under the Code Napoléon of 1810, which provided that : 'Il n'y a ni crime ni délit, lorsque le prévenu était en état de démence au temps de l'action ... ' (Article 10).

Although the Code may have been interpreted in such a way that in practice there was little difference between the French and the English law, Article 10 prescribes only a temporal relationship, and does not require a causal relationship between the insanity and the deed. The M'Naghten Rules stipulate both. These comparisons can be used to show the significance of the causal requirement. If 'idiocy' and 'démence' are taken to refer to mental deficiency rather than to mental disease, it is clear that the causal requirement may be superfluous. It is at this point that the analogy with children is helpful. If a person is so defective that he has the mental age of a very young child, it is unnecessary to enquire into the relationship between his mental state and his conduct. If on the other hand he is of average mental capacity but temporarily deranged, the relationship is clearly crucial. If any significant line is to be drawn between those who are and those who are not responsible on grounds of mental disorder, it would seem that it can only be drawn on the basis either that the disorder was such that it did as a matter of fact affect a person's conduct, or that it was so great that it must be presumed to have affected it. To omit the causal requirement might therefore lead to a more restirictive test of responsibility.

The special verdict

Of course, a successful plea of insanity under the M'Naghten Rules was not in all respects tantamount to an acquittal for lack of *mens rea*. Above all, it did not automatically entitle the accused to his liberty. It is true that before 1800 the jury appears to have had a choice in such cases between returning a simple acquittal and acquitting on the ground of insanity. This special verdict is described by Hale in his chapter on infancy : [19]

' ... in all cases of infancy, insanity, &c., if a person uncapable to commit a felony be indicted by the grand inquest, and thereupon arraigned, the petit jury may either find him generally not guilty, or they may find the matter specially, that he committed the fact, but that he was non compos, or that he was under the age of fourteen ...'

But as late as 1800 it was open to argument at Hadfield's trial whether a person who had been found insane by the jury could be confined by order of the court. Following Hadfield's trial the Criminal Lunatics Act 1800 provided that the only verdict open to the jury in such cases was 'not guilty on the ground of insanity', and that on the return of this special verdict the court should order the accused 'to be kept in strict custody, in such place and in such manner as to the court shall seem fit, until His Majesty's pleasure be known;' whereupon it would be for His Majesty to give orders for his custody. Since 1964, the form of the order is for the accused to be admitted to such hospital as may be specified by the Home Secretary.

The significance of the 1800 Act is well explained by Dr Walker :

'From the jurisprudential point of view the statutory special verdict was an attempt at a compromise between two traditional alternatives. It purported to be an acquittal, for it used the words 'not guilty'. On the other hand, it resembled the old special verdict in two ways, by adding the finding that the accused had been insane at the time of his act, and thus enabling the judges to return him to custody. It was an acquittal in name only, for it tacitly admitted that the doctrine of *mens rea* could not safely be applied to the insane. A criminal lunatic might be as morally innocent as a man who had done harm by accident or in self-defence, but the danger of treating him as innocent was too great. The solution was to pay lip-service to his innocence but use the law to make sure he remained in custody. Hitherto it had been the civil law that had been used for this purpose; henceforth it was to be the criminal law.' [20]

The special verdict could not therefore be regarded as a complete acquittal. Indeed it has been argued that there was every justification for the change introduced by the Act of 1883, whereby the verdict was to be 'that the accused was guilty of the act or omission charged against him, but was insane . . . at the time when he did the act or made the omission', or, as it became popularly known, 'guilty but insane'. The Trial of Lunatics Act 1883 was passed at the instance of Queen Victoria, who had been the victim of a succession of murderous attacks by assailants found to be insane. The royal patience was exhausted after one Roderick Maclean fired a pistol at her as she was about to descend from her carriage at Windsor Station, was tried for treason, and was acquitted on grounds of insanity.

In support of her view that the law was in need of reform, the Queen argued as follows :

'Punishment deters not only sane men but also eccentric men, whose supposed involuntary acts are really produced by a diseased brain capable of being acted upon by external influence. A knowledge that they would be protected by an acquittal on the grounds of insanity will encourage these men to commit desperate acts, while on the other hand certainty that they will not escape punishment will terrify them into a peaceful attitude – towards others.'

Dr Walker is no doubt correct in defending the Queen against the particular illogicality with which she was later charged. [21] But her argument does appear to confuse two different things : responsibility for the act, and capacity to be deterred. Capacity to be deterred is hardly an index of responsibility, although no doubt there is some relationship between the two.

Further it could be doubted whether a person who was capable of appreciating the significance of the form of verdict provided by the 1883 Act would ever have been likely to be acquitted on grounds of insanity. Finally, it is to be noted that although the Act did not provide for any change in the form of treatment, as opposed to the form of verdict, in such cases, Queen Victoria was apparently relying on the threat of punishment to deter the insane.

A further illogicality resulted from the practice of instructing juries, for the sake of brevity, to return a verdict of 'guilty of the act but insane at the time', or even of 'guilty but insane'. This practice obscured the fact that it was not with insanity *simpliciter* that the law was concerned, but with the question whether the accused was insane so as not to be responsible according to law for his actions. This confusion may have contributed to the popular belief that the law was attempting to determine insanity, which was properly a medical question ; and even to the belief that no insane person is responsible in law, quite the opposite of the effect intended by Queen Victoria !

Despite Victoria's views, the verdict came to be treated as an acquittal in substance. At one time it seemed possible that an accused could appeal against the special verdict. In Ireland's case in 1910, [22] an epileptic who did not set up the defence of insanity was found 'guilty but insane'. The Court of Criminal Appeal, while not upholding his appeal, accepted that the special verdict amounted to a conviction, and could therefore be the subject of an appeal. This view of the law, if it had been maintained, would have raised a host of problems. Was an appeal to be available only if the accused had not himself raised the issue of insanity ? If not, he would be able to appeal against the verdict which was the result of his own plea. Yet it would have been arbitrary to make the right of appeal dependent on what plea he had put forward at the trial. An attempt was soon made to escape from this dilemma when the Court of Criminal Appeal decided, in the case of Machardy, [23] that what could be the subject of an appeal was the finding that the accused had done the act charged, but not the finding that he was insane This otherwise admirable solution unfortunately ignored the fact that it was precisely the question of insanity which had been at issue in the earlier case.

In Felstead's case in 1914, however, these doubts were finally resolved when the House of Lords laid it down *pace* Queen Victoria that the special verdict was an acquittal against which there was no appeal.[24]

In Kemp's case in 1957 Devlin J suggested a modification of this view. He described the special verdict as a 'qualified' rather than an 'absolute' acquittal. He considered that the Act of 1883 altered the common law position that 'if a man is not responsible for his actions he is entitled to be acquitted by the ordinary form of acquittal, and it matters not whether his lack of responsibility was due to insanity or to any other cause.' [25] But before 1883, as we have seen, the special verdict was not 'the ordinary form of acquittal', and even before the Act of 1800 the common law had provided for a special verdict. [26]

In describing the special verdict as a qualified acquittal, however, Devlin J was proved right, and Queen Victoria wrong, by the Criminal Procedure (Insanity) Act 1964. On the one hand, the Act restores the position as it was prior to 1883 by providing for a special verdict of 'not guilty by reason of insanity', which is clearly an acquittal in form. This had been recommended forty years before by the Atkin Committee on Insanity and Crime. [27] On the other hand, the Act recognises the qualified character of the acquittal by empowering the prosecution in certain cases to bring evidence of insanity and by conferring a right of appeal on any person in whose case a special verdict is returned.

Because a successful plea of insanity always carries with it the risk of a permanent loss of liberty, it has not generally been regarded as a plea worth making except where the alternative was the death penalty. With the rapid contraction in the incidence of capital punishment in the nineteenth century, it came to be confined in practice to charges of murder and treason; and following the distinction between capital and non-capital murders introduced by the Homicide Act in 1957, which also made available the alternative plea of diminished responsibility, it was restricted further to capital murders. Finally, the suspension of the death penalty for murder in 1965 seems likely to lead to the virtual extinction of the plea of insanity. In all trials at Assizes and Quarter Sessions in 1967, only three persons were found not guilty by reason of insanity. Of these one had been charged with murder, one with attempted murder, and one with felonious wounding. [28]

Extension to M'Naghten
On the issue of responsibility the principal criticism of the M'Naghten Rules has always been that they do not allow for the person who, although he knows what he is doing and may in some sense know that it is wrong, nonetheless seems unable to help himself. On the basis that 'ought' implies 'can', a person is not responsible for what he cannot help doing ; yet a person who has the requisite knowledge cannot under the M'Naghten formula escape responsibility for his acts. Stephen produced an ingenious argument to show that the Rules could be interpreted to cover this case ; he argued that a person who cannot control his actions necessarily does not know what he is doing. 'Knowledge and power are the constituent elements of all voluntary action, and if either is seriously

impaired the other is disabled. It is as true that a man who cannot control himself does not know the nature of his acts as that a man who does not know the nature of his acts is incapable of self-control.' [29] But he did not persuade his brother judges, who were generally highly sceptical of such pleas as irresistible impulse, and his views represented the law only when he himself directed the jury accordingly. The gap remained ; many formulas were proposed to meet the defect, and in other jurisdictions various statutory amendments to the Rules were introduced. Thus the criminal codes of Queensland and Tasmania have added a third limb to the M'Naghten test : in the Queensland code, 'capacity to control his actions' [30] and in Tasmania, irresistible impulse. [31] A recent Northern Ireland statute extends to any person 'who suffers from mental abnormality which prevents him ... from controlling his own conduct'. [32] In the United States the American Law Institute has adopted the following formula for its Model Penal Code : [33]

'A person is not responsible for criminal conduct if at the time of such conduct as a result of mental disease or defect he lacks substantial capacity either to appreciate the criminality of his conduct or to conform his conduct to the requirements of law.'

Where the legislature has not intervened, judicial techniques have been used to achieve similar results. The High Court of Australia has adopted Stephen's argument that 'the absence of the power of self-control would involve an incapacity to know right from wrong'. In one case in South Australia, where the M'Naghten Rules applied without modification, the defendant had shot and killed his employer for no apparent reason. He raised a defence of insanity and there was medical evidence that he had a schizoid personality. He said that he felt he could not help doing what he did, but admitted that he would not have shot at the deceased if a policeman had been present. The trial judge directed the jury that if the true explanation of the accused's conduct was that he was unable to control his impulse to kill his employer, he had no defence to the charge; but the High Court of Australia allowed his appeal on the ground that the jury should have been directed to consider whether his inability to control his impulse to kill the deceased had prevented him from knowing that what he was doing was wrong. [34]

A similar interpretation was consistently rejected by the English Court of Criminal Appeal, and attempts to legislate were equally unsuccessful. Thus in True's case in 1922 the Court, in dismissing True's appeal against conviction, rejected the view of the trial judge that the jury could return a finding of insanity if they thought that he had been deprived of the power of controlling his actions. [35] Here the Court of

Criminal Appeal seemed in tune with popular opinion, for when True was subsequently reprieved there was a public outcry, and the Atkin Committee on Insanity and Crime was appointed as a result.

The Committee, however, supported an extension of the M'Naghten Rules; their Report recommended that it should be recognised that a person charged with a criminal offence is irresponsible for his act when the act is committed under an impulse which the prisoner was by mental disease in substance deprived of any power to resist. [36]

Their proposed amendment was eventually adopted in Tasmania, but the English law remained unchanged. In 1924 Lord Darling introduced in the House of Lords a Criminal Responsibility (Trials) Bill which would have added to the M'Naghten Rules a provision that the accused is entitled to a verdict of not guilty on the ground that he was insane 'if at the time the act was done or omission made he was suffering from such a state of mental disease as therefrom to be wholly incapable of resisting an impulse to do the act or make the omission.' The Bill met with strong opposition from the judges, and no support at all from other members of the House, and Lord Darling eventually withdrew it.[37] The aversion of the judges to this defence is illustrated by a case of the same period, in which counsel for the appellant argued that the judge should have directed the jury that a person under an impulse which he cannot control is not criminally responsible. This was described by Lord Hewart CJ as a 'fantastic theory ... which if it were to become part of our criminal law, would be merely subversive'. [38] It is interesting to compare this view with the actual consequences, discussed below, of the introduction of 'diminished responsibility' in the 1957 Homicide Act.

Meanwhile committees continued to make recommendations to no effect. In 1930 the Select Committee on Capital Punishment recommended that the death penalty should be suspended for five years, but that, if it were retained, the M'Naghten Rules should be revised 'so as to give full scope to general medical considerations and to extend the area of criminal irresponsibility in the case of the mentally defective and those who labour under some distinct form of Insanity.' Neither recommendation was implemented.

Finally the Royal Commission on Capital Punishment, which examined the whole question in greater depth than any other body before or since, proposed the following formula in 1953 : [39]

'The jury must be satisfied that, at the time of committing the act, the accused, as a result of disease of the mind or mental deficiency, (a) did not know the nature and quality of the act or (b) did not know that it was wrong or (c) was incapable of preventing himself from committing it.'

D

This proposal, together with the rest of the Report, was ignored.

The M'Naghten Rules have however been defended by some on the ground that for all their defects the criteria they employ are at least logically secure in a sense in which alternative tests are not. Thus Baron Bramwell said: [40] 'I think that although the present law lays down such a definition, that nobody is hardly ever really mad enough to be within it, yet it is a logical and good definition.' Lord Devlin used an argument that recalls the earlier justifications of *mens rea:*[41]

'As it is a matter of theory, I think there is something logical – it may be astringently logical, but it is logical – in selecting as the test of responsibility to the law, reason and reason alone. It is reason which makes a man responsible to the law. It is reason which gives him sovereignty over animate and inanimate things. It is what distinguishes him from the animals, which emotional disorder does not; it is what makes him man; it is what makes him subject to the law. So it is fitting that nothing other than a defect of reason should give complete absolution.'

Baroness Wootton, using a different argument and with different motives, reaches a similar conclusion. [42] She holds that once the M'Naghten test is extended there is no logically secure resting-place short of the total abandonment of responsibility. In the final chapter it will be suggested that these arguments are fallacious. But they may have been encouraged by the fact that some of the proposals for amending the M'Naghten Rules are indeed logically defective. Some of them have shown a permanent and apparently ineradicable tendency to confuse under the heading of responsibility what are essentially distinct questions: the legal question what are the conditions of liability to legal penalties; the moral question what are the criteria of responsibility outside the law; and the medical question of the effect of mental disease, disorder, and defect on a person's capacity to understand and control his conduct.

An example of this confusion is to be found in the recommendation of the Medico Psychological Association to the Atkin Committee on Insanity and Crime whose report has already been referred to. The Association proposed *inter alia* that the legal criteria of responsibility expressed in the M'Naghten Rules should be abrogated and that the responsibility of a person should be left as a question of fact to be determined by the jury on the merits of the particular case. [43] The authors of the proposal failed to see that responsibility in law cannot be solely a question of fact. Simply to ask whether a person was responsible in law, without providing any criteria of responsibility, would be a wholly vacuous question. One might as well ask whether a person was civilly liable, without providing any test of civil liability.

A less extreme approach on similar lines was in fact followed by the State of New Hampshire which adopted the following rule:[44]

'There is no legal test of irresponsibility by reason of insanity. It is a question of fact for the jury in each case whether the defendant had a mental disease, and if so, whether it was of such character or degree as to take away the capacity to form or entertain a criminal intent.'

A minor difficulty is caused by the use of the words 'criminal intent' which seems to require definition if the formula is not to be circular, But the major difficulty is that the rule is so illogical as to be self-contradictory. Having stated that there is no legal test of irresponsibility, the rule proceeds to provide one, namely, that a person is not legally responsible if his mental disease was such as to deprive him of the capacity to form or entertain the requisite intent. But the inconsistency is not surprising. It is difficult to see how the concept of criminal responsibility could be of any use at all in the absence of any criteria for its application.

Stephen saw this point and expressed it with characteristically forthright clarity:[45] 'The question "What are the mental elements of responsibility?" is, and must be, a legal question. It cannot be anything else, for the meaning of responsibility is liability to punishment; and if criminal law does not determine who are to be punished under given circumstances, it determines nothing.'

Other substitutes for the M'Naghten Rules have been equally defective in different ways. The most famous recent example is the Durham rule[46] in the United States that 'an accused is not criminally responsible if his unlawful act was the product of mental disease of defect'. One difficulty here derives from the very simplicity of the wording. The simplicity is deceptive.[47] When can an unlawful act be described as the 'product' of mental disease or defect? If it prevents a person from realising what he is doing? Or if as a result of the disease he has an impulse he is unable to resist? The new test does not allow us to escape from the old criteria, and does not answer the old questions. In the end it raises more problems than it solves.

The same criticism can be made of the proposal of the Royal Commission on Capital Punishment.[48] Their suggested amendment to the M'Naghten Rules has already been quoted. But this was only in their view a last resource. The best course would be to abrogate the Rules and leave the jury to determine 'whether at the time of the act the accused was suffering from disease of the mind or mental deficiency to such a degree that he ought not to be held responsible'. Again, the criteria are not specified; but they cannot be omitted, if the test is to be of any value.

The Mental Deficiency Acts

From an early date the law had distinguished between a 'lunatic' or 'person of unsound mind' on the one hand and an 'idiot' or 'natural fool' on the other hand. The distinction is recognised in the statute *de praerogativa regis* which dates from the fourteenth century. No consistent use, however, was made of this terminology and the terms were frequently used interchangeably. The statute asserted the wardship of lunatics and idiots and of their property to be a prerogative of the Crown; the principle of the law was that the property of a lunatic must be preserved intact and returned to him on recovery, subject only to the maintenance of the lunatic and his family meanwhile out of the estate, whereas the profits of the property of an idiot, beyond what was spent on his maintenance, might be appropriated for the enjoyment of the Crown or of the person entrusted with the custody of the idiot.

During the late eighteenth and nineteenth centuries a series of Lunacy Acts was enacted to provide for the care of 'lunatics' in 'asylums' and elsewhere. Admission to asylums and other institutions was regulated by the use of procedures which became known as 'certification'; these procedures gave authority for the admission and detention of the patient for as long as his mental disorder lasted, and could be used only for the categories of persons to whom the Act applied. The consolidating Lunacy Act of 1890 applied to all 'lunatics' and defined the term 'lunatic' as meaning 'an idiot or a person of unsound mind'. In 1904 the Royal Commission on the Care and Control of the Feeble-Minded was appointed to consider the needs of the feeble-minded and other mentally disordered persons who were not considered certifiable under the Lunacy Acts, and the need for special forms of treatment for them and for idiots. In their Report [49] published in 1908 this Royal Commission recommended new legislation which would cover all forms of 'mental defect', a term which was used in the wide sense in which the Mental Health Act of 1959 used the term 'mental disorder'.

The Report led to the Mental Deficiency Acts of 1913 and 1927. Both these Acts were repealed in their entirety by the Mental Health Act 1959, which also introduced a new terminology, but they are important as showing the main developments in the law relating to the mentally abnormal between the M'Naghten Rules and the 1959 Act.

The Report classified all the mentally afflicted as follows:-

1. Those who once were normal, but have become abnormal; whether (a) through disorder of the mind, i.e. 'lunatics';   or

(b) through decay of mind (e.g. in senility), i.e. the 'mentally infirm'.

2.   Those who never had full mental power; these were together classed as 'mental defectives', and special provisions were made for those who committed offences punishable by imprisonment, in the Mental Deficiency Acts.

Mental defectives were classified in four groups, idiots, imbeciles, feeble-minded persons, and moral imbeciles, which were defined by the Act of 1913 as follows:—[50]

a)   Idiots: persons so deeply defective in mind from birth or from an early age as to be unable to guard themselves against common physical dangers.

b)   Imbeciles: persons in whose case there exists from birth or from an early age mental defectiveness not amounting to idiocy, yet so pronounced that they are incapable of managing themselves or their affairs, or, in the case of children, of being taught to do so.

c)   Feeble-minded persons: persons in whose case there exists from birth or from an early age mental defectiveness not amounting to imbecility, yet so pronounced that they require care, supervision, and control for their own protection or for the protection of others, or, in the case of children, they, by reason of such defectiveness appear to be incapable of receiving proper benefit from the instruction of ordinary schools.

d)   Moral imbeciles: persons who from an early age display some permanent mental defect coupled with strong vicious or criminal propensities on which punishment had little or no deterrent effect.

Under the Mental Deficiency Acts, the courts were empowered, in-stead of passing sentence on a mental defective, to place him under guardianship or to send him to an institution for mental defectives. These powers could be used in the case of offences which would other-wise have been punishable with imprisonment; in the case of murder, the jury would have had to find not merely that the accused satisfied the definition of mental deficiency contained in the Acts, but that the deficiency rendered him insane within the meaning of the M'Naghten Rules. But although it is arguable that mental deficiency is not a 'disease of the mind' in the ordinary sense of the term, that is, 'a pathological change arising *de novo* in the mind of an individual who has already progressed some way towards maturity or has attained it',[51] nevertheless the Royal Commission on Capital Punishment found that 'in practice the M'Naghten Rules have often been so interpreted as to include mental deficiency, at least in cases where the other conditions laid down by the Rules are fulfilled'.[52]

Mental defectives, as defined by the 1913 Act, included a class of persons described as 'moral imbeciles', a term that was changed by the Act of 1927 to 'moral defectives'; and the provisions relating to this class of persons may be regarded as crucial to the issue of responsibility. The type of persons intended to be included by this term corresponds approximately to what is now described by reference to a psychopathic personality; the significance of the change of terminology was the intention of showing that there need not be in such cases any defect of the understanding. The concept of mental defectiveness was thus expanding beyond the cognitive limits which were so pronounced a feature of the previous law relating to the responsibility of the mentally abnormal.

'Mental defectiveness' itself was defined by the 1927 Act as 'a condition of arrested or incomplete development of mind existing before the age of eighteen years, whether arising from inherent causes or induced by disease or injury.' The language of this definition, which was to be adapted to cover cases of murder under the doctrine of diminished responsibility in the Homicide Act of 1957, thus serves to distinguish the mental defective from the person who is insane so as not to be responsible within the M'Naghten rules in part by the fact that whereas in an insane person faculties which were originally normal have been impaired by mental disease, mental defectives include those who have never possessed a normal degree of intellectual capacity.

The Acts of 1913 and 1927 went some way towards remedying the defects of the M'Naghten Rules in their application to offences other than murder, but it is questionable whether they had any significant implications for the concept of criminal responsibility. They did not purport to provide a new test of responsibility, but only to provide new methods of treatment for those who were responsible under the old tests. To argue that this implies the abandonment of responsibility is to imply that responsibility and 'treatability' are mutually exclusive alternatives, and also posits a rigid distinction between punishment and treatment which is perhaps unjustified by modern penal policy.

It is true that in some cases a conviction was not required. The Act of 1913 provided that the court's powers could only be exercised after conviction; but this was subject to the proviso that 'if the court is a court of summary jurisdiction and the case is one which the court has power to deal with summarily, the court, if it finds that the charge is proved, may give such directions or make such order as aforesaid without proceeding to a conviction, and such a person shall for the purposes of this Act be deemed to be a person found guilty of an offence.'[53] But it is not possible to attach much significance to this somewhat formal distinction, the main object of which must have been to avoid harming the character of the accused.

One significant feature emerges from a comparison of the two Acts, if their respective definitions of the moral defective are constrasted. In 1913, moral defectives were defined as 'persons who from an early age display some permanent mental defect coupled with strong vicious or criminal propensities on which punishment has had little or no deterrent effect.' In 1927, the criterion is less severe; they are 'persons in whose case there exists mental defectiveness coupled with strongly vicious or criminal propensities and who require care, supervision and control for the protection of others.'[54] The disappearance of the earlier requirement that punishment should have been tried and failed is evidence of a more humane approach to the problem of the moral defective, but is no evidence of the elimination of responsibility. It may be true in particular cases that persons who are not responsible for their actions are also less susceptible to the influence of methods appropriate to a system of punishment, but such susceptibility is neither a necessary nor a sufficient condition of responsibility. There are in fact two quite separate grounds for holding that such persons should be absolved from the usual processes of the criminal law. One is the practical ground that punishment may be less effective in such cases than some form of treatment. But it may be equally or more effective; and this raises a consideration of principle: that punishment, whatever its practical consequences, is not morally justified where the person is not responsible for his acts.

Only on one interpretation, perhaps, could the Acts of 1913 and 1927, in their attempts to supplement the deficiencies of the M'Naghten Rules, be construed as tending towards an elimination of responsibility from the criminal law. It might be argued that, for all its failings, even in the light of the psychiatric knowledge of the nineteenth century, a cognitive test is for some reason the only logically reliable criterion of responsibility. The argument has been advanced that however unsatisfactory the M'Naghten Rules may have been in other respects, they did at least provide a test of responsibility that was logically consistent, and that the departure from this test has undermined the whole basis of the concept. Evidence of a train of thought along such lines as these is to be found in the lectures of O.W. Holmes in 1881, which are discussed more fully below. In recent years a similar but independent position has been adopted by Lady Wootton. Such a view is not, of course, entirely novel. Reference has already been made to Lord Bramwell's view that, 'although the present law lays down such a definition, that nobody is hardly ever really mad enough to be within it, yet it is a logical and good definition.' Since this argument has been developed by later writers in the specific context of the doctrine of diminished responsibility, it will be examined shortly in that context; but it is clear that its implications extend to a far broader field than that to which it is generally confined. The wider implications of the argument will therefore also be considered in the concluding chapter.

It is possible to point to illogicalities in any compromise, and to argue that it is in some respects less satisfactory than a radical measure, however extreme. Any attempt to divide into clear categories people with so indeterminate a characteristic as mental abnormality must have consequences which will in some cases necessarily appear arbitrary. But criticisms of this kind are of dubious theoretical validity; for the difficulty of applying criteria in border-line cases does not necessarily cast doubt on the value of the criteria or on the validity of the distinction. It is a familiar problem in the application of any system of rules. Nor are such criticisms helpful in practice, since the difficulties to which they draw attention are not consequences of a specific solution but rather inherent in the problem itself. Any rational programme for the treatment of offenders, whether or not it incorporates a concept of responsibility, must distinguish between different types of treatment on the basis of different types of abnormality.

Infanticide

The first departure from the fixed penalty for murder in cases where the mental abnormality was insufficient to exonerate under the M'Naghten Rules entered English law with the Infanticide Act of 1922 (later replaced by the Act of 1938). The problem of the mother who kills her own child when mentally disturbed as a result of the processes of the birth had long been recognised but previous attempts to legislate were unsuccessful. The Act passed in 1922 provided that a woman charged with killing her newly-born child should not be convicted of murder but might be convicted instead of the new offence of infanticide, punishable in the same way as manslaughter, if at the time of the act the balance of her mind was disturbed as a result of the birth or of lactation.

On the issue of responsibility the significant feature of this legislation is that, although it requires a temporal connection between the mental disturbance and the deed, it does not require any causal nexus. The question whether the mental disturbance caused the act is by-passed. In this respect it may be contrasted with some of the earlier legislative proposals; two Bills, for example, introduced in 1872 and 1874 included a requirement that the mother was deprived of self-control by the effects of the birth.[55] But the significance of this departure from the traditional concept of responsibility is limited. The truly significant requirement in this type of case is the temporal link; for if the disturbance existed, as the Act requires, at the time of the deed, it would generally be unreasonable to suppose, in a case of this sort, that there was no causal nexus. It is best to treat infanticide, therefore, as a very special case, comprising situations which would virtually always on their facts justify this limited exception to the general rule.

The changing attitudes of the courts are reflected in the figures for the treatment of women convicted of infanticide. In the five-year period immediately following the passage of the 1922 Act, approximately half the women convicted of infanticide were sentenced to imprisonment; of the remainder, most were released on recognisance or discharged. In the five-year period from 1961-5, the proportion sentenced to imprisonment had fallen to a mere 1.3%, and most of those convicted were put on probation.[56] In 1967, none of the seventeen women convicted of infanticide was sentenced to imprisonment; fourteen were put on probation, two hospital orders were made under section 60 of the Mental Health Act, and one woman was conditionally discharged.[57]

The Criminal Justice Act 1948

Broadly speaking, it can be said that before 1948 no provision was made by the criminal law for the compulsory treatment of convicted persons. This, of course, is true subject to the provisions for the transfer of a person serving a sentence of imprisonment to another institution; the powers of the Secretary of State in such cases are now regulated by section 72 of the Mental Health Act 1959. Subject to this one exception, which does not affect the course of the argument, it can be said that before 1948 all mental treatment was voluntary, or was involuntary only to the extent to which persons who submitted to it did so in the belief that the alternative to such treatment was prison. Section 4 of the Criminal Justice Act 1948, provided a more effective means of procuring mental treatment, by empowering the courts to make mental treatment a condition of a probation order. Section 3 (1) of the Act empowered the court, where 'having regard to the nature of the offence and the character of the offender, it is expedient to do so', to make a probation order in respect of all offences other than those for which the sentence was fixed by law; and section 4 (1) provided that 'Where the court is satisfied, on the evidence of a duly qualified medical practitioner appearing to the court to be experienced in the diagnosis of mental disorders, that the mental condition of an offender is such as requires and as may be suceptible to treatment but is not such as to justify his being certified as a person of unsound mind under the Lunacy Act, 1890, or as a defective under the Mental Deficiency Act, 1913, the court may, if it makes a probation order, include therein a requirement that the offender shall submit ... to treatment ...'

This was the first recognition by the legislature of a fact which had long been taken into consideration by the courts, that there are persons guilty of crime whose mental condition is relevant to their guilt, although they cannot be classified as either insane or defective. It may therefore be regarded as carrying one stage further the principle introduced by the Mental Deficiency Acts.

It is less clear what the effect of these provisions may be on the concept of responsibility. It has indeed been argued that the adoption of the criterion of susceptibility to treatment represents a step in the direction pointed by those who wish to see the idea of responsibility somehow replaced in the criminal law by the idea of 'treatability'. It is not easy to see how these ideas can be regarded as interchangeable, but an argument of this type is familiar from the writings of social scientists.

Lady Wootton, for example, in her Hamlyn lectures on *Crime and the Criminal Law* writes of the 1948 reform in terms of an antithesis between responsibility and 'treatability'. She argues:[58]

'Such a provision represents a very whole-hearted step in the direction of accepting the criterion of treatability. For, although those to whom this section may be applied must be deemed to be guilty — in the sense that they have been convicted of offences involving *mens rea* — the only question to be decided is that of their likely response to medical or other treatment.'

It is doubtful whether the conclusion of this argument, that the relevant section does adopt a new criterion, is fully supported by its premises. In any case, if the statute is interpreted against the background of the Act of 1927, its innovations in this respect appear far less radical, since the term 'moral defective' was defined, as we have seen, largely in terms of susceptibility to treatment. There are, further, the qualifications mentioned by Lady Wootton herself, that the provisions of the 1948 Act operate only after a conviction involving a finding of *mens rea.* It could be argued on these grounds that they do not affect the question of responsibility at all.

Finally, certain other aspects of these provisions are important. It should be noted, in the first place, that, although the courts are required to take into account the offender's susceptibility to treatment, they are authorised to do so only in deciding whether such treatment is suitable; and it is difficult to see, in deciding this question, what other criteria could be satisfactorily used. An order of this type can in any case only be made on the evidence of a psychiatrist and with the consent of the accused person. These qualifications on the exercise of the powers conferred on the courts make it additionally difficult to interpret the provisions as in any way displacing the notion of responsibility.

Diminished responsibility

One hundred and fourteen years after the promulgation of the M'Naghten Rules, the law of murder was amended by the Homicide Act 1957. The Rules were retained, but (against the advice of the Royal Commission on Capital Punishment) the Scottish 'defence' of diminished responsibility was introduced. The 1957 Act was essentially a compromise solution to the controversy over capital punishment. It appeased the retentionists by retaining as capital offences certain categories of murder, including murder by shooting and murder in the course or furtherance of theft; but the remainder, numerically more significant, carried a mandatory sentence of life imprisonment. The Murder (Abolition of Death Penalty) Act 1965, by suspending capital punishment for five years, made all murders punishable by life imprisonment alone.

Section 2 of the Homicide Act 1957 introduced the 'defence' of diminished responsibility. Strictly speaking it is not a defence but operates to alter the category of the crime; the section provides that where a person kills or is a party to the killing of another, he shall not be convicted of murder but shall be convicted of manslaughter, 'if he was suffering from such abnormality of mind (whether arising from a condition of arrested or retarded development of mind or any inherent causes or induced by disease or injury) as substantially impaired his mental responsibility for his acts and omissions in doing or being a party to the killing.' The effect was to give the court the widest discretion in passing sentence. Instead of a mandatory penalty of death or life imprisonment, the court could impose imprisonment for life or any lesser period, a fine, or a conditional or unconditional discharge under the Criminal Justice Act 1948. But the effect was not to exclude responsibility. On the contrary, at least before the Mental Health Act enabled the courts to make a hospital order, the large majority of cases were given prison sentences, most of them for life or long fixed terms of more than three years. [59] Some commentators observed that the only unmistakable change in penal practice which resulted from the new defence was that some murderers who would presumably have been committed to mental hospitals were now sent to prison instead. In one case the Court of Criminal Appeal stated that a verdict of manslaughter based on a finding of diminished responsibility implies that a 'residue of responsibility' rests upon the accused in such circumstances and that this 'residue of criminal intent may be such as to deserve punishment.'[60] If this interpretation of the Act is correct, then the doctrine which it introduces into the law is not really diminished responsibility, but is rather a doctrine of diminished culpability. This interpretation is confirmed by the number of cases of mercy killings where verdicts of diminished responsibility have been returned.[61] In these cases there is often of course no previous record of mental abnormality, and it may well be that some have escaped conviction for murder under the Homicide Act who could not have been brought within the M'Naghten Rules by the most sympathetic of juries.

The sentencing picture has however changed dramatically in recent years, no less than in cases of infanticide. Whereas in the early years of the Homicide Act only about two a year escaped imprisonment, in recent years there has been a growing use of hospital orders under the Mental Health Act. Thus in 1967, out of a total of forty-nine persons convicted under section 2 of the Homicide Act, only thirteen were sentenced to imprisonment. No fewer than 29 restriction orders were made under section 65 of the Mental Health Act; a hospital order under section 60 was made in one case; four were put on probation, one was required to enter into recognisances, and one was otherwise disposed of.[62] The changing pattern is illustrated by Table A.

Table A.

Sentences on finding of diminished responsibility: the first ten years.[63]

	Number Convicted	Imprisonment *	Hospital orders +	Otherwise dealt with
1957	11	10 (3)	–	1
1958	25	22 (6)	–	3
1959	21	20 (2)	–	1
1960	23	21 (6)	–	2
1961	36	19 (3)	15	2
1962	34	12 (1)	19	3
1963	46	21 (3)	24	1
1964	41	13 (2)	23	5
1965	47	16 (2)	24	7
1966	51	18 (1)	31	2

*   The figures in brackets are of the number of persons who have been transferred to hospitals under section 72, Mental Health Act 1959, or under corresponding provisions in force before that Act came into effect.

The relevant provisions of the Mental Health Act 1959 came into force on 1 November 1960.

The extent to which the law had departed from the traditional conception of *mens rea* was first apparent in Byrne's case[64] in 1960, when the Court of Criminal Appeal gave a lucid and liberal interpretation of the obscure wording of the Act which was subsequently described as 'authoritative and correct'.[65] The Court said of the expression 'abnormality of mind' that it appeared to be 'wide enought to cover the mind's activities in all its aspects, not only the perception of physical acts and matters, and the ability to form a rational judgment whether an act is right or wrong, but also the ability to exercise will-power to control physical acts in accordance with that rational judgment'; and the expression 'mental responsibility for his acts' pointed to 'a consideration of the extent to which the accused's mind is answerable for his physical acts, which must include a consideration of the extent of his ability to exercise will-power to control his physical acts'. Although it is perhaps unfortunate that the court was led by the language of the Act to draw a dubious distinction between the mental and physical ingredients of an act, the judgement is valuable for its clear and categorical assertion that a person's capacity to control his actions, as well as his purely cognitive capacities, are to be considered in assessing his responsibility.

Two principal criticisms have been advanced against the introduction of diminished responsibility. First, it has led Lady Wootton to deny the possibility of making any meaningful judgments about responsibility;[66] her general arguments are discussed in the concluding chapter. A more specific criticism is made by Dr Richard Sparks.[67] He argues simply that either a person could have helped breaking the law, or he could not have helped it.

'If we believe that the offender could have helped committing his crime, despite some mental impairment, there would surely be nothing unfair in punishing him in the normal way. On the other hand, if we believe that a mentally impaired person could *not*, on that account, have helped breaking the law we should, according to our usual principles, excuse him *completely* from blame or punishment (properly so-called), though perhaps taking steps to see that he does not cause harm in the future. In neither case is there any reason merely to *reduce* his punishment.'[68]

But this objection appears to overlook the fact that, while a person either could or could not have helped breaking the law, it may have been possible, but very difficult indeed, for him to avoid breaking it. If this is so, then it may be that diminished responsibility is after all an appropriate term to describe those who, while not totally irresponsible, cannot be credited with the responsibility of a normal person. Dr Sparks himself recognises that the term 'mental responsibility' must be taken to refer to the capacity to control one's conduct;[69] but this is clearly something which does admit of degrees, and which can, in the words of the Act, be 'substantially impaired'. On this interpretation, therefore, the Act does not merely provide a wider test to include those who could not control their conduct, without satisfying the M'Naghten test; it also extends to those who have abnormal difficulty in controlling their conduct.

The wider test of responsibility introduced by the Homicide Act might have been expected to lead to a considerable increase in the proportion of persons charged with murder who escaped conviction on grounds of mental abnormality. No such increase has in fact occurred; as compared with the position before 1957, this proportion has remained remarkably constant. The large and rapidly increasing proportion of persons found to be suffering from diminished responsibility has done no more than to compensate for a decline in the numbers both of those found insane on arraignment and of those found insane after trial. So far as the decline in the first category is concerned, Dr Walker suggests that the explanation may lie in two factors.[70] One is the increasing importance attached to allowing the accused a trial, at which he has the opportunity of establishing his innocence, before he is committed to indefinite detention; the importance of this is now recognised by the Criminal Appeal Act 1968, which establishes the right of appeal against a finding of unfitness to plead.[71] The other factor is the increasing availability of certain tranquillising drugs which make it possible for mentally disordered persons to be rendered fit for trial. These factors, of course, would be expected to lead to an increase in verdicts showing a finding of insanity or diminished responsibility, and such an increase is reflected in the statistics. What is most significant, however, so far as the impact of diminished responsibility is concerned, is that the proportion of persons who have escaped conviction, under one head or another, on grounds of mental abnormality, has hardly changed at all. The increase in the number of findings of diminished responsibility has done no more than to keep this proportion constant, at a little under 50%. Thus in 1967, 63 persons were found guilty of murder, 49 of manslaughter under section 2 of the Homicide Act; eight persons charged with murder were found unfit to plead, and one not guilty by reason of insanity.[72]

It is clear that in effect the Homicide Act has replaced the verdict of insanity under the M'Naghten Rules with a finding of diminished responsibility. But the question remains why the wider test introduced by the Act has not led to a greater number of such findings.

A number of explanations may be suggested. It seems clear in the first place that the M'Naghten Rules themselves must have been given a liberal interpretation, and that they were extended to include persons who, while not fully responsible, should not have been committed to indefinite detention. Many such cases arising since 1957 will have benefited from the more flexible policy of the Homicide Act, or, since it came into force, of the Mental Health Act 1959.

Other explanations have been advanced by Dr Walker; he suggests, in particular, that prison medical officers may not have succeeded in adjusting to the new criterion. [73] But what is especially puzzling about the statistics is that, as already mentioned, there have been some cases, e.g. of mercy killings, where there is no previous record of mental abnormality, which have resulted in a finding of diminished responsibility although they could hardly have come within the M'Naghten Rules on any interpretation. It is true of course that there was a greater incentive before 1957 for lawyers, judges, juries, and medical witnesses to construe the Rules in favour of the accused; and since the special verdict was treated as an acquittal against which the prosecution could not appeal, there was no means of challenging a broad interpretation of the Rules. Between 1957 and 1965, when about 85% of murders were non-capital offences, and still more after 1965, when capital punishment for murder was suspended, it may be surmised that the accused was less likely to raise a defence of mental abnormality, that the prosecution was more likely to resist it, that witnesses would be less helpful and judge and jury more sceptical. It is not impossible, therefore, that the overall effect of the Homicide Act has been paradoxically to narrow rather than to widen the test of mental abnormality. The additional cases of 'diminished culpability' would have served to keep the proportionate figure constant.

The exact place at which the line is drawn may not, however, be of so much significance. There is one very simple but very plausible explanation of why the cases of mental abnormality have not risen proportionally by any significant amount. This is that the persons who before 1957 came within the M'Naghten Rules or were found unfit to plead already included most serious cases of mental abnormality; and that the remaining murders — little more than half the total — simply did not suffer from any form of recognised mental disorder.

This explanation is supported by the fact that there are few cases in which a plea of insanity is unsuccessful; and that there appear to be relatively few cases in which a plea of diminished responsibility fails. [74] But its implications, if correct, are highly significant. For those who criticise legal tests of responsibility often argue that there is no reliable dividing line between offenders who are and those who are not mentally 'normal'; and that any distinction is arbitrary and unfounded. If this were so, one would expect to find a very large category of border-line cases, and very considerable fluctuations in the statistics. The evidence, however, shows the position is exactly the reverse.

The reform introduced by the 1957 Act should therefore be understood as a modification less in the practice of the criminal law than in its conceptual structure. [75] It enlarges the concept of responsibility as understood by the law, and brings it more closely in line with contemporary thought.

This trend of the criminal law in departing from an older 'all-or-nothing' approach to questions of responsibility and fault is one to which parallels can be found in twentieth century developments in the civil law. In the law of contract, the older view that in the event of frustration the loss lay where it fell has been progressively modified to the extent that it is now possible for the loss to be apportioned equitably between the parties. [75] In tort, the old injustice that the victim of an injury had no redress if the injury was to any degree the result of his own fault has in the same period been remedied so that the responsibility can be shared between the parties in proportion to their degree of fault. [76] In the criminal law the recognition that there is an intermediate stage between the denial of all responsibility and the attribution of full responsibility does not constitute an abandonment of the primary distinction.

It has however been argued that this innovation, even if it does not itself constitute an abandonment of responsibility, does at least represent a stage in the process which cannot logically stop short of that goal. The strongest of the arguments advanced in support of this position is perhaps this : that with the acknowledgment that the question whether a person is responsible does not always admit of a yes-or-no answer and with the recognition of degrees of responsibility, juries and judges have been faced with problems which seem to defy common sense as well as science. This difficulty can be illustrated by a number of the cases and has evoked outspoken criticisms from the judges themselves. But some of the arguments which have been based on this difficulty appear to be less plausible, and, apart from being less well supported by evidence from the cases, often also seem to be structurally unsound. No one who was familiar with the operation of a legal system, or indeed with the application of any system of rules to concrete situations, would be tempted to argue that difficulties of demarcation where two categories merge into one another necessarily cast doubt on the validity of the classification or make impossible any division into categories. Nor can it be argued that arguments about responsibility are vitiated by any unique logical flaw. But since at this stage the immediate concern is with the present position of the law, rather than with the question whether that position is logically tenable, and since these arguments have a general importance apart from their application to the specific doctrine of diminished responsibility, a full consideration of their logic must be left to the concluding chapter.

The Mental Health Act 1959

Those who argue, however, that the concept of responsibility is changing, or disappearing altogether, under the impact of recent legislation, derive their strongest arguments from the Mental Health Act of 1959, which attempts to start afresh not merely in questions of the criminal respons- ibility of the mentally abnormal, nor only in the treatment of the mentally abnormal offender, but over the whole field of mental health and among all the social services dealing with mental illness. Even if the changes in the concept of responsibility may not be as far-reaching as they might at first sight appear, an examination of this legislation is a valuable study in the general implications of that concept in those areas where it has its most complex applications.

The new approach of the 1959 Act is marked first of all by an over- haul of the terminology, some of which is directly relevant for our present purposes. Most important, no attempt is made to define mental illness; instead, the term 'mental disorder' is given a comprehensive significance. It is defined as 'mental illness, arrested or incomplete dev- elopment of mind, psychopathic disorder, and any other disorder or disability of mind'. The term 'mental deficiency' is replaced by 'sub- normality' and 'severe subnormality'; and the terms 'subnormality' and 'severe subnormality', as well as 'psychopathic disorder', are defined by section 4 of the Act: severe subnormality is defined as a state of incomplete or arrested development of mind which includes subnormality of intelligence and is of such a nature or degree that the patient is incapable of living an independent life or of guarding himself against serious exploitation, or will be incapable when of an age to do so. This expression was intended to cover those who were previously called idiots and imbeciles, and some of those classified as feeble-minded. [77] Sub- normality is defined as a state of arrested or incomplete development of mind (not amounting to severe subnormality) which includes subnorm- ality of intelligence and is of a nature or degree which requires or is susceptible to medical treatment or other special care or training of the patient. [78]   This covers those formerly described as higher-grade defectives, and others of the feeble-minded. Psychopathic disorder is defined as a persistent disorder or disability of mind (whether or not including subnormality of intelligence) which results in abnormally

E

aggressive or seriously irresponsible conduct on the part of the patient, and requires or is susceptible to medical treatment. [79] It is provided that a person is not to be regarded as mentally disordered by reason only of promiscuity or other immoral conduct. [80]

The principal implication of this classification is to be found in the civil procedure for committing a person who is mentally unsound, whether for observation, or for treatment, or for guardianship. In practice there may be available compulsory powers which can be exercised without resort to prosecution for any criminal offence. A person is subject to compulsory detention for a period initially of one year, but renewable, if suffering from mental illness or severe subnormality, or (in the case of a patient under twenty-one) psychopathic disorder or subnormality.

More important, however, from the criminal aspect are the provisions contained in section 60 of the Act relating to those brought before the criminal courts. By section 60 (1) of the Act, a person who is convicted by a higher court (or by a magistrates' court if the offence is punishable with imprisonment) may, instead of being sentenced in the ordinary way, be compulsorily detained in hospital or made subject to a guardianship order, if certain conditions are fulfilled. The court must be satisfied, on the evidence of two doctors, one of whom must have had special experience in the diagnosis or treatment of mental disorders, that the offender is suffering from mental illness, psychopathic disorder, subnormality or severe subnormality, and that this is in all the circumstances the most appropriate way of dealing with him. The only offences to which the provisions do not apply are those which are not punishable by imprisonment and those for which the penalty is fixed by law; thus they do not apply to murder, but can be used where a charge of murder leads to a finding of diminished responsibility.

The great merit of these provisions is that the mentally abnormal offender who might before the Act have submitted to a sentence of imprisonment because the alternative (if he raised a plea of insanity) would lead to indeterminate detention in Broadmoor, might now be encouraged to bring forward his mental condition after conviction in the hope of obtaining a hospital order rather than a sentence of imprisonment. A further incentive stems from the fact that his freedom is better protected. The Act gives a certified patient far greater safeguards against prolonged confinement and abusive treatment than existed previously. He cannot be detained for more than a year unless he is re-certified, and he has a right of periodic appeal to an independent tribunal.

These provisions may be regarded as to some extent dispensing with responsibility. They do not in the first place require the existence of a causal relationship between the mental abnormality and the commission of the offence. [81] They may be contrasted in this respect not only with section 2 of the Trial of Lunatics Act 1883, but also with section 2 of the Homicide Act 1957. The former Act provided for a special verdict if 'it is given in evidence on the trial of such person for that offence that he was insane, so as not to be responsible, according to law, for his actions at the time when the act was done or omission made'. The Homicide Act also looks to a relationship between the abnormality and the offence: 'if he was suffering from such abnormality of mind ... as substantially impaired his mental responsibility for his acts and omissions in doing or being a party to the killing'.

Further, the provisions of the Mental Health Act do not even require that the abnormality should have existed at the time when the offence was committed. In this respect, it may again be contrasted both with the Homicide Act, and with the Trial of Lunatics Act, which explicitly provided that 'the jury shall return a special verdict to the effect that the accused was guilty of the act or omission charged against him, but was insane as aforesaid at the time when he did the act or made the omission'. And the subsequent legislation changing the form of the verdict to 'Not guilty by reason of insanity' has, of course, retained the temporal link.[82]

To some extent the Mental Health Act does represent a change in the approach of the criminal law to the responsibility of the mentally abnormal. It explicitly adopts the criterion of 'treatability', and it does not stipulate a restrospective inquiry into the state of mind of the offender at the time of the offence. But before the impact of these provisions can be properly assessed, several important qualifications must be observed.

In the first place, the novelty of this approach should not be exaggerated. Although a clear advance on the older provisions relating to insanity, the Mental Health Act was anticipated in some respects by the Mental Deficiency Acts and also by the Criminal Justice Act of 1948. The Mental Deficiency Act 1913, although it required a conviction in some criminal cases, did of course confer powers of civil committal. [83] The 1913 Act, too, dispensed with the need for a conviction in certain summary offences, [84] although when this provision was re-enacted in 1946, it was provided that 'such a person shall for the purposes of this Act be deemed to be a person found guilty of an offence.' [85] The Criminal Justice Act 1948, anticipated the 1959 Act in dispensing, in some cases, with a retrospective inquiry; it too adopted, although perhaps in less unequivocal terms, the criterion of treatability. The effect of these earlier provisions has already been examined. It remains to be seen to what extent the 1959 Act does represent a move towards the ultimate elimination of responsibility.

The provisions of section 60(1), for these purposes the most important provisions of all, do not dispense altogether with the notion of responsibility. On the contrary, it can be argued that they do in a number of ways either explicitly retain or implicitly presuppose the notion of responsibility. First, and most important, the sub-section applies only to an offender who has been convicted of an offence. Under the existing system, of course, this is inevitable, since it would otherwise represent only an extension of the special provisions made for those who are found unfit to plead. But it is significant that the Act is applied within the framework of the existing system, and does not substitute the alternative possibility of a procedure whereby a person suffering from mental abnormality could be made subject to an order by the court without the necessity for a formal conviction. Such powers would be analogous to the civil jurisdiction exercised by the courts in respect of children and young persons, which are discussed in the following chapter. But the Mental Health Act operates within the existing framework; it presupposes a distinction between civil and criminal procedures and retains the requirement of a conviction by a criminal court before the procedure it introduces can operate. Even under section 60 (1) of the Act, a person who was suffering from one of the specified forms of mental abnormality would not be eligible for treatment under that subsection if he were acquitted on the ground that he did not have *mens rea.* To this extent responsibility is retained. Further, the interpretation of the Act by the courts suggests that the issue of responsibility must still be considered, even in the case of a person who has been convicted and is found to have a mental disorder, in deciding whether an order under section 60 should be made. In some cases, it was stated by the Lord Chief Justice in 1961, the prisoner may on the facts be shown to have some responsibility for which he must be punished. [86]

Lady Wootton argues that, even where an order is made under the Act, the court may take into account considerations which she regards as involving a punitive element. A hospital order made by a higher court may be accompanied by a restriction order of either specified or indefinite duration, during the currency of which the patient may only be discharged on the order of the Home Secretary; while a magistrates' court, although it has no similar power itself to make a restriction order, may commit an offender to sessions to be dealt with, if it is of opinion that, having regard to the nature of the offence, the antecedents of the offender, and the risk of his committing further offences if set at liberty, a hospital order should be accompanied by a restriction order.

'The restriction order is thus professedly designed as a protection to the public; but a punitive element also, I think, still lingers in it. For if the sole object was the protection of the public against the premature discharge of a mentally disordered dangerous offender, it could hardly be argued that the court's prediction of the safe moment for release, perhaps years ahead, is likely to be more reliable than the judgment at the appropriate time of the hospital authorities who will have had the patient continuously under their surveillance. If their purpose is purely protective all orders ought surely to be of indefinite duration, and the fact that this is not so suggests that they are still tainted with the tariff notion of sentencing — that is to say, with the idea that a given offence 'rates' a certain period of loss of liberty.' [87]

Lady Wootton's argument is open to a number of objections. In the first place, it cannot be assumed that the purpose of a restriction order is necessarily punitive simply because its duration is predetermined. It is argued elsewhere that the antithesis between a 'punitive' and a 'preventive' system does not in any case present the clear-cut choice between alternatives which she suggests. Even if there were a clear alternative, several objections could be made to the imposition of an indeterminate restriction order which would not themselves entail a 'punitive' approach. It could justifiably be maintained that such an order would confer too wide a discretion on the administrative authorities and run counter to the values of the rule of law. At the same time there is no guarantee in the present state of medical knowledge that such a procedure would offer adequate protection to the public. Finally, it must be observed that even if a clear alternative were presented between a 'punitive' and a 'preventive' approach, a choice between them would have no necessary implications for the principle of responsibility, whose retention can be justifed within a purely 'preventive' system.

In some respects the provisions of the second sub-section of section 60 go further than those of the first. It has already been observed that under the first sub-section a magistrates' court has no power itself to make a restriction order, although it may under certain conditions commit an offender to sessions. Wider powers are conferred on these courts by section 60 (2). By this sub-section, when magistrates are dealing summarily with a person suffering from mental illness or severe abnormality, they may make a hospital order without convicting, if they are satisfied that he did the act or made the omission charged. Since this sub-section dispenses altogether with the requirement of a conviction, it may be regarded as to that extent dispensing with responsibility; although it does not of course absolve the courts from what Lady Wootton describes as their primary job, that of determining responsibility in a wider sense which refers only to what she calls the authorship of the act. [88]

It is not immediately clear why there should be no need under section 60 (2) for a conviction; but two alternative explanations of these provisions may be tentatively advanced. On one possible explanation, a conviction is not required simply because the effect of the mental illness is to preclude a conviction. On this interpretation, the purpose of the provisions would be that the mental illness should have the same effect as a plea of insanity within the M'Naghten Rules is now recognised as having, namely, that it should operate as a defence that would entitle the accused to an acquittal. This is a perfectly plausible and innocuous explanation. But there is an alternative possibility suggested by the phrasing of the sub-section which would be more revolutionary in its implications, if not in its immediate consequences. It is possible that a conviction is not required on the ground that there is no need to investigate the question of *mens rea;* it is necessary to find only that the accused did the act or made the omission charged. It might be argued that, if the requirement of *mens rea* were retained, a person who was so mentally disordered as to be incapable of forming the necessary intent could not be said to have done the act, with the consequence that precisely those people whose needs the provisions were primarily designed to meet would be deprived of their benefit. Therefore, the argument would run, the words 'the act' must be taken to refer only to the physical movements of the accused and not to include his state of mind. In this respect it may be thought that this sub-section takes the process of dispensing with responsibility a stage further than the provisions of section 60 (1).

On the other hand it differs from the first sub-section in that it is confined to persons suffering from mental illness or severe subnormality. It is not available in the case of persons suffering from either of the two other forms of mental disorder recognised by the Act, namely psychopathy, or simple, as distinct from severe, subnormality.

Conclusions

The question has so far been considered whether, and to what extent, recent legislation on the position of the mentally abnormal offender, and in particular the provisions of the Mental Health Act 1959, are symptoms of a trend towards the elimination of responsibility from the law. This is one aspect of the general question of what their implications may be for the evolution of the concept of criminal responsibility. It appears that the idea itself is a complex one, and that although there are some senses in which it has been affected, the consequences of recent changes in the law are different from what they have often been taken to be.

The Mental Deficiency Acts of 1913 and 1927, the relevant provisions of the Criminal Justice Act 1948, and of the Homicide Act 1957, and finally the new powers conferred by the Mental Health Act 1959, do at various points and in various ways affect the traditional link between criminal responsibility and punishment. Secondly, it is questionable whether any general conclusion from the legislation for the mentally abnormal can validly be argued to justify a progressive elimination of responsibility. The fundamental question is whether the newer procedures are tending to obliterate the previously more or less clearcut distinction between those who are and those who are not considered responsible for their actions. Is the line of demarcation between the two categories in the process of being altogether obliterated, or are the categories becoming blurred at the edges? On the evidence of recent legislation, neither of these descriptions would be entirely accurate; instead, they have had a different effect, which itself appears to provide a conclusive argument against the view that they are tending to the elimination of responsibility. The effect of these changes has not been to obliterate the line between the two classes, or even to blur the edges; what they have intended to do (with the possible exception of homicide) is rather to draw the line in a different place, and to exempt a wider class of persons from criminal liability. To this extent, of course, there has been what might be described as a reduction of responsibility; but far from this being an attempt to disregard extra-legal notions of responsibility, it has been an attempt to recognise changing standards of responsibility outside the law. It may therefore be said to reflect a greater rather than a lesser recognition of *mens rea*. Some attempt has been made by this means to put into practice a principle whose justification was most clearly stated in a similar context in the Report of the Royal Commission on Capital Punishment:

'A just and adequate doctrine of criminal responsibility cannot be founded on legal principles alone. Responsibility is a moral question; and there is no issue on which it is more important that the criminal law should be in close accord with the moral standards of the community. There can be no pre-established harmony between the criteria of moral and of criminal responsibility, but they ought to be made to approximate as nearly as possible.' [89]

The effect of recent legislation on the mentally abnormal offender, as of that on the juvenile offender, has been that a higher proportion of persons is now regarded as not legally responsible. Both of these trends may therefore be said to have resulted in a reduction in the incidence of criminal liability. But although as a result of these trends more mentally disordered persons charged with offences against the law may be found not to be responsible in law for their actions, this consequence can hardly be interpreted as a move towards the ultimate elimination of responsibility. Such legislation constitutes rather a clarification of the concept of responsibility and represents an attempt, prompted by advances in medical knowledge and changes in social attitudes, to reflect more faithfully in the criminal law the distinctions made by ordinary people as well as by specialists outside the law between those who are and those who are not responsible.

Chapter 3

The Young Offender

In an earlier age a child was regarded as a miniature and rather imperfect adult, and young children who broke the law were treated as criminals to be tried and punished for their crimes in the same way as adults. Today the traditional concepts of the criminal law are increasingly accepted as inappropriate to young offenders. 'Constructive training' and 'remedial treatment' are advocated as alternatives to 'punitive measures', and so it is argued that these ideas should replace the concept of criminal responsibility in dealing with the child, if not with the young adult offender. (The term 'child' is used throughout this chapter except where a distinction is necessary between those under fourteen who are 'children' for the purposes of this branch of the law and those of fourteen and under seventeen who are legally 'young persons'. 'Young adults' are those between seventeen and twenty-one.) The main problem is to examine the implications of new attitudes and new measures for the concept of criminal responsibility. How far can a distinction be maintained between 'punishment' and 'treatment', or between 'penal' and 'preventive' measures? To the extent that the line can be drawn, is the concept of responsibility superfluous? Or does it still fulfil a valuable if somewhat altered function of protecting personal liberty from the possibility of arbitrary executive action?

The problem is not, of course, confined to the young. An enlightened penal system attempts to apply positive and constructive measures to all offenders, adults as well as juveniles. The Criminal Justice Act 1948 declares that 'the purpose of training and treatment of convicted prisoners shall be to establish in them the will to lead a good and useful life on discharge, and to fit them to do so'.

But, for several reasons, the problem has arisen in an acute and striking form in the case of young offenders. Even apart from purely humanitarian considerations, there is clearly greater justification in their case for the use of remedial measures. Penalties which may be necessary for adults have proved ineffective, and the prospects of reclamation are greater at a more formative stage of development.

It is taken for granted in our own society that the legal system will necessarily make special provisions for children, just as it will make special provisions for those who because of some mental abnormality are not fully capable of managing their own affairs.

In all branches of the law the rules relating to infancy are partly designed to protect those not able to protect their own interests. An infant cannot, for example, be held to a contract into which he enters unless it falls into a class of recognised exceptions; he may make a binding contract for the supply of goods regarded as necessaries, or a beneficial contract of service; but outside this class a contract made by an infant may be void or voidable. [1] Thus an infant may find it difficult to borrow money, to obtain goods on hire purchase, or to buy a house. If the infant is to be protected the inevitable corollary is to deny him the equality before the law which is otherwise its fundamental principle and to deprive him of some of the advantages which it affords to the sane adult. In the law of tort, on the other hand, infancy as such is not a defence; but like all other defendants, an infant is not liable for a specific tort if it is shown that he lacked the required state of mind. Nor can he be sued if to hold him liable would indirectly bind him to a contract by which he would not otherwise be bound. The principle here is that he cannot be sued for improper performance of an act contemplated by such a contract; but he can be sued for an independent tort. [2] Subject to this single exception, however, it seems that an infant's liability in tort is determined on the same principles as are applicable to adults; and it will be shown that the same was true, until quite recently of the criminal law. There is also a notable disparity between the age of criminal responsibility, which is currently ten, and the position of the infant in the civil law, where before the Family Law Reform Act 1969 'infancy' ceased, and full responsibility was attained, only at the age of twenty-one. The Act reduced the age, for most purposes, to 18.

It may be said that no exact parallel is possible here because the rights conferred by the civil law are necessarily correlative to obligations so that the infant cannot have one without the other; whereas the criminal law consists primarily of obligations. But even in the criminal law there can be said to exist certain rights. The rights here include such procedural rights as are involved in, for example, the right to a fair trial and the right not to be arbitrarily deprived of one's liberty. Just as the infant is deprived by law of the benefits of certain civil transactions, so there is a danger that he may be deprived also of the safeguards of the normal criminal process. We must consider how far the reforms of the past decades, designed primarily to protect his interests, have contributed to this danger.

Criminal responsibility
The principle of equality before the law was reflected a hundred years
ago in the fact that the general principles of criminal responsibility
were, for the most part, applied indifferently to adults and children alike.
These general principles were taken to include the requirement that a
person could not be convicted of an offence unless at the time when the
act was done he had a guilty mind or *mens rea;* and they were taken to
include also an interpretation of guilt which made a necessary condition
of *mens rea* the capacity to distinguish between right and wrong. Thus
in the case of an adult a person was not and would not now be considered legally responsible for his actions if he did not know what he
was doing, and the offence required *mens rea;* nor would he be responsible although he knew quite well what he was doing if as a result of
some defect of reason he did not know that he was doing wrong. One
application of this principle is to be found in the formulation in the
M'Naghten Rules of the criteria of legal insanity which have already been
discussed. But these requirements were also relevant to the young
offender who was otherwise normal; for it is important to notice that
such special provisions as were made for children in the criminal law of
the nineteenth century were only incorporated into the law by reference
to the general principles of liability applicable to adults. These principles
do not recognise any exception on grounds of age, and infancy alone
did not exempt an offender from liability. Thus a child under the age
of seven was immune from conviction of a crime not simply because of
extreme youth, but on the ground that he was presumed by the law not
to be capable of having a guilty mind — to be *incapax doli.* Infancy in
itself was no defence, for even if a child was under seven, and therefore
below the age of criminal responsibility, he was not exempt simply on
grounds of infancy; he was deemed incapable of committing a crime
because there was an irrebuttable presumption that he did not have the
necessary *mens rea.* The absence of any automatic exemption of infants
from criminal liability is shown by the fact that at one time the presumption applied only to felonies — a fact vividly illustrated in the
incident recorded by one writer of a child of two being sentenced for a
misdemeanour as late as the nineteenth century to fine or imprisonment.[3]
It was not only in the principles of liability that the juvenile was in
the same position as the adult. There was in the case of a young
offender, too, the same clear-cut alternative between conviction and
acquittal, with their respective consequences; and the consequences of
either were the same as for an adult. If exempt from liability, for
example, through ignorance of right and wrong, the child was entitled
to an acquittal and there were no further steps that a court could take,

however much the child might be seen to be in need of care or protection.

Conviction on the other hand entailed liability to punishment for a young offender as for an adult; and the penalties inflicted on children were penalties designed for adult criminals. The punishment was fixed by law or determined within fixed limits by judicial discretion. If there was not a fixed penalty, the youth of the offender might be treated by the court as a mitigating factor; but often, especially in the case of the more serious offences, the penalty was mandatory, so that in practice the principle of equality before the law meant that children were liable to hanging, transportation or imprisonment on the same basis as adult criminals. Children were executed even for theft as late as the nineteenth century, and in 1849 over 10,000 children were sentenced to transportation.[4] If they escaped execution or transportation they were confined in the same penal institutions as adults. In 1844 there were in prison over 11,000 persons between the ages of ten and twenty. [5]

Only gradually in the course of the present century, has the situation improved. In 1907 the Probation of Offenders Act provided a means of reinforcing parental control in the child's own home through the agency of trained social workers. Shortly afterwards, by the Children Act 1908, the practice of sentencing children to imprisonment was abolished; and the same enactment instituted the first juvenile courts. These courts, sitting at a different time or place from the ordinary courts, their proceedings attended by fewer formalities and less publicity, and staffed to some extent by magistrates with special experience of juvenile offenders, have adapted the ordinary procedures of the criminal law to the special needs of the young. A child under fourteen on a charge of any offence except homicide must be tried summarily in the juvenile court, unless he is charged jointly with an adult, when special rules apply. A young person over fourteen but under seventeen may be tried summarily for an indictable offence if he consents and if the prosecution and the court agree; but he has the right, like an adult, to be tried by jury at assizes or quarter sessions, and the court may if it thinks fit send him for trial. After the institution of juvenile courts the greatest step forward was taken with the Children and Young Persons Act 1933, which though substantially modified by the Acts of 1963 and 1969, remains the principal legislation in this field; the implications of some of the main provisions of these Acts are considered in detail in the following pages.

The 1933 Act enshrined the principle that the court should have regard to the welfare of the child, and subsequent legislation has been largely directed to improving the methods available for dealing with young offenders. The borstal system had been recognised for this purpose since the beginning of the century, and in 1948 detention centres and attendance centres were introduced with a view to replacing the use of imprisonment for the young offender. By section 17 of the Criminal Justice Act 1948, no person under seventeen could be sentenced to imprisonment by a court of summary jurisdiction, or by a court of assize or quarter sessions if under fifteen; and no court was to impose imprisonment on any person under twenty-one unless the court was of the opinion that no other method of dealing with him was appropriate; in order to answer this question, the court was to obtain and consider information about the circumstances, taking into account anything relevant to his character and his physical and mental condition. This policy was continued by subsequent legislation. The Magistrates' Courts Act 1952, laid down by section 107 (2) that a magistrates' court should not impose imprisonment on any person under seventeen. Section 107 (4) provided for the eventual prohibition of the imprisonment of persons up to twenty-one by magistrates' courts when the Home Secretary was satisfied that adequate alternative methods of dealing with them were available. Finally, the Criminal Justice Act 1961 completely abolished imprisonment for anyone under seventeen; for those aged seventeen to twenty-one it restricted imprisonment to sentences of up to six months or more than three years ; and it contained provision for the abolition by order of sentences of up to six months.

It is only in the context of these reforms in methods of dealing with juvenile delinquency that we can usefully examine the controversial question of the age of criminal responsibility and its significance for the nature of criminal responsibility in general. We have seen that at common law children below the age of seven were deemed incapable of committing a crime. In an earlier period the age was as high as twelve,[6] but after some fluctuations it was finally settled at seven probably through the influence of Coke. [7] The apparent arbitrariness of this age was not mitigated by the fact that it was shared by the Roman law and Canon law, and was scarcely qualified by the decision to raise the age to eight in 1933. The Children and Young Persons Act 1933 provided that 'it shall be conclusively presumed that no child under the age of eight years can be guilty of an offence.' [8] The Ingleby Committee which examined the question in 1960 recommended that the age of criminal responsibility should be raised to twelve with the possibility of raising it to thirteen or fourteen at a later date.[9] An attempt was made in the House of Lords on the initiative of Lady Wootton to incorporate this recommendation against the advice of the government into the Children and Young Persons Act 1963; the result was a compromise by which the age was raised from eight to ten. The effects of the 1969 Act on the age of responsibility are examined below.

But the age of criminal responsibility cannot be considered in isolation; for children below this age could still be brought before the juvenile court in the exercise of its civil jurisdiction if they were beyond control or in need of care or protection. It is important to note that in such cases, although the child is exempt from criminal proceedings, nevertheless the evidence that he is beyond control or in need of care and protection may well be evidence of substantially the same type as would in the case of an older child amount to evidence of crime. For other reasons too, which will shortly be mentioned, some consideration of the civil powers of the juvenile courts is essential to an appreciation of the juvenile's criminal liability.

Civil proceedings

The civil procedure of the courts in regard to neglected children dates from 1857, when the first Industrial Schools Act was passed. Its provisions were amended in 1866 and further amended by the Children Act 1908. Section 58 of the 1908 Act empowered a court of summary jurisdiction to send to an industrial school a child under the age of fourteen who fell within one of certain categories. They included children who were found begging; or 'wandering and having no parent, or a parent or guardian who does not exercise proper guardianship'; or who were destitute; or whose parents had criminal or drunken habits or were in prison; or who were associating with reputed thieves or common prostitutes. Further, parents could themselves apply to the court to have their child sent to an industrial school. The powers of the juvenile courts are now governed by the Children and Young Persons Act 1933, but were altered and somewhat extended by amending statutes and by the Acts of 1963 and 1969.

Children and young persons brought before the court by their parents or guardians as beyond their control could be removed, with their parent's consent, from their homes under section 64 of the 1933 Act and sent to an appropriate establishment. Alternatively, a child or young person could be brought before the courts under section 62 of the Act by the local authority, by the police, or by an authorised person if there were reasonable grounds for believing that he was in need of care and protection. He might be regarded as in need of care and protection under section 61 if, having no parent or guardian, or one who failed to exercise proper care or guardianship, he was falling into bad associations, or was exposed to moral danger, or was beyond control; or if certain offences, including sexual offences, had been committed. In these 'care and protection' cases, appropriate treatment might be ordered even against the wishes of the parent or guardian.

Finally, persistent truancy could bring a child before the juvenile court, even though no offence had been committed. If a parent had failed to comply with a school attendance order, the court which had convicted the parent could, under section 40 (3) of the Education Act 1944 as amended, direct the local education authority to bring the child before the juvenile court. It could do so also if satisfied that the child had failed to attend the school at which he was a registered pupil, whether it convicted the parents or not. Further, where the local authority was satisfied that such a step was necessary to secure the child's regular attendance, it could of its own motion bring the child to the juvenile court. Whether the child was brought at the direction of the court before which the parent had appeared, or by the education authority of their own motion, the court, if it considered it necessary to do so to secure the child's regular attendance at school, could make any order it had power to make in regard to a child in need of care and protection.

Thus, the difference between the civil and criminal cases was never so pronounced as it might at first sight appear. In practice the factors which brought children within the civil jurisdiction of the court were very similar to the factors which led to delinquency. As one writer has summarised the position,

'The commission of an offence is frequently a symptom of the delinquent's need of care and protection, and the moral danger of those brought before the courts as beyond control or in need of care and protection is often greater than that of those accused of some minor offence. While truancy might at first sight seem unconnected with juvenile crime, experienced magistrates have stressed the close relationship between it and delinquency. Truancy at the least gives the young child time to get into mischief; at the worst it is a sign that something is wrong, either with the child himself or with his home, and is a warning that something must be put right. It is reasonable, therefore, that such cases should fall within jurisdiction of the Juvenile Courts.[10]

Important changes in the civil jurisdiction of the juvenile courts were introduced by the Children and Young Persons Act 1963. Section 2 of the Act widened the definition of a juvenile in need of care or protection under the 1933 Act with the object of including children under ten who, under the old law, might have been charged with offences. The category was also renamed: 'care or protection' has been abolished in favour of 'care, protection or control'. The definition of children and young persons 'in need of care, protection or control' in this section includes two classes of case. The first corresponds to that of children and young persons who, under the 1933 Act, were found in need of care or protection. Under the later Act two conditions must be satisfied if a child or young person is to be found in the first class of those in need of care, protection or control. First, it must be found that he is not receiving such care, protection and guidance as a good parent may reasonably be expected to give. Secondly, one of the other conditions set out in the Act must be satisfied; for example, that he is falling into bad associations or is exposed to moral danger, as under the 1933 Act.[11] The second class of children and young persons in need of care, protection or control comprises any child or young person who is beyond the control of his parent or guardian.[12] The parent, however, is deprived of his power to initiate proceedings; instead, under section 3, he may request the local authority to do so. Alternatively, proceedings may be brought by the police or by an authorised person.

Again, the two categories of children cannot be kept entirely separate. There is no great difference in practice between children who are beyond control and those who are neglected or in need of care or protection for other reasons; and by its new classification the 1963 Act appears to recognise explicitly what was implied in the 1933 Act. An experienced magistrate has written that 'so far as concerns the adolescent, particularly the adolescent girl, there is often little in the facts to distinguish a child said to be "beyond control" from another who is said to be "falling into bad associations or exposed to moral danger." More often than not, the two things go together. ... Whether, under the 1963 Act, a boy or girl who runs away from home and gets into trouble is brought to the court as being beyond control or in moral danger is often fortuitous; as indeed it was under the 1933 Act where the wording of section 61 enabled the authorities to proceed on either ground.'[13]

Similarly, the distinction between the delinquent and the non-delinquent child is disappearing, and the 1969 Act, considered below, takes the process further; but it will be seen that some aspects of the distinction still survive and that its partial retention can be justified even in modern conditions and after the adoption of more enlightened policies.

In fact the processes for dealing with young offenders represent an undisguised compromise. While the old principle of equal responsibility has long been abandoned, to a considerable extent the concept of criminal responsibility has nevertheless been preserved. Although there are some important respects in which the trial of a young offender differs from that of an adult, there are also significant differences between the civil and criminal procedures of the juvenile courts. Against the advice of the Ingleby Committee, the presumption that a child under fourteen is *incapax doli* still exists, and the prosecution still has to go through the form of showing that the child knew he was doing wrong. This requirement is the clearest indication of a punitive conception of the law's function, since the need for remedial measures would presumably be all the greater in cases where it was not satisfied. The prosecution must also produce evidence, in such a case, of the child's state of mind at the time of the offence; it is not permissible, as it may sometimes be on a charge against an adult, to infer *mens rea* from the circumstances of the case. In some respects, it is true, the penal approach was modified. Thus, under the Children and Young Persons Act 1933, the terms 'conviction' and 'sentence' were replaced in the juvenile courts by the terms 'finding of guilt' and 'order made upon such finding'. Further, under the 1963 Act, such findings do not count towards the criminal record of an adult. Section 16 (2) provides that, in any proceedings for an offence committed or alleged to be committed by a person of twenty-one or over, any offence of which he was found guilty while under fourteen should be disregarded for the purposes of any evidence relating to his previous convictions. However, both of these provisions still imply a distinction between civil and criminal proceedings.

In a criminal case, the commission of an offence must be proved beyond reasonable doubt. Although on a finding of guilt the court is directed to act with regard to the child's welfare, he is still entitled to the protection which the criminal law affords to the adult. Only if he is proved guilty can the court exercise its powers. Where a child is alleged to be in need of care, protection or control under section 2 of the 1963 Act the allegation need only be established on the balance of probabilities. The implications for the concept of criminal responsibility of the 1969 Act, and of the surviving distinctions between the civil and the criminal jurisdictions of the courts, are examined at the end of this chapter.

Apart from these distinctions, which are primarily procedural matters designed to protect the child's rights, there is now little difference of approach to a civil or criminal case. We shall see that with the increasing similarity in the forms of treatment available, the difference between measures which might be described as 'treatment' and measures which might be described as 'punishment' depends largely on the intention with which the measures are imposed and on the attitudes of those concerned; and the objects which the courts have in mind are now broadly similar whether the proceedings are civil or criminal. The Departmental Committee on the Treatment of Young Offenders observed as long ago as 1927 that 'there is little or no difference in character and needs between the neglected and the delinquent child. It is often a mere accident whether he is brought before the court because he was wandering or beyond control, or because he has committed some offence. Neglect leads to delinquency.'[14]

Accordingly it recommended that the principle of guardianship should

F

be at the root of all juvenile court procedure. The Act of 1933 implemented this recommendation by providing a general principle to guide
the courts whether acting in the exercise of their civil or criminal jurisdiction: 'Every court in dealing with a child or young person who is
brought before it, either as being in need of care and protection or as an
offender or otherwise, shall have regard to the welfare of the child or
young person and shall in a proper case take steps for removing him
from undesirable surroundings, and securing that proper provision is
made for his education and training.'[15] Nor is this assimilation surprising;
for clearly an offender on the one hand may be in need of remedial
treatment, while one of the primary aims of the civil jurisdiction is to
obviate the need for any subsequent criminal proceedings. It is therefore to be expected that the methods used by the courts in dealing with
juvenile offenders closely resemble those used for non-delinquent
children. These methods must be analysed in some detail if we are to
appreciate their full significance for the concept of criminal responsibility
in its application to young offenders.

Methods of treatment
In considering the wide range of measures available to the juvenile courts,
we shall be able to detect six significant features. The first, and most
important feature, which has already been referred to, is the great similarity between the measures available for the offender and for the non-
offender. We may say at this stage, to anticipate our conclusions, that
before the 1969 Act there were five measures available for dealing with
the juvenile offender which were not available, or not available in a similar form, in the case of the non-offender. The non-offender could not be
fined; he could not be sent to a remand home *as a punishment* under
section 54 of the 1933 Act, although he could be sent there for other
purposes; and he could not be sent to an attendance centre, to a detention centre, or to borstal. The 1969 Act, as will be seen, carries the
process of assimilation much further. |

Secondly, there is the emphasis which is placed on the positive
objects of the forms of training available for all children. Thus we shall
see that the object of borstal training, which was confined to offenders,
has always been regarded as remedial rather than punitive. But it will
also be suggested that there are difficulties both in theory and in practice in classifying institutions on this basis; and we shall ask how far any
distinction between treatment and punishment can now be maintained.

Thirdly there must be considered the problem of selecting the appropriate institution. It will appear that this task has to some extent
been taken away from the courts. This indeed is a natural consequence

of the new approach. The problem arises at two stages. There is the initial selection, where if it is to be made in the light of the child's needs rather than on the basis of his offence, a classifying centre of some type may be better equipped than a court; and there is the need to leave open the possibility of transferring him to another institution, which can only be done in the light of his response to training.

A fourth and closely connected consideration is the principle of the indeterminate sentence. Here again there has been an increasing tendency to deprive the court of the power to impose a sentence of pre-determined length; and again the chief justification is that the appropriate term cannot be decided in advance. A further argument is that if a fixed sentence cannot terminate before a known date (and the objection to the indeterminate sentence is precisely that a person ought to know when he can expect his release) then it provides him with little incentive to respond to training.

A fifth factor to be taken into account in an examination of the antithesis between treatment and punishment is the system of after-care. After-care is now regarded as a vital part of the system of training provided by prisons, borstals, detention centres and approved schools, and has been considerably extended in accordance with the provisions of the Criminal Justice Act 1961. This is extremely significant, since it will be seen that the system, like the comparable system of probation, was previously regarded as incompatible with any sentence that was considered punitive rather than remedial.

Finally, it is important to consider the liability to recall of the juvenile who has been released from custody. If it were possible to pursue the distinction between punitive and remedial measures, liability to recall would be the clearest sign of the latter, since unless recall is to be regarded simply as a penalty imposed without recourse to the court, it can only amount to an indication that the 'cure' is after all incomplete and further 'treatment' necessary. In either case, it entails the greatest departure from the traditional function of the court as the sole authority for less of liberty.

Where a child or young person is found to have committed an offence the court could, before the 1969 Act, simply make a probation order. Such an order might be made only to a probation officer and might be for any period of not less than one and not more than three years. Where he was found to be in need of care, protection or control the court could make a supervision order, placing him under the supervision of a probation officer or of some other person appointed for the purpose for a period not exceeding three years. Although the legal provisions differed, the practical consequences in both cases were substantially similar. Thus, a probation order, although it could be imposed compulsorily on a child, required the prior consent of a young person, while a supervision order did not require consent in any circumstances, unless in the case of a young person it was to contain a requirement as to residence or mental treatment. If probation proved ineffective and the officer felt that in the probationer's interest some alternative form of treatment was desirable, such as training in an approved school, he had to prove that the probationer had committed a breach of one of the requirements of the order. If he could not prove a breach, the court had no powers. But no duties were imposed on the juvenile under a supervision order. Nevertheless, the sanction in both cases was in effect the same, for by section 66 (1) of the 1933 Act the supervisor was empowered to bring him before the court whenever it appeared necessary in his interests to do so, and the court might then send him to an approved school or commit him to the care of a fit person. Alternatively, under the 1963 Act, it might permit the order to continue but bind over the parent or guardian to exercise proper care and guardianship. [16]

It is significant that to justify committal to a fit person or approved school, or the binding over of the parent or guardian, there was no need for the supervisor to prove that the child in his care had committed an offence or acted in any particular way. As one authority said, 'The court is concerned with the interests of the child or young person, and his conduct is only one of many matters to be considered. If his conduct be exemplary but his associations and environment bad, it may be in his interests to be sent away.' [17] Thus, a child who had committed no offence but was placed under supervision as being in need of care, protection or control, was subject to the same restraints as a child who had committed an offence and had been put on probation.

The same was true where a child was sent away by the court to a probation home or hostel. If the child had to be removed from home for a short period, then again there was little difference between the offender and the subject of guardian proceedings. In the former case the probation order might require residence in a probation home or hostel. In the latter case the supervision order might contain a provision for such residence. In both cases he was subject during his period of residence, which was for a maximum of twelve months, to supervision by a probation officer or, in the case of a supervision order, by the person charged with the duty of supervision. In both cases again no requirement of residence might be imposed on a young person who did not voluntarily accept it.

Similar considerations were evident in the use of the remand home. The three classes of children and young persons who might be brought before the juvenile courts, namely, offenders, children in need or care, protection or control, and truants, might all be sent to a remand home. Before the Children Act 1908, there was no provision for the accommodation of juveniles on remand or awaiting disposal except prison. The 1908 Act required the provision of 'places of detention', superseded under the 1933 Act by 'remand homes'. The 1933 Act also introduced a new form of punitive detention by providing that children and young persons might be committed to the custody of a remand home for a term not exceeding one month, but only in cases where an adult could be sent to prison and only where no other method of treatment was considered suitable.[18] But a child or young person in need of care, protection or control, might be sent to a remand home for a number of purposes, but might not be sent there as a punishment. Again a distinction seems to be implicit between punishment and what might be described as mere custody. But here too the practical application of the distinction created difficulties and it too has been affected by the 1969 reforms, discussed below. It has been found undesirable to mix offenders who are undergoing punishment with juveniles who are in the home for care and protection, while they await hearing by a juvenile court, or further observation. The Care of Children Committee (the Curtis Committee) recommended in 1946 that no children should be sent to a remand home for punishment,[19] and the system was substantially modified by the 1969 Act,

There remained, however, alternative methods of detention for young offenders which did appear to imply a distinction between punitive and non-punitive measures. For these measures were confined to offenders, and could not be imposed by a court on a child in need of care, protection, or control. Even here, however, we shall see that the distinction could never be fully preserved.

Two new forms of detention for youthful offenders were introduced by the Criminal Justice Act of 1948. First, detention centres were introduced for those between fourteen and twenty-one.[20] These were intended to replace custody in remand homes and it was also hoped, in accordance with the general policy of the Act, to reduce the number of young offenders committed to prison. The period of detention was ordinarily three months, and no one might be committed there if he had already served a term of imprisonment of six months or more or had undergone a period of borstal training. When these proposals were introduced the regime was described as one of brisk discipline and hard work, both mental and physical, and was meant to be a short, sharp reminder to offenders that they were getting into ways that would land them in disaster.[21] Experience showed, however, that it was possible, even in the short period of detention which the offender served, to include some positive form of training. [22]

The second innovation was the attendance centre [23] for those between twelve and twenty-one (the minimum age has since been lowered to ten)[24] who had been found guilty of a breach of probation or of an offence for which an adult could be imprisoned. They might be ordered to attend one of the attendance centres for a number of hours not normally exceeding twelve, the object being to deprive them of their leisure without depriving them of their liberty. It is questionable, however, whether the purpose of the attendance centre could be described as one of punishment or of treatment. A rule made under the Act provided that 'the occupation and instruction given at a centre shall be such as to occupy persons attending there . . . in a manner conducive to health of mind and body.' [25] Similarly, in the case of detention centres, it was said that, while the living conditions in such centres might be better than those in prisons, the regime would certainly be more exacting.

The controversy as to the purpose of the attendance centres was summarised by one writer as follows :

'Opinions vary upon what the nature and underlying purpose of the treatment should be. Lord Templewood described it as a "short sharp punishment". Earlier in the debate he had said its object was "to deprive young offenders of a half-holiday, to prevent their going to a football match or a cinema and, perhaps not less important, to make them ridiculous to their friends and relations." Some people, including many magistrates, think that in an attendance centre the emphasis should be mainly upon punishment, the discipline should be of the strictest, and the tasks uncongenial. There are others who claim that the emphasis should be mainly upon reformation; they would like to see the statutory maximum period of detention as high as possible and have suggested thirty-six hours – the object being to give time for the reformative influences of the attendance centre to be brought to bear. My own view lies between these extremes, with a strong leaning towards the punitive purpose. I am fully in agreement with the Ingleby Committee when they recommended that "the main purpose of attendance centres is to impose punishment through loss of leisure", and that twelve hours were enough.' [26]

The fact that detention centres and attendance centres were nevertheless regarded as forms of punishment was well illustrated by one unfortunate consequence of this attitude, that it rendered impossible any effective system of compulsory after-care. From the point of view of the antithesis between 'punishment' and 'treatment', it will be seen that one of the most significant features of both approved school training and borstal training, to be discussed shortly, was the system of after-care, which clearly seems to presuppose a 'remedial' approach, and was not available in conjunction with 'punishment'. Some courts tried to circumvent this difficulty where a person had committed two offences by making a detention order on one offence and imposing a probation order in respect of the other offence. But section 3 of the Criminal Justice Act 1948, clearly envisaged probation as an alternative to any form of punishment; in 1958 the Court of Criminal Appeal finally ruled that the practice was not permissible, [27] and after-care was altogether excluded. This defect in the scheme was finally remedied by the Criminal Justice Act 1961, which provided for compulsory supervision for a period of twelve months after the date of release, during which time failure to comply with the requirements of supervision would render the offender liable to recall. [28] After January 1964, when the provisions for after-care became effective, every person committed to a detention centre was on his release subject to supervision for twelve months by such society or person as the Prison Department might direct, and had to comply with any requirements they made. If he responded to supervision the Prison Department might shorten the period or modify the requirements. If he failed to respond, they might recall him to the detention centre for such part of the period of detention ordered by the court as was remitted for good conduct, or for fourteen days, whichever was the longer. It has already been suggested that the provisions for recall, envisaging as they do a further period of detention without the authorisation of the court (and a period which may be longer, although only fractionally, than that originally ordered by the court), constituted the most significant departure from the traditional division of functions. They might be described as establishing in effect a system of probation without reference to the courts.

Again, there might be little difference, even before the 1969 Act, between the offender and the non-offender where a long term remedy away from home was thought necessary; here the court might make a fit person order or an approved school order. A fit person order committed the child to the care of a private individual or more usually a local authority. Quite apart from committal by the court, a local authority was obliged by section 1 of the Children Act 1948, to receive into care any child in its area under seventeen who had no parent, or whose parent was prevented from looking after him properly, or who was abandoned or lost. Section 5 of the Children Act 1948, obliged the local authority to accept any child a court might desire to place in its care by a fit person order. The general duty of the authority towards a child in care was 'to exercise their powers with respect to him so as to further his best interests, and to afford him opportunity for a proper development of his character and abilities.' The powers and responsibilities of the local authority were the same whether the child was a delinquent or a non-offender; and they were the same whether the child had been committed under a fit person order by a court, or had been received into care under section 1.

Alternatively the child might be sent to an approved school. Approved schools were the descendants of the earlier reformatories and industrial schools of the nineteenth century and were so called before the 1933 Act. However, the courts had long been empowered to commit children to these institutions and in 1908 the Children Act placed the schools under the supervision of a special department of the Home Office.

As to the form of training, approved schools differed greatly among themselves, and an important task was to find a school which would provide the most suitable training. The appropriate school might be selected by a special classifying school and it is important to notice that whereas at one time the selection of an approved school was entirely a matter for the court, it later had little say in determining what form of treatment the child would receive. Before 1963 the approved school selected by the court had to be specified in the committal order; but after 1942 instead of naming the school the court might simply commit the child to a school 'to be named', and then forward particulars of the juvenile to the Home Office. The Home Office would then select a suitable school and later the court would endorse its name on the committal order. The 1963 Act provided that the name of the approved school should no longer be stated in any order of the court; the order was merely for detention in an approved school. The responsibility for this choice was that of the classifying school, if there was one; if not, of the Home Secretary.

Further, the court had no power to specify any period of training; the date of release was determined by the managers of the school, though no one might be released in the first six months without the consent of the Home Secretary. There were also maximum periods: for those under fifteen, three years or until four months after their fifteenth birthday, whichever was the longer; and for those over fifteen, three years or until their nineteenth birthday, whichever was the shorter; in practice a juvenile rarely remained for the maximum statutory period. The significance of the indeterminate sentence is discussed further below.

Again it is necessary to observe that the two principal classes of case where such orders could be made before the 1969 Act were, first, where the juvenile had been found guilty of an offence punishable in the case of an adult by imprisonment, or, secondly, on a finding that he was in need of care, protection or control.

When a juvenile was released from an approved school, the managers were responsible for his supervision for two years from the date of his release or until he reached twenty-one, whichever was the shorter period. In the meantime he had to live where the managers directed. If his progress was unsatisfactory, and he was under nineteen, they might recall him to the school for further training until the expiry of the full statutory period of detention or for six months from the date of recall, whichever was the later. At the end of the period of supervision they might, at his request, give him further assistance, so providing a further measure of after-care after his release from the school. If he had no satisfactory home to return to, they had to arrange for him to enter a hostel or had to find lodgings for him; and if he was over school-leaving age they had to try to find him a job.

Perhaps the only principal method of dealing with young offenders which is confined to offenders yet acknowledged to be non-punitive was borstal training. As long ago as 1902 Rochester Prison at borstal was turned into an institution for boys, but borstal training did not become a separate feature of the penal system until the enactment of Part I of the Prevention of Crime Act 1908. By section 20 of the Criminal Justice Act 1948, when a person had been convicted on indictment of an offence punishable by imprisonment, then if he was not less than sixteen and under twenty-one, the court might pass a sentence of borstal training in place of any other sentence, provided the court was satisfied that it was expedient to do so for his reformation and for the prevention of crime. In coming to this conclusion the court would have regard to the offender's character and previous conduct and to the circumstances of the offence. A magistrates' court could not generally sentence to borstal but had normally to commit to assizes or quarter sessions with a recommendation for borstal. They had first to be satisfied 'having regard to the circumstances of the offence and after taking into account the offender's character and previous conduct, that it is expedient that he be detained for training for not less than six months.'[29] The minimum age was lowered to fifteen by the Criminal Justice Act 1961, but an offender under seventeen may not be sent to borstal unless the court is satisfied that no other method of dealing with him is appropriate. The 1969 Act envisages the eventual abolition of borstal for those under seventeen.

It has been said that the purpose of borstal is training rather than punishment. We have already seen that the system is described as training and that the purpose of sending the young offender for such training is 'for his reformation and for the prevention of crime'. Further guidance is given by the Borstal Rules: 'The objects of training shall be to bring to bear every influence which may establish in the inmates the will to lead a good and useful life on release, and to fit them to do so by the fullest possible development of their character, capacities, and sense of personal responsibility.' [30] But even here no clear distinction can be draw between punitive and non-punitive measures. Borstal training, which is supposed to be corrective training rather than punishment, with provisio for vocational training and encouragement of outside activities, still involves compulsory separation from home and friends, considerable loss of liberty, and so forth; and it is, of course, as we have seen, unlike other non-punitive measures, confined to offenders. The difficulty of drawing a distinction in practice was well illustrated by the problem of classifying borstal institutions and young prisoners' centres. Closed borstals, it is clear, necessarily involve punishment, whereas young offenders in prison were given remedial and educational treatment. It was said that 'The regime in these prison centres has been based on borstal principles so far as is compatible with the security and atmosphere of a prison. It includes industrial training for those with long enough sentences; physical, mental and moral education; and personal attention from the staff, including assistant governors who fill a similar role to that of borstal housemasters.' [31]

The Advisory Council on the Treatment of Offenders argued in 1959 that

'If it is accepted that the regime provided for young offenders should in all cases be remedial and educational, and should be carried out in institutions separate from ordinary prisons, it is in principle no longer necessary for the law to provide a separate form of sentence, such as the borstal sentence, to secure those ends. The present system of two forms of sentence makes for difficulties which are unnecessary and tend to hinder rather than help the training of young offenders as a whole. Some young persons are sentenced to borstal training whose needs could better be met by the type of regime provided at a young prisoners' centre, and some are sentenced to imprisonment who would benefit from the type of training provided at a borstal institution. It is also impossible to make the most advantageous and economical use of the establishments available.' [32]

Accordingly the Criminal Justice Act 1961, placed restrictions on the imprisonment of young offenders which have already been described and at the same time established the borstal system as the principal form of medium-term institutional treatment for offenders between the ages of seventeen and twenty-one, as well as for those aged fifteen and sixteen who are not considered suitable for committal to an approved school.

The type of training provided in borstal institutions, however, still varies from one borstal to another, as in the case of approved schools; and here too the need arises of selecting the appropriate borstal. They vary from the open borstal making available a wide range of outside activities to the correction centre for those whom the training borstals have been unable to control. The job of classification which could be done in the case of approved schools by the classifying school already mentioned, may be done in the case of borstal by the borstal reception centre.

The maximum borstal sentence has been reduced from three to two years but the Prison Department may in their discretion release a trainee earlier, subject to his remaining under supervision for two years from the date of release. The period he spends in the training borstal is decided by the Prison Department in the light of his progress and training and of his apparent readiness to return to normal life.

Supervision after the boy (or girl) leaves borstal is undertaken by the Central After-Care Association. They do this work on behalf of the Prison Department and are answerable to it. On discharge a boy is helped to find work, the necessary tools, and if he has no home somewhere to live. Supervision continues as long as required up to two years and if necessary he is liable to recall.

We have now surveyed the wide range of measures available to the courts for dealing with children whether as offenders or otherwise. We have seen that the law and administration in this field starts from some conception of a distinction between punitive and non-punitive measures. Sometimes punishment and treatment are contrasted; sometimes punishment and other measures are simply regarded as different forms of treatment. We have seen also that especially with recent developments in this field the distinction has become increasingly difficult to maintain either in theory or in practice. The conclusion must be that any attempt to classify the law's function in this area at least in terms of a distinction between punitive and remedial measures is necessarily over-simplified and is likely to distort a description of the actual operation of the system. In the final chapter the further implications of this distinction, which have a general importance outside the area of juvenile delinquency, are more fully examined.

The elimination of responsibility

The reforms which have been so far analysed in methods of dealing with juvenile delinquents have operated within the framework of the criminal law, adapting it to the special requirements of the young, and providing greater flexibility. Past reforms may be said to have substituted a principle of modified responsibility for the nineteenth-century principle of equal responsibility. But recent proposals have gone far beyond this. What has been envisaged in some proposals is the total abolition of the criminal liability of the young. These proposals, which clearly have far-reaching implications for the concept of responsibility, must now be considered in outline.

Briefly, it can be said that these proposals have been advanced in two principal forms, one an extreme, and one a more moderate form. In its extreme form, the proposal is to abolish the juvenile courts altogether, and to transfer their functions to the welfare services administered by the central and local government. In its less extreme form, the proposal is to retain the juvenile courts but to abolish their criminal jurisdiction by raising the age of criminal responsibility at any rate to the minimum age of leaving school.

A proposal of the latter type was advanced by one authority, Sir William Clarke Hall, as long ago as 1926:

'Juvenile courts should have power to assume.guardianship over all children who have either committed offences or are living under conditions likely to lead them into delinquency or immorality. The courts in the exercise of such guardianship would have full powers of placing their wards under the care of a probation officer, sending them to certified schools, or transferring their custody to others. This guardianship would continue until the age of 16, or until his improved conduct or circumstances justified his liberation. Under such a system no delinquent child would be "convicted" of a "crime", but he would be a wrongdoer whose conduct had necessitated a stricter supervision and in some cases punishment, whilst the child whose parents had been unable or unwilling to exercise proper control over him would be given a new parental authority with full power to secure such control.' [33]

It will be observed that although Clarke Hall was prepared to assimilate the civil and criminal jurisdiction of the juvenile courts, he did not propose to exclude from that jurisdiction the punishment of a young wrongdoer in an appropriate case.

Proposals of this type were examined by the Departmental Committee on the Treatment of Young Offenders which reported in 1927. [34] Comparison was made with the American system of juvenile courts, which were older than their English counterparts but which had operated from the beginning under what was described as a 'Chancery procedure' rather than as criminal courts and aimed at the protection rather than the punishment of the child. There was also available the precedent of the New Zealand Child Welfare Act of 1925, which provided that when a child was brought before a Children's Court charged with an offence, it should not be necessary for the court to hear and determine the charge, but it could act after taking into consideration the child's environment, history, mentality, and so on.

Reforms of this kind were rejected by the Committee on two grounds. It was argued first that there are occasions on which the alleged offender pleads his innocence, and that he should have an opportunity of establishing this. Secondly it was said that if a serious offence were proved against a young person, it was desirable that its seriousness should be brought home to him in order to induce a respect for the law.

These proposals were therefore rejected. Instead, the Committee compromised. They proposed to retain the criminal jurisdiction of the juvenile courts, but they made three recommendations, all of them implemented by the 1933 Act, which had the effect of modifying the borderline between civil and criminal cases. First, they advocated raising the age of criminal responsibility by one year from seven to eight. Secondly, they recommended an extension of the civil jurisdiction of the juvenile court; sections 62 and 64 of the Act, which have already been referred to, were based on the Committee's proposals. Finally, as we have seen, the Committee proposed that the principle of guardianship should be at the root of all juvenile court proceedings.

This principle has had great influence on the criminal jurisdiction of the juvenile courts and much subsequent legislation has been concerned, as we have seen, to apply the same principle to the treatment of juvenile offenders. In all these ways the criminal jurisdiction of the courts has been increasingly modified, until in 1960 the Ingleby Committee recognised that existing methods of dealing with juvenile delinquency represented a compromise between a legal apparatus and a welfare service. It recommended that this compromise should continue, although with some further adjustment in the balance between the two. The juvenile court system would be retained, but greater power would be conferred on local authorities; they would be empowered to assist a family in difficulties either in cash or in kind. In this way it was hoped that some progress might be made in the prevention of delinquency. At the same time the Committee recommended that the age of criminal responsibility should be raised to twelve with the possibility of raising it to thirteen or fourteen later. This recommendation, however, as we have seen, was not accepted.

In spite of these recommendations, the Committee's Report and the subsequent legislation presupposed a distinction between the functions of the court and those of the social services. The juvenile courts thus retain in England their traditional role of independence of the welfare agencies. It is the responsibility of the executive to provide the services of which the court can make use; but it is the function of the court to protect the individual against unwarranted intervention by the executive and it is significant in this connexion that the probation officer is responsible primarily to the court.

In Scotland, a less compromising approach was adopted by the Kilbrandon Committee, constituted to advise the Secretary of State for Scotland on the treatment of young offenders. In their Report, published

in 1964, the Committee argued that a court of law was not an appropriate method of dealing with juvenile delinquency, whatever its value
as a safeguard of individual liberty. The Committee's conclusions are
epitomised in the following extracts from its Report:

'Ultimately the question must be decided on practical grounds. Delinquency is
predominantly an activity of the young. On purely practical grounds it would
therefore appear that emphasis ought to be given to preventive and remedial
measures at the earliest possible stage if more serious delinquencies are not to
develop. That implies above all the application of an educative principle . . .

The task . . . calls for skills quite different from those involved in adjudicating
legal issues and it is quite inappropriate that the new body should be expected
to combine the two functions.

It must finally be a matter of judgment how far . . . the application of an
educative principle would in fact and in practice represent an appreciable inroad
into personal and family life, amounting to loss of liberty or freedom from inter-
ference such as to be unacceptable in our society. For our part we do not believe
that a retention of the present system . . . is susceptible of modification in any
way which would seem likely to make any real impact on the problem.' [35]

Accordingly, the Report recommended the abolition of juvenile
courts and their replacement by specialised agencies or 'panels' whose
function would not be to adjudicate on any question of guilt or innocence. but solely to determine the appropriate treatment. The Committee
found that in approximately 95 per cent of cases coming before the
juvenile courts in Scotland, there was no dispute as to the facts alleged,
those concerned pleading guilty. Only in 5 per cent of the cases did
those concerned plead not guilty so that the case proceeded to trial. In
the light of these findings, the Committee proposed a procedure whereby
juvenile offenders would in all cases be brought before a specialised
agency whose sole concern would be the measures to be applied:

'on what amounts to an agreed referral. Under such a procedure, on appearance
the child and his parents would be asked whether they fully understood the
nature of the allegation and in the parents' presence the child would then be
asked whether or not he admitted to having done the acts alleged. If this was
admitted, the agency would then proceed to deal with the child. If the child
denied the act in question, action by the agency would be stayed, and the case
would immediately be referred to the Sheriff Court, which would thereupon
have jurisdiction to determine under criminal procedure the disputed allegation
of fact. Where the Court found the facts established, the case would thereupon
revert to the agency, which would then be empowered to consider measures of
treatment in the same way as on an 'agreed' case. The agency would thus exercise
jurisdiction only on the basis of facts established by admission of the child in the
parents' presence and with their agreement, or after an adjudication by a court
of law. It would have no concern whatsoever with the determination of legal

issues, its sole function being the consideration and application of training measures appropriate to the child's needs. Such an agency would clearly not be a criminal court of law, or indeed a court in any accepted sense. It would be the duly constituted public agency authorised to deal with juvenile offenders, where necessary by the application of compulsory measures. Within the range of methods authorised by law, it would have the widest discretion in their application appropriate to the needs of the individual child, who would thereafter remain within its jurisdiction for as long a period as was judged to be necessary, subject to whatever upper-age limit might be fixed by statute. During that period the agency would have the widest discretion to vary or terminate the measures initially applied, and where appropriate to substitute others.'

The Report's recommendations, as the extract shows, envisaged that the 'panel' should have coercive powers. It would, for example, be empowered to remove a child from its home. But its decisions would be subject to a right of appeal to the Sheriff. Indeed, the coercive powers of the panel would in one respect be considerably wider than those of the juvenile court it replaced, since it would be able, if the Committee's recommendations were implemented, to vary its initial decision and to substitute other measures for those originally prescribed. Although this was not envisaged as anything but an exceptional procedure, the power to impose an indeterminate custodial order would confer on the panel a wider discretion than a court of law had possessed. In addition to an initial right of appeal against an order of the panel, the Committee recommended that there should be a right of appeal against any subsequent order involving a greater measure of deprivation of parental rights, and a recurring right of appeal in every case against the continuance of an order at annual intervals. [36]

In a White Paper on *Social Work in the Community* [37] the Government announced its acceptance of the main principles of the Kilbrandon Committee's proposals and put forward its own proposals for reorganising the social services provided by the local authorities in Scotland. There were two main departures from the Kilbrandon Committee's system; it was proposed that the reorganised services should be vested in a new local authority Department of Social Work and not in a Social Education Department of the Education Authority; and it was proposed that the new Department should serve all age groups and not only children and their families. These reforms were given statutory effect by the Social Work (Scotland) Act 1968.

It will be seen that these proposals, while preserving the child's right to establish his innocence before a court, envisage a complete separation of functions between the court and the panel; the court would only be concerned in the exceptional case to decide disputed questions of fact and would have no say in determining the appropriate form of treatment, while the panel would have no concern with questions of law or fact but would be solely required to decide the question of treatment. To this extent it can be said that the requirement of criminal responsibility is still retained.

Similar proposals adapted to the English scene were published in 1965, in a White Paper setting out 'the Government's provisional proposals for practical reforms to support the family, to forestall and reduce delinquency, and to revise the law and practice relating to offenders up to 21.' [38] These proposals, too, envisaged that the appropriate treatment should be decided upon wherever possible by agreement; they too recognised the importance of treating juvenile delinquency in the context of the family; and they involved the abolition at any rate in their existing form of the juvenile courts.

The principal and most controversial of the White Paper's proposals was to remove young people so far as possible from the jurisdiction of the court, and to empower each local authority, through its children's committee, to appoint local family councils to deal with each case, so far as possible in consultation and by agreement with the parents. Where the facts were disputed or agreement could not be reached, the case would have to be referred to a family court. The family court would be a magistrates' court specially constituted to deal with those under sixteen, and would also sit as a Young Offenders' Court to exercise criminal jurisdiction in offences committed by those over sixteen and under twenty-one. The right to trial by jury for those between fourteen and sixteen would be abolished; and all courts, when passing sentence on an offender under twenty-one, would be required, as juvenile courts already are, to have regard to his welfare.

Reforms in methods of treatment were also proposed. For those under sixteen in need of long-term training, the wide range of residential establishments would be extended to include approved schools; for those over sixteen youth training centres would be established by merging borstals and senior approved schools and reorganising them under the administration of the Home Office, and for periods over two years special young offenders' institutions would be provided. One effect of these changes would apparently be the abolition of imprisonment, at any rate in name, for all under twenty-one; another would apparently be the abolition of the fine as a method of dealing with juvenile offenders, although the family council could agree that compensation should be paid for harm done by a child.

Four reasons were given for minimising the role of the court. First, it was argued that children should be spared the stigma of criminality.

Secondly, it was observed as the Kilbrandon Committee had found, that in most cases the facts were not in dispute, and the sole question was what form of treatment was appropriate; this should be discussed with the child's parents and with the relevant social services. Thirdly, the parents should assume a greater personal responsibility; and finally, a court order was not sufficiently flexible to meet the child's response to treatment and his changing needs.

The response to the White Paper was somewhat critical, and some attempt must be made to examine its merits and defects in the context of its implications for the criminal law. It is evident that the proposals, like those of the Kilbrandon Committee, do not altogether dispense with the court, even in the case of the offender under sixteen; for they preserve his right in the last resort to establish his innocence. Nevertheless they are open to a number of objections.

First it can be said that while they may remove the stigma of criminality to some extent, some stigma may still attach to the proceedings of the family council and to the measures it adopts. Nor is this altogether undesirable; for it can be argued that social attitudes are important influences, while there is still some force in the converse of the objection to stigma, that it is desirable to inculcate, if not respect for the law, at least some acknowledgement of the anti-social quality of the offender's conduct.

Further, the difficulty arises on these proposals of deciding what criterion to adopt in dealing with children who previously would have been found guilty of an offence. Objections can be made against a suggestion which would attempt to apply to all children the criterion already accepted in the case of those in need of care, protection or control. This is the suggestion that the measures taken should be appropriate to the 'needs' of the child. It is argued that this criterion, although quite intelligible and perhaps adequate in 'care or protection' cases, becomes alarmingly vague and perhaps wholly inapplicable to those who without being in need of care and protection have committed an offence. Such a criterion, it is argued, being quite indeterminate, would lead both to wide discrepancies in dealing with similar cases and in some at least to unnecessary and potentially harmful action.

This difficulty is of course reflected in the related problem of what measures to apply to children who previously would have been found guilty of an offence. The statistics [39] show that quantitatively the problem is an enormous one and throw some doubt on the practicability of the proposals. In 1965, no fewer than 25,060 persons under fourteen were found guilty of indictable offences by magistrates' courts; the total of those over fourteen and under seventeen was as high as 36,980. At

G

the same time it is clear that the great majority of those offences were of comparatively trivial proportions, and it may be doubted whether at any rate in these cases the proposed reforms provide an appropriate solution. Thus in 1965, of those under fourteen found guilty of an indictable offence, no less than 30% were discharged altogether, whether absolutely or conditionally. A third were put on probation, and nearly a fifth were fined. Only one in twenty was sent to an approved school, and rather more to an attendance centre. Of every ten offenders aged between fourteen and seventeen, approximately two were discharged, three were put on probation, and three were fined. Approved schools and attendance centres together accounted for 13% of the total.

Although the value of the fine as a method of dealing with juvenile offenders is not universally accepted, it is arguable that it is still the most effective as well as the most economical method of dealing with a large number of offenders, which it would be undesirable to abolish. In the case of a child it must, and in the case of a young person it may be imposed not on the child but on the parents, unless the court is satisfied that they have not conduced to the offence by failing to exercise due care of the child. The chief disadvantages of the fine are generally said to be that the imposition of a fine on parents who are responsible for the child's offence by virtue of their neglect is unlikely to remedy the situation or improve their relationship, and that the fine is merely a punishment providing no positive remedy. But the whole validity of the distinction between punitive and remedial measures is open to question, and there may well be cases where further remedial measures are considered inappropriate and the fine provides an adequate solution.

One of the principal merits of the fine illustrates the difference between treating young offenders by means of the juvenile courts and substituting methods for dealing with juvenile delinquency in the context of the social services. Fears have been expressed that these services, already stretched far beyond their capacity, might break down altogether if the proposals of the 1965 White Paper were implemented. The White Paper itself estimated that children's departments might need something like 1,000 additional social workers, and suggested optimistically that some of these might be transferred from the probation and after-care services. The courts have at least made more discriminating use of these scarce resources. From the figures already quoted it can be seen that approximately half the offenders were disposed of by discharge or fine, and therefore imposed no further strain on the welfare services — though it should be mentioned that when ordering a child or young person to pay a fine by instalments, magistrates sometimes make use of their powers under section 71 of the Magistrates' Courts Act 1952 to place him under the supervision of a probation officer while he does so.

A final advantage of the fine which is closely related to the characteristics just described is that it does at least avoid the danger of exposing the child to undesirable contacts which he may make if sent for training. And this feature may be used to illustrate what is perhaps the most important of all criticisms of the more extreme proposals for dealing with juvenile delinquency, and in particular with attempts to anticipate delinquency. The great problem is that failure may lead to the child becoming a confirmed criminal. But it is perhaps insufficiently realised that proposals which emphasise a preventive approach may have quite the opposite effect to that intended. These proposals seem to assume that it is possible to make more successful predictions of criminal conduct than the experimental evidence warrants. Lady Wootton, in her analysis of 'Studies in Criminological Prediction', came to the unsurprising conclusion that prediction of recidivism was generally more accurate than prediction of delinquency generally. [40] But it must not be forgotten that only a small proportion of juvenile offenders do in fact go on to record convictions as adults. [41] It cannot be assumed, on the evidence so far avilable, that this proportion can be identified in advance. Still less is it possible to identify the so-called 'pre-delinquent'.

The danger in the light of these facts is that the proposals may have the effect not of preventing but of promoting delinquency. It is trite knowledge that many children have engaged in the types of activity which bring some of their number before the courts, and that such activities do not lead in the majority of cases to a career of crime. Yet all too many of those dealt with by the courts, above all of those sent for training, have a subsequent criminal record. Thus it has been found that one of the best predictors of recidivism among borstal boys is previous residence in an approved school: [42] and in another survey it was found that over half, the boys committed to detention in remand homes were afterwards found guilty of an indictable offence. [43] For obvious reasons this argument cannot be taken too far; and no doubt if it were carried to its logical conclusion it might be taken to preclude any official action against juvenile delinquency. But it does at any rate weaken the case for preventive measures where there is no clearly proved need for treatment; and in doing so it may perhaps also strengthen the case for the retention of the juvenile courts.

The conclusions to be drawn from this survey of the development of policy and practice in this area, of the implications of recent reforms and of possible future trends, have a general importance beyond the limits of the special problems posed by juvenile delinquency. First, it is doubtful how far a distinction between punishment and treatment can be maintained. It seems unreasonable to suppose that a minor difference of emphasis in the form of training provided in the course of a custodial sentence, for example, should be held to justify any modification of the fundamental principles of criminal responsibility.

Secondly, if it is possible to distinguish between punishment and treatment, it is doubtful how far punitive methods can in all cases be discarded. We have seen that many of the reforms and proposals for change still retain measures which may be regarded as having a punitive element; while those proposals which like the recommendations of the 1965 White Paper would abolish such punitive sanctions as the fine are open to serious objections on practical grounds. It is perhaps significant in this context that the Ingleby Committee, in recommending that the age of criminal responsibility be raised to twelve, proposed a new category of children and young persons 'in need of protection or discipline' which would have included any child who, while under the age of twelve years, acts in a manner which would render a person over that age liable to be found guilty of an offence. The Committee recommended that for the treatment of children in this category certain minor punishments should be available in addition to those forms of treatment which under the existing law might be ordered for children in need of care or protection. The forms of treatment available under the existing law were committal to an approved school, committal to the care of a fit person, a supervision order, and an order binding over the child's parent or guardian to exercise proper care and guardianship. The Committee recommended that there should also be made available detention in a remand home, attendance centre, and pecuniary penalties. One experienced magistrate has written that 'the recommendation was only common sense; but the government, in providing for the treatment of children between eight and ten years of age found in need of care, protection, or control as the result of misbehaviour, ignored it'[44]

In response to the criticisms of its more extreme proposals, the White Paper was considerably modified in a further White Paper, 'Children in Trouble'[45] published in April 1968, which set out some of the main legislative proposals subsequently enacted in the Children and Young Persons Act 1969. These proposals were less revolutionary. The proposal for family councils disappeared. Juvenile courts were retained, and their existing jurisdiction and age limits preserved. The upper age limit for the juvenile court system remained the seventeenth birthday. There were no changes in the procedures for offenders over seventeen, or in the system of courts for offenders whether over or under that age; and the procedure for children under ten was to remain as before.

There was, however, to be a new procedure for offenders aged ten and under fourteen which in the words of the White Paper 'represents a half-way stage between care, protection or control proceedings and prosecution.'[46] Under the new procedure, as embodied in the Act, the commission of an offence ceases to be, by itself, a sufficient ground for bringing a child before a court. Instead, the conditions on which a child or young person might under the 1963 Act have been found in need of care, protection or control, have been widened to include as an alternative the condition that the child 'is guilty of an offence, excluding homicide'. However, this condition, described in the Act as 'the offence condition', is not by itself sufficient; the court must be of the opinion also that the child is in need of care or control.[47]

Under the provisions of the Act, apart from the offence condition, the court before which a child or young person is brought may make an order if it is of the opinion that:

(a) his proper development is being avoidably prevented or neglected or his health is being avoidably impaired or neglected or he is being ill-treated; or,

(b) it is probable that the condition set out in paragraph (a) will be satisfied in his case, having regard to the fact that the court or another court has found that the condition is or was satisfied in the case of another child or young person who is or was a member of the household to which he belongs; or,

(c) he is exposed to moral danger; or,

(d)   he is beyond the control of his parent or guardian; or,

(e) he is of compulsory school age and is not receiving efficient full-time education suitable to his age, ability and aptitude.

Thus the grounds on which the court may act have now been formulated in such a way as almost to obliterate the distinction between civil and criminal proceedings. Almost, but not quite. For although the Act prohibits criminal proceedings for all offences except homicide committed under the age of fourteen,[48] and thus in effect raises the age of criminal responsibility to that age, it appears from the wording of the offence condition that a child below the age can still commit an offence and even 'be guilty' of it. Further, the Act does not dispense with the traditional safeguards of the criminal process; for it provides *inter alia* that the court shall not find the offence condition satisfied unless it would have found him guilty of the offence on a criminal charge.[49] Since the Act contains no provisions to the contrary, it must be presumed that the old rules, including the requirements of proof both of *mens rea* and of knowledge of wrong, are intended to survive.

Since the requirements for proof of an offence remain unchanged, more significance may be thought to lie in the fact that the court is also required to find that the child is in need of care or control. Existing procedures will presumably be combined; the police will adduce evidence of the offence, and if it is admitted or proved, the local authority or the police will bring evidence that he was in need of care or control. In practice, no doubt the evidence of the offence will in some cases suffice for both purposes, and overlapping will be inevitable. But the aspect of this legislation which aroused the strongest criticism is that its effect seems to be that a child from a good home who commits an offence is not brought before the court at all. Even where two children have jointly committed an offence, one may be brought before the court while no proceedings at all are taken against the other; and this inequality, it was objected by critics of the Act, is different in principle from a difference of treatment by the court which could be justified by differences in the children's circumstances.

In the case of young persons between fourteen and seventeen criminal proceedings are retained, but the policy of the Act is to establish the principle of dealing with offenders in this age group outside the courts so far as possible, and to lay down criteria for the decision whether to prosecute in each case. It was originally provided that the consent of a juvenile court magistrate would be required for the prosecution of a young offender, but after considerable opposition to this proposal the Bill was amended to leave the decision to the police after consultation with the local authority. However, the Act provides that no one but a 'qualified informant', normally a police officer, may lay information against a young person, and that he may do so only if the case falls within one of the categories to be specified by regulations by the Home Secretary, and if the case cannot be dealt with by other means set out in the Act. [50] A young person over fourteen but under seventeen may also, of course, be brought before the court under the same procedures as a child under fourteen, when the court will have to find that the prescribed conditions, already referred to, are satisfied.

Where the prescribed conditions are satisfied the court is empowered to make one of a number of orders. [51] First, it may make an order requiring the child's parent or guardian to enter into a recognisance to take proper care and exercise proper control of him. It may, as under the older law, make a supervision order, placing him under the supervision of a local authority or of a probation officer; [52] but it can no longer make a probation order as such. Probation orders could be made only in the case of offenders over seventeen. [53] The distinction between probation orders for offenders and supervision orders for those found in need of care, protection or control is thus abolished. The court could make a hospital or guardianship order within the meaning of the Mental

Health Act 1959. Finally a care order could be made committing the child to the care of a local authority. Approved schools, [54] remand homes, [55] and fit person orders [56] are abolished under the Act; Part II makes provision instead for regional planning of accommodation for children in care in 'community homes'.

It is significant that, except for orders under the Mental Health Act, the 1969 Act provides that the above measures shall also be available for a young person found guilty of an offence punishable in the case of an adult with imprisonment. [57]

With regard to treatment, independently of the question of whether the person concerned has committed an offence, the general policy of the Act is to end the sharp distinction between forms of treatment which involve complete removal from his home and those which do not. Section 12 of the Act makes possible the development of new forms of intermediate treatment, to be used in conjunction with supervision. Wide powers may be conferred by the supervision order on the supervisor to give directions as to where, for example, the person supervised should reside for certain periods, or requiring him to participate in certain activities on specified days; and it is envisaged that such supervision orders will replace junior attendance orders and junior detention centres.

Further, with the abolition of approved school orders [58] and the raising of the minimum age for borstal training from fifteen to seventeen, [59] all children and young persons requiring continuing treatment away from home will be placed in the care of local authorities. Some of the residential institutions known under the generic term community homes will be maintained by the local authorities themselves, while others will be run on a voluntary basis in co-operation with the local authorities. In any case the new system is intended to provide for better co-ordination of the different forms of treatment available for offender and non-offender alike.

But such a system, by reason of its very flexibility, was clearly open to the charge of depriving the infant of necessary safeguards. Thus, it was objected when the Bill was before Parliament that once a court had made a care order to a local authority, which could have effect unless discharged earlier until the age of eighteen, [60] there would be no judicial authority with power to review the order or interfere in any way. Under the old law a child who was committed to the care of a local authority under a fit person order could not be transferred to an approved school or even to a remand home without being brought before the court. Under the Act the local authority has complete discretion and there is no provision for any remedy by the infant or his parents or guardian.

The debate on the Act continues, and no answers, however tentative, can be expected to the many questions it raises until it has been in operation for a considerable time and the effects of the new measures can be assessed. The principal object of this necessarily brief survey, however, has been more limited: it has sought to throw some light on the concept of responsibility by exploring an area where the criminal process itself is in issue.

Chapter 4

Strict Liability

There are many offences in English law today where there is no need for *mens rea*. In these cases a person may be convicted, not merely if he did not intend the prohibited consequences, but even though the conduct which led to them was not negligent. Strict liability, which disappeared almost totally from the criminal law at an early stage of its development, reappeared in the nineteenth century; but its precise ambit and implications are still uncertain today.

Subject to a few minor qualifications, the general principle remains that common law crimes always require *mens rea,* but that in the case of crimes which have been created or defined by Act of Parliament, the existence and extent of the requirement of *mens rea* depend upon the construction of the relevant statutory provisions. A clear example is the definition of theft contained in the Theft Act 1968; 'A person is guilty of theft if he dishonestly appropriates property belonging to another with the intention of permanently depriving the other of it';[1] the Act further specifies that a person's appropriation of property belonging to another is not to be regarded as dishonest, among other cases, if he appropriates the property in the belief that he would have the other's consent if the other knew of the appropriation and the circumstances of it.[2] Similarly, the requisite *mens rea* could be altered by statute. An Act of Parliament could explicitly exclude, for example, the defence that the person charged with the offence was reasonably mistaken as to the circumstances of the case; it could, by the use of such terms as 'knowingly', 'maliciously', or 'wilfully', vary the specific mental element required; it could transfer the burden of proof from the prosecution to the defence.

Often, however, the statute is silent on the question of *mens rea*. It may, for example, make it an offence for a person to 'permit' a certain act or event, without specifying that knowledge is a condition of liability. If it is an offence for a person to permit an invoice of fertilisers sold to a purchaser to be false in a material particular, should a person be convicted who believed the invoice to be true?[3] If it is an offence for a person to permit a motor-vehicle to be used as an 'express carriage,' is the owner of a vehicle liable if he did not know that it was so used?[4] Examples could be multiplied indefinitely of cases where the statute gives no clear guide. It then becomes necessary for the courts to interpret the statute by reference solely to the general principles of the criminal law as they have been developed through the cases.

The old principle was stated by Coke: 'Acts of Parliament are to be so construed, as no man that is innocent or free from injury or wrong be by a literal construction punished or endamaged.'[5] In the course of the nineteenth century, as will be seen, a more literal approach to the interpretation of statutes was adopted. The view was taken that if nothing was said of *mens rea* no *mens rea* was required. But the decisions were not always easy to reconcile. In *Cundy* v. *Le Cocq*[6] the charge was brought under section 13 of the Licensing Act 1872, which provided that 'if any licensed person ... sells any intoxicating liquor to any drunken person, he shall be liable to a penalty.' These words were held to create strict liability so that ignorance by the licensee that his customer was drunk was no defence. In *Sherras* v. *De Rutzen*[7] the charge was laid under section 16 (2) of the same Act: 'If any licensed person ... supplies any liquor ... to any constable on duty ... he shall be liable to a penalty.' These words were held to imply the requirement of *mens rea* so that ignorance by the licensee that the constable was a policeman on duty was a defence.

By the end of the century it could be said that 'in construing a modern statute this presumption as to *mens rea* does not exist';[8] but this view has since been repudiated,[9] and recent decisions have reaffirmed the general requirement. There has at no time, however, been much consistency in the approach of the courts and the law can only be stated in the most general terms.

It can be said that in the majority of cases there remains a presumption that *mens rea* is required; but, in the course of the last hundred years, this presumption has been displaced in two categories of offence which have come to be regarded as offences of strict liability. In certain serious offences, such as abduction, bigamy, and carnal knowledge, the courts have adopted the anomalous doctrine of what might be described as partially strict liability, which excludes some but not all of the defences generally accepted. It will be argued later that strict liability never excludes all the defences based on *mens rea*, but the anomaly here is greater because knowledge of the material circumstances is generally required yet ignorance of a particular element is no defence. Thus, for example, in the classic case of *Prince*[10] in 1875, the accused was charged with taking a girl under sixteen out of the possession of her parents, contrary to section 55 of the Offences against the Person Act 1861. The girl in the case, although only fourteen, looked very much older than sixteen, and the jury found that the accused *bona fide* believed the girl's statement that she was eighteen. The court held that his assertion that he was mistaken as to her age was not a good defence. The decision was based in part, as will be seen, on a literal interpretation of the relevant statutory provisions which made no reference to *mens rea* and did not require as a condition of liability the knowledge or belief that the girl was under the age of 16. But he would not have been guilty if he had no reason to know that she was under the lawful charge of her parents,[11] and Holmes has suggested [12] that he would not have been guilty if he had reasonable cause to believe that she was a boy.

The offence of bigamy, defined by the same Act, illustrates the illogical results which follow from the conflict between the common law principles of *mens rea* and the literal application of the words of a statute. In the celebrated case of *Tolson* [13] the court held that the accused, a woman, had a defence to a charge of bigamy if, at the time of the second ceremony of marriage, she reasonably though mistakenly believed that her husband had died; whereas in *Wheat and Stocks,* [14] where a man was charged with the same offence, it was held that the accused should still be liable to conviction if he reasonably but erroneously believed that his marriage had been terminated by divorce.

The accused in the first case, Mrs Tolson, was married in 1880. In 1881 her husband deserted her. As a result of enquiries made about him from his brother, Mrs Tolson was led to believe that her husband had been lost in a ship bound for America which had gone down with all hands. In 1887 she married again, believing herself to be a widow. Later the same year, her first husband reappeared on the scene. Section 57 of the Offences against the Person Act 1861, defined the crime of bigamy as follows: 'Whosoever, being married, shall marry any other person during the life of the former husband or wife shall be guilty of felony'. The statute provided three exceptions, the first of which alone is relevant to the present case. By this proviso, the offence is not committed by any person who marries a second time whose husband or wife shall have been continually absent from such person for the space of seven years then last past and shall not have been known by such person to be living within that time. On a literal interpretation of the definition of the offence the same result would have been reached as in the case of *Prince,* concerned with an offence against section 55 of the same Act. No mention is made of *mens rea* and *prima facie,* therefore , bigamy would appear to exclude any requirement of knowledge or belief except in so far as this was contained in the proviso. The proviso could not be applied because the former husband had not been absent for seven years, but a majority of the court were of the opinion that the legislature could not have intended in cases of bigamy to exclude the principle requiring a guilty mind. Stephen J. said:'It could not be the object of parliament to treat the marriage of widows as an act to be if possible prevented as presumably immoral. The conduct of the women convicted was not in the smallest degree immoral, it was perfectly natural and legitimate. Assuming the facts to be as they supposed, the infliction of more than a nominal punishment on them would have been a scandal. Why, then, should the legislature be held to have wished to subject them to punishment at all .. . .' Yet in the later case of *Wheat and Stocks* the court said: 'We are of the opinion that a *bona fide* belief on reasonable grounds that the person accused has been divorced, when in fact he has not been divorced, affords no defence in law to the charge of bigamy.' The latter decision was finally overruled in a recent case by the Criminal Division of the Court of Appeal. [15]

Such anomalies constitute, perhaps fortunately, exceptions of comparatively minor significance to the general rules relating to criminal responsibility and are by no means characteristic of the specific doctrine of strict liability as it normally operates. The majority of offences of strict liability appear to be concerned in the first place with particular trades, businesses and professions including for instance the distribution of food and drugs; and, secondly, with certain other standard types of activity, notably the driving and use of motor vehicles. In these cases, although the imposition of strict liability may result in a person being penalised for an infringement of the law which he had no opportunity to avoid while engaging in an activity which may well be socially beneficial, yet it can be said in defence of the doctrine as it operates here, first, that in these cases the individual still has the ultimate choice not to engage in the activity at all and, secondly, that if he does so they may be such as require a higher standard of care. It is perhaps significant that the origins and development of strict liability were remarkably similar in England and the United States. The doctrine reflects the rise of industrialisation, and the earliest American statutes and cases come from the New England states, particularly Massachusetts, where the industrial revolution had its roots.

The chief general justification of strict liability is usually based on the difficulty of proving *mens rea* and the abuse which would follow from any other rule. We shall meet the same problems later in the discussion, and the relevant arguments are examined in the concluding chapter. The present chapter is primarily concerned to consider two related themes; the question how far the doctrine of strict liability may be justified in terms of the changing functions of the criminal law, and the relationship between the specific doctrine and the general issue of criminal responsibility.

In considering the evidence for the elimination of responsibility, we have in previous chapters discussed one sector of suggested evidence; we have discussed the suggestion that the classes of persons exempt from liability are being widened, or indeed that new categories of exemption have evolved. Hence, it is argued either that the doctrine of *mens rea* cannot survive, or that it should be abrogated, or both. The second part of the argument rests not upon the increasing exemption from liability of the young and of the mentally disordered, but upon the development of principles of liability which, in the standard case where the accused is an adult of not abnormal mentality, no longer necessitate an inquiry into his state of mind at the time when he did the act with which he is charged. In this case, what is advocated is an extension of strict liability.

We have already noticed a number of important differences between the two sectors of the argument. In examining the evidence on which they rely, there is a further difference to be observed. The evidence in the first part of the argument is based on the work of the legislature, whereas the principles of liability are still largely the creation of the judges. We have seen that, in the case of the mentally disordered, the main changes were introduced by a series of statutes culminating in the Mental Health Act 1959; while in the case of children the modern law is again largely statutory, the most important enactments being the Children and Young Persons Acts of 1933 and 1963. So far as the principles of liability concern the normal adult, however, it is necessary to turn to the case-law. It was the courts which, in the nineteenth century, evolved the doctrine of strict liability, and the extent to which the doctrine operates today still depends largely upon the attitude of the criminal courts. It is true that the doctrine arose, and has since developed, out of the construction of statutes whose form is determined by the legislature, and that it was in part the adoption of a more literal approach towards the interpretation of penal legislation which gave rise to strict liability. But the principles of statutory interpretation are themselves to a large extent the creation of the judges.

It is in fact one of the most impressive criticisms of the institution of strict liability that it appears to be based upon unrealistic and unjustified assumptions about the intention of the legislature. The argument which is open to criticism is that if the legislature has not specifically enacted the requirement of *mens rea*, it is not the function of the court to read it into the statute. To do so is to usurp the function of the legislature and can only confuse the systematic development of the law. The fallacy in this argument was exposed in the clearest terms by Professor Glanville Williams. Writing in 1961, he pointed out that

'Every criminal statute is expressed elliptically. It is not posssible in drafting a statute to state all the qualifications and exceptions that are intended. One does not, for instance, when creating a new offence, enact that persons under eight years of age cannot be convicted. Nor does one enact the defence of insanity or duress. The exemptions belong to the general part of the criminal law, which is implied into specific offences ... . Where the criminal law is codified ... this general part is placed by itself in the code and is not repeated for each individual crime. Now the law of *mens rea* belongs to the general part of the criminal law, and it is not reasonable to expect Parliament every time it creates a new crime to enact it or even to make reference to it.' [16]

Similarly in *Tolson's* case Cave J argued that the defence of a mistake of fact could be read into a statute in the same way as the defences of infancy and insanity.

'At common law an honest and reasonable belief in the existence of circumstances, which, if true, would make the act for which a prisoner is indicted an innocent act has always been held to be a good defence. This doctrine is embodied in the somewhat uncouth maxim *actus non facit reum, nisi mens sit rea*. Honest and reasonable mistake stands in fact on the same footing as absence of the reasoning faculty, as in infancy, or perversion of that faculty, as in lunacy. Instances of the existence of this common law doctrine will readily occur to the mind. So far as I am aware it has never been suggested that these exceptions do not equally apply in the case of statutory offences unless they are excluded expressly or by necessary implication.'

We shall see that this principle has had considerable influence in a number of recent English and Australian cases where the courts have rejected the argument from silence for excluding the requirement of *mens rea*.

Assumptions about the intentions of the legislature have concealed, here as elsewhere, the important questions of policy which have faced the courts. In fact it can be shown that, except in the very rare cases where the requirement of *mens rea* has been expressly excluded by an Act of Parliament, the question often turns upon the individual attitudes of the judges, and developments can often be traced to the influence over a period of a particular judge. Many judges in the nineteenth century, for example, and again in the nineteen thirties, took a view of the purposes of the criminal law, and of the function of the courts, which led them to adopt a narrowly literal interpretation of Acts of Parliament. Conversely, in the period since the last war (during which special considerations influenced the courts), we shall find considerable evidence that individual judges have adopted consistent policies allowing them more scope in the application of penal legislation.

It can be said that some of these policies are based on the premise that *prima facie* a criminal offence requires *mens rea* even where this is not explicitly stipulated; and this makes increasingly implausible, although difficult to refute outright, the suggestion that strict liability is actually increasing. On the contrary, although it may not be possible to quantify the incidence of strict liability, it may be argued that the courts over the last twenty years have to a great extent re-introduced *mens rea*. Thus we shall see that some judges, notably Lord Goddard and Lord Devlin in this country and others in the Supreme Courts of Australia and the USA, differing from their counterparts a hundred years ago, have consistently criticised and where possible rejected or modified the doctrine of strict liability.

If the case-law on the topic appears to contradict the view that strict liability is increasing, a variety of other factors may have tended to encourage this belief. These factors might be regarded as including not only the effects of changes in legislative policy, to be examined below, but also some looseness in the idea of strict liability itself.

This lack of precision may be illustrated by Professor Fuller's remark in his lectures on *The Morality of Law:* 'It is a kind of cliché that there exists today "a general trend" toward strict liability. It seems, indeed, often to be assumed that this trend is carrying us remorselessly toward a future in which the concepts of fault and intent will cease to play any part in the law'.[17] It is necessary to observe first in relation to this remark that there are other principles of liability, one of which will be examined in the next chapter, capable of being regarded as dispensing with fault and intent. For the present, from the point of view of strict liability, it is sufficient to distinguish between civil and criminal liability. It would indeed be interesting to speculate on the implications for, say, the law of contract if the concept of intention were to disappear. In the law of tort, however, the idea of strict liability has come to be widely accepted as serving a useful though limited purpose, and one explanation of the suggestion that it is increasing might be sought in the modern development of the civil law.

There are, however, a number of reasons for rejecting the analogy. In the first place, we have already seen that the justification of strict liability in tort is quite different from that in crime. A main function of the law of tort, the redistribution of losses which one party has caused the other, itself provides a justification of strict liability to which there is no analogue in criminal theory. An interesting illustration of this difference is provided by the case of *Prince* already referred to, where the charge was brought under section 55 of the Offences against the

Person Act 1861. One of the two arguments in the majority judgment
in that case was that section 55 replaced earlier legislation, the object of
which was stated in the preamble to be the recognition of a legal right
in the father to the possession of the child, and it was said that 'the
object of the legislature being to protect this legal right to possession
would be baffled, if it was an excuse that the person guilty of the taking
thought the child above 16.' But it is difficult to regard the imposition
of strict liability in the criminal law as a method of protecting rights.
Even if the protection of private rights could be regarded as one of the
objects of the criminal law, this object would not be achieved by strict
liability. In the law of tort strict liability can be regarded as protecting
a right because it results in compensation.

The difference of functions between civil and criminal law can be
further illustrated by contrasting the criteria for requiring a degree of
fault as a condition of liability. In the civil law the requirement of intention is a sign that the interest protected is valued less highly; it is for
this reason that only the deliberate infringement of it is actionable.
Rights to the security of person and property are protected by the civil
law even in the absence of fault; liability for financial loss is in many
cases based on negligence; while at the other extreme, the right to
protection from malicious prosecution is so circumscribed that it is
necessary to show malice as a condition of liability. The reverse is true
of the criminal law. Here the arguments against strict liability are
stronger the more serious the offence, since the importance of protecting
the individual against penal sanctions is correspondingly increased. Thus,
in the case of *Tolson,* Wills J gave the gravity of the offence of bigamy
as one reason why it was not a crime of strict liability.

But it could also be said, independently of these arguments, that it is
by no means self-evident, even if there is a better case for strict liability
in tort, that it is increasing even in this branch of the law. Many examples
could be given of developments in quite the opposite direction. An
interesting illustration is afforded by the law of defamation. The aim of
this branch of the law is to compensate the plaintiff for injury to his
reputation; but the principles of liability are no longer determined solely
by this aim. The injury to his reputation will not ordinarily be affected
in its extent if the defamation was not intended nor even negligent but
simply accidental. Yet even here the law has now attempted to mitigate
the consequences to the defendant of his unintentional conduct. Proof
of the absence of malicious motive and intention has always been
allowed in mitigation of damages; and since the Defamation Act of 1952
special provisions have enabled a newspaper, for example, which has
unintentionally published a defamatory statement to avoid the normal

consequences of its action. Previously it could be held liable for a quite innocent publication;[18] but by section 4 of the Act, if it makes an offer of amends, together with an offer to publish an apology, then if the offer is accepted it will form a bar to any action by the aggrieved party, while if it is refused and the aggrieved party proceeds to sue, proof of the innocence of the statement will be a defence. This particular example is simply an illustration of what appears to be a general tendency of the modern law of tort of which other instances may be briefly mentioned. The introduction of contributory negligence by the Law Reform (Contributory Negligence) Act 1945 enabled liability to follow more closely upon fault than the doctrine of the 'last opportunity' which it replaced; section 1 (1) of the Act provides that 'Where any person suffers damage as the result partly of his own fault and partly of the fault of any other person or persons, a claim in respect of that damage shall not be defeated by reason of the fault of the person suffering the damage, but the damages recoverable in respect thereof shall be reduced to such extent as the Court thinks just and equitable having regard to the claimant's share in the responsibility for the damage.' And as a final illustration it may be mentioned that the test of foreseeability is not only now of increasing importance to the question of liability but is also generally accepted in place of the rule in *Re Polemis* on the question of remoteness of damage.[19]

Indeed, a convincing argument could be developed for the view that the whole history of the law of torts has shown a gradual progression away from an absolute duty of restitution of which few traces now survive except for occasional isolated instances of liability, for instance, in cases falling under the rule in *Rylands* v. *Fletcher,* in some cases of liability for damage done by animals, in other cases of liability for the breach of a statutory duty, and so on. The general trend of English law, it could be maintained, has been away from the imposition of an absolute duty, independent of fault, in a few specific situations, towards the concept of a general duty of care where liability is imposed only in the event of a specified degree of negligence. This trend was well illustrated by the speech of Lord Atkin in the classic case of *Donoghue* v. *Stevenson,*[20] and is further exemplified in such recent cases as *Hedley Byrne* v. *Heller.*[21] A detailed discussion of this topic would, however, lead beyond the scope of the immediate inquiry. Discussion has taken place elsewhere of the decrease of strict liability in the civil law.[22] It is doubtful how far the suggestion that strict liability is increasing may be due to a confusion of different branches of the law; for present purposes, it may be sufficient to compare the principles of liability in civil and in criminal law in terms of their respective purposes and to

H

observe that, in a branch of the law where different considerations may apply, there is no evidence of any parallel development to the alleged increase of strict liability in the criminal law.

Legislative policy, coupled with the changing patterns of criminal statistics in recent years, may nevertheless suggest a quantitative increase, even in real terms, among offences of strict liability. But, of two arguments which may be used at this point, one appears to be of dubious validity, while the other if valid has little significance. The first argument takes the form that strict liability is mainly found, as had been observed, in minor statutory offences; that the number of minor offences created by Parliament, particularly in the field of what is described as public welfare legislation, is notoriously increasing; from which the conclusion is drawn that strict liability is increasing. Although the truth of the premises is indisputable, and the reasoning apparently sound, this argument is of dubious validity, since, although strict liability was at its inception more readily introduced in public welfare offences, it must be remembered in the first place that it was at no time confined to these offences and secondly that it has never been uniformly incorporated in them. There is certainly now, whatever the position may have appeared to be in the past, no evidence of any general principle of interpretation that offences created by statute do not require *mens rea:* on the contrary, that available evidences suggest, as we shall see, that the contrary presumption is now more firmly established than at any period in the last hundred years.

Nor should it be said that the development of minor statutory offences reflects a transformation in the function of the criminal law which makes unnecessary the concept of *mens rea.* We shall several times meet the argument that strict liability is justified at least in the so-called 'regulatory offences' which since the beginning of the nineteenth century have formed an ever increasing part of the criminal law. But it will be suggested in the concluding chapter that the appropriate response to this change in the law is not strict liability but a different justification of *mens rea.*

A better argument takes a rather different form. It is said that strict liability is extremely common, not so much in statutory offences as a whole, but in particular categories of offence (motoring offences are the best example) which at the same time constitute an ever-increasing proportion of the total number of offences committed. The conclusion is the same as that of the previous argument, that at any rate the incidence of strict liability is growing; the incidence of strict liability being based in this case not on the proportion of statutory offences, but on the proportion of individual cases, in which the doctrine may be applied.

But although this argument has a greater validity, it surely has less significance as evidence of the elimination of responsibility from the law. It is true that in a motorised society concentrated in congested conurbations, with a system of communications seriously out of date, motoring is bound to create a whole range of social problems which the legal system and the criminal statistics are likely to reflect. It may be true also that one cannot accept the formerly popular view that motoring offences are not 'real crimes'. But a number of important qualifications are necessary before motoring offences can be treated as paradigm cases of crime.

In the first place it must be observed that not all motoring offences are in any case offences of strict liability. Two cases may be used to illustrate this. In one case before the Divisional Court [23] the appellant company had been convicted of permitting to be used on the road a trailer, the brakes of which were not in efficient working order. The appellant's lorry and trailer had left their premises with the connecting cable in position and in good working order. It was necessary to un-couple the trailer to load some goods but the driver's assistant forgot to re-connect the brake cable. The appeal against conviction was allowed, the Divisional Court arguing that a charge of 'permitting' at once imports *mens rea*. In a later case, that of *Spurge,* [24] the appellant had been con-victed of driving a motor vehicle in a manner dangerous to the public, contrary to section 11 (1) of the Road Traffic Act 1930 [25] This section provided that an offence was committed 'if any person drives a motor vehicle on the road recklessly, or at a speed or in a manner which is dangerous to the public, having regard to all the circumstances of the case, including the nature, condition and use of the road, and the amount of traffic which is actually at the time, or which might reason-ably be expected to be, on the road.' The appellant, while driving a sports car round a sharp and dangerous left-hand bend, went over the double white lines in the middle of the road on to the wrong side and collided with an oncoming motor scooter. He had taken delivery of the car only a few days before the accident and had been told by the vendor that the brakes had been overhauled. The brakes were in fact defective and their application, when the car was going at a moderate speed, pulled it to the offside of the road. The appellant was aware of this tendency. He contended that the accident was caused by the faulty brake mechanism and not by the manner in which he was driving. The Court of Criminal Appeal, sitting with five judges, recognised the principle that it is a defence to a charge of dangerous driving and to a charge of careless driving that the driver, without fault of his own, was deprived of control of the motor vehicle by a mechanical defect in the vehicle, of which he did not know, and which was not such as he should have discovered if he had exercised reasonable prudence. The appeal was dismissed on the ground that since the appellant was aware of the car's tendency to move to the right when the brakes were applied it was dangerous for him to drive the vehicle, as he did, with knowledge of this mechanical defect. But the case establishes the existence of the defence and places the burden of proof on the prosecution.

Even where the offence is apparently one of strict liability a complete loss of control may still be a defence. Dangerous driving is still, in one se an offence where liability is strict; for 'if a driver in fact adopts a manner of driving which the jury think was dangerous to other road users in all the circumstances, then on the issue of guilt it matters not whether he was deliberately reckless, careless, momentarily inattentive or even doing his incompetent best.' [26] But this must be read subject to the decision in *Hill* v. *Baxter*,[27] where the defendant had been acquitted of charges of dangerous driving and of failing to conform to a traffic sign under sections 11 and 49 (b) of the Road Traffic Act 1930, respectively. His defence was that he did not remember anything about the driving and that he had become unconscious as a result of a sudden illness. Allowing the prosecutor's appeal, the Divisional Court appeared to accept that a complete loss of control, such as might be induced by automatism or by other causes, could be a defence even on a charge of an offence of strict liability. Lord Goddard CJ said: 'I agree that there may be cases where the circumstances are such that the accused could not really be said to be driving at all. Suppose he had a stroke or an epileptic fit, both instances of what may properly be called acts of God; he might well be in the driver's seat even with his hands on the wheel, but in such a state of unconsciousness that he could not be said to be driving.'[27] Similarly in *Burns* v. *Bidder,* [28] where the charge was of failing to accord precedence to a foot-passenger on an uncontrolled crossing, contrary to regulation 4 of the Pedestrian Crossing Regulations 1954, the court said: 'The regulation does not impose an absolute liability, come what may, and there is no breach of the obligation under the regulation in circumstances where the driver fails to accord precedence to a foot-passenger solely because his control of the vehicle is taken from him by the occurrence of an event which is outside his possible or reasonable control and in respect of which he is in no way at fault'.

These cases may be reconciled with the doctrine of strict liability by the argument that what is lacking here is not *mens rea* but the more fundamental requirement of an act, so there is no *actus reus.* But however convenient this may be as an argument to persuade the courts to accept such defences in spite of strict liability, it is somewhat specious insofar as it draws an arbitrary line between the 'mental' and 'non-mental' ingredients of an act. It is also difficult to apply to cases of omission, such as *Burns* v. *Bidder* itself. It seems better to say that the exclusion of *mens rea* is always partial, never total, and to justify the exception made in each case on its own facts.

One argument which cannot now be accepted is that offences of strict liability are not 'real crimes'. It could hardly be suggested that these offences should be excluded from the criminal statistics. But it has been argued that the justification for *mens rea* is less when the offence is a minor one and the penalty only a small fine, and there is some evidence that this argument has influenced the thinking of the judges. We have already seen that the gravity of the crime of bigamy was given as a reason for the requirement of *mens rea*; and it was natural that the converse argument should also be advanced. In the case of *Sherras* v. *De Rutzen*,[29] already referred to, Wright J spoke of 'acts not criminal in any real sense ',[30] and some years later Channell J described them as 'quasi-criminal offences'.[31] The courts have sometimes suggested that, where the defendant is morally innocent, the penalty could be merely nominal; but many factors are involved apart from the actual penalty or the possible penalty (in *Yeandel* v. *Fisher*, discussed later, the maximum penalty on conviction on indictment was ten years imprisonment or a fine of £1,000 or both). It can now be seen that many of the offences of strict liability are no less serious in their social consequences than many offences requiring *mens rea*; and it can be argued that the case for *mens rea* is strong, however small the harm.[32] But, to take motoring offences by way of illustration, a distinction must still be drawn between those occasions where the machinery of the criminal law seems appropriate to the nature of the offence, and the occasions where it is cumbersome and unnecessary. In the first category would be placed both the use of a motor vehicle for an unlawful purpose and its use for a lawful purpose in a manner actually or potentially dangerous to the public. It is true also that the criminal law may be necessary not only, for example, to deter drunkenness in drivers, but also to maintain a very high standard or care. But the justification for the use of the criminal law in this area as a technique of social control does not necessarily validate any principles of liability of general application in the criminal law. Motoring offences, as the law stands at the moment, have many special features which differentiate them from other types of offence; and these special features can largely be explained not by any legal principle but simply by the fact that motor cars are both exceptionally dangerous and virtually ubiquitous. The resulting administrative complexities have already made essential the transfer of some of the problems away from the competence of the courts, and administrative rather than legal solutions are being sought to still more of them. Although it cannot be forgotten that some types of motoring offence are as paradigmatic breaches of the law as were highway robberies in an earlier age, the ultimate solution to the strict liability aspects of motoring offences may be found not in the total abolition of the concept of responsibility but in the elimination of traffic regulations from the criminal law.

A safer guide to the role of strict liability may be afforded by an examination of judicial attitudes. It has already been remarked that the general principles of liability have largely been fashioned by the courts. We shall see that even today the influence of individual judges has been considerable. But there is a further reason for trying to discover the philosophy of the judges, if it may be described as such. Many reasons have been advanced for the origin and development of strict liability. These include the social and economic changes precipitated by the industrial revolution and the increasing intervention of the State in the areas of public health and social welfare. But important also, if on a different level of explanation, are the attitudes of the judges themselves. The nineteenth century in particular was an era of changing beliefs about the relation of law and morality, the relation of the courts to Parliament, and the purposes of punishment. And if we are to attempt to relate the principles of liability to the function of the law, it may be useful to examine the changing and often conflicting attitudes of the judges themselves to the aims of the law which they were fashioning. Lawyers and legal theorists were by no means agreed on these aims.

There appear to have been three principal theories which have evolved over the past one hundred and fifty years as to the role of the courts in the administration of the ciminal law, and which still have their adherents today. One view we may call 'moralism'; for this view is based on the idea that the underlying purpose of the criminal law is to punish the morally guilty and to acquit the morally innocent. No doubt the belief that this should be the object of the framing and administration of the criminal law has always been very widely accepted; but moralism would appear to go further in that it would seem to justify the extension of the criminal law by the courts to punish immorality even where this is not expressly covered by the wording of an existing rule. The moralist approach was recently illustrated by the notorious case of *Shaw* v. *D.P.P.*, where Viscount Simonds said:[33]

In the sphere of criminal law I entertain no doubt that there remains in the courts of law a residual power to enforce the supreme and fundamental purpose of the law, to conserve not only the safety and order but also the moral welfare of the State, and that it is their duty to guard it against attacks which may be more insidious because they are novel and unprepared for.

The House of Lords thus appeared to affirm that 'the fundamental purpose' of the criminal law includes the conservation of 'the moral welfare of the State'; and that to achieve this purpose it is the task of the courts to apply the law to cases which were not previously envisaged as being within its scope. But moralism may also justify restricting the ostensible scope of the criminal law; for it would justify reading *mens rea* into a statute which does not expressly require it. Here the effect is to equate moral and legal guilt by restricting the apparent ambit of the law rather than extending it; for moralism is based on the belief that moral guilt is a necessary as well as a sufficient condition of legal liability.

A second view holds, contrary to the first, that the criminal law should never be extended beyond the terms of the rule as laid down by the legislature. To extend the law, adherents to the second view maintain, would be contrary to the principles of legality. They would criticise the ruling in *Shaw* v. *D.P.P.* on the ground that it infringes one aspect of the principles of legality, the rule *nulla poena sine lege*. The legalists, as they may be called, deny that there is a necessary connexion between legal and moral guilt. On the other hand, since the principles of legality themselves are based on moral considerations, they do not deny that certain moral principles may and should be invoked when the courts are required to interpret the wording of a statutory offence. They would argue that wherever possible the words should be so interpreted as to include the requirement of *mens rea*. They, like the moralists, would regard it as wrong to omit *mens rea*, but for different reasons. They would regard it as wrong not because it would involve punishing the innocent (since, as we have seen, there is for them no necessary connexion between legal and moral innocence). It would be wrong because this would contravene another, related aspect of the principles of legality: it would involve convicting a person for an act which he did not realise at the time was a criminal offence. The legalists would argue that *mens rea* is a necessary condition of legal liability because it would be contrary to legality as well as to moral justice to deny it. But they would deny that moral guilt is sufficient because to admit this, though in accord with moral justice, would be contrary to the principles of legality. The principles of legality in effect require, not that the morally guilty be punished and the morally innocent acqitted, but that no one be found guilty without due process of law.

A third legal theory would differ from both the others. Holders of the theory would not interfere with a statute either to extend or to limit its *prima facie* application. Like the legalists they deny that there is a necessary connexion between moral and legal guilt, but, unlike them, they would not make use of any moral principle to interpret the will of the legislature. They would apply the words which the legislature has adopted. They might regret any resulting injustice, for they may, without inconsistency, recognise the possibility of injustice, but they can be described as positivists, not because they believe the law to be immune from moral criticism, but in the sense that they believe with Austin that the question of what the law is, is one thing, the question of its rightness and wrongness, another. If they are judges they may excuse their decisions by saying that if the law is unjust it is for Parliament to remedy it. Again, this theory may be connected with a particular doctrine or parliamentary sovereignty and with certain assumptions about the intentions of the legislature.

All the theories, of course, pay lip-service to the principle that the existence and extent of the requirement of *mens rea* depend upon the interpretation of the statute and the legislative intention. But because they start from different assumptions, they lead to different results, and to anomalies and contradictions in the cases. In the case of *Prince* already mentioned, traces of all three attitudes can be detected. Balckburn J, with whom nine other judges agreed, adopted the positivist approach. He considered that the sole question for determination was the intention of the legislature. Rejecting the suggestion that the word 'knowingly' should be inserted into the section, he said that it was impossible to suppose that the legislature meant the issue to depend on the knowledge by the prisoner of the girl's actual age. It is significant that the same judge not only wrote the principal judgement in both *Prince* and *Fletcher* v. *Rylands*, perhaps the leading cases on strict liability in crime and tort in the nineteenth century, but also rejected the need for *mens rea* in a number of other influential cases[34]. The second judgement, delivered by Bramwell B, with the support of seven other members of the court, appears to exemplify the moralist doctrine. He refused to insert the word 'knowingly' into the section on the ground that 'the act forbidden is wrong in itself if without lawful cause; I do not say illegal but wrong'. What was wrong was the taking of an unmarried girl under the age of 16 which, he said 'gave full scope to the doctrine of *mens rea*'. Yet only two years before, Bramwell himself had criticised a similar argument in another jurisprudential *cause celebre, Middleton*, where he said that the judges 'seem to me to reason thus: the prisoner was as bad as a thief (which I deny) and, being as bad ought to be treated as one (which I deny also)'. Of the sixteen judges constituting the Court of Crown Cases Reserved in the case of *Prince*, Brett J alone stood his ground, perhaps on the basis of legality, in maintaining the necessity for *mens rea*. His closely argued judgement led him to the conclusion 'that a mistake of facts on reasonable grounds, to the extent that, if the facts were as believed, the acts of the prisoner would make him guilty of no offence at all, is an excuse, and that such an excuse is implied in every criminal charge and every criminal enactment in England.'[37]

Yet undoubtedly the prevailing attitude of the period was a scarcely disguised moralism. A typical case is one in which Lord Campbell upheld the justices in a refusal to convict consignors who had sent for carriage a quantity of 'oil of vitriol' without notifying the nature of the goods as required by statute.[38] The consignors had reasonably believed that the goods were adequately marked. 'The justices were perfectly right,' said Lord Campbell, *'actus non facit reum nisi mens sit rea . . .* what they have done it very satisfactory to me. . . . The act with which the respondents were charged is an offence created by a statute and for which the person committing it is liable to a penalty or to imprisonment. . . . There was neither negligence nor moral guilt of any kind on their part'. Some judges, however, went out of their way to repudiate the moralist philosophy. Apart from the case of *Middleton* already mentioned, the case of *Ashwell*[39] provides a useful illustration. In that case the accused asked a person to lend him a shilling. He was given a coin which both believed to be a shilling but which was in fact a sovereign. The accused went away with the coin in his pocket, and when he later realised that it was a sovereign he decided to keep it for himself. It seemed that he could not be convicted of stealing the sovereign unless he could be said to have acquired possession of it at the time it was handed over to him. But could he be said to be in possession of a sovereign when he believed it to be a shilling? The dilemma has recently recurred on charges of possessing drugs. In Ashwell's case the jury found a special verdict in which they described his conduct as fraudulent and added that ' if it were competent to them to find the person guilty they meant to do so'. A verdict of guilty was entered and the case reserved for the Court of Crown Cases Reserved. Two of the judges, Matthew and Field J J, expressly dissented from the assumption that, because the defendant had been dishonest, it was their duty to find some legal excuse for convicting him of a crime.

If we turn now to the case of *Tolson*, there is an apparent conflict between the evident moralism of Wills J, the legalism of Cave J, and the qualified positivism of Stephen J. Wills J drew a distinction between an act 'wrong in itself and apart from positive law' and an act 'merely prohibited by statute or by common law'[40]; while Cave J, as we have seen, argued that a requirement of *mens rea* must be read into a statute unless excluded expressly or by necessary implication. So far as Stephen is concerned, attention had already been drawn by Holmes to his apparent *volte face* between the time when he said in *A General View of the Criminal Law of England* (1863) that the state of mind required in criminal law is generally 'malice' and that malice stripped of technical accretions was simply wickedness, and the time when he prepared his *Digest of Criminal Law* (1877), when he seemed to cast out *mens rea* even in cases of murder.[41] In his *History of the Criminal Law* (1883) he expressed the view that '. . . as all crimes (except crimes of omission) must be voluntary actions, intention is a constituent element of all criminal acts.'[42] There was an inconsistency between his acceptance of strict liability in *R.v. Bishop* (1880)[43] and *Cundy* v. *Le Cocq* (1884) and his insistence on *mens rea* in *Tolson* (1889). In *Tolson* itself he rejects the crude moralist view that *mens rea* means that 'by the law of England no act is a crime which is done from laudable motives, in other words that immorality is essential to crime'; following Brett J in *Prince* he asserts as a rule without exception that reasonable mistake is a defence in crime, yet he relates, without explaining the contradiction, his own previous decision in the case of *Bishop*[44].

These decisions illustrate the diverse assumptions which the judges held about the proper scope of the criminal law. It is therefore hardly surprising that no agreement could be reached on the circumstances in which a statute should be construed as imposing strict liability, or whether, and to what extent, it should be read as importing *mens rea,* so that the reported decisions are individually paradoxical and mutually inconsistent.

In recent years, however, although the actual cases still show little consistency, there is evidence of mounting criticism among both scholars and judges of the doctrine of strict liability. This criticism has been accompanied by an attempt to approach the problem with a coherent philosophy. To appreciate the full significance of recent developments, it is only necessary to go back thirty years to the classic account by Sayre of 'Public Welfare Offences'[45] and the article by Dr Stallybrass significantly entitled 'The Eclipse of *Mens Rea*'[46]. In the first article Sayre attempts a justification of strict liability which is now generally rejected[47]. Dr Stallybrass came to the reluctant conclusion that although the maxim *actus non facit reum nisi mens sit rea* was still applicable to the older statutes, it had no application at all to modern enactments, and that unless such an enactment made specific reference to a mental requirement, there was no need of *mens rea.*

In the past thirty years there has been hardly noticed a radical change of opinion and of judicial policy. Ever since the classic articles of Sayre and Stallybrass, academic opinion has been almost unanimously hostile to any degree of strict liability[48] and recent cases show that, although the courts are not entirely agreed on the circumstances in which they should interpret a prohibition strictly, many judges have been increasingly reluctant to impose strict liability unless it is unambiguously required by the wording of the legislation. The reversal of judicial policy can be clearly illustrated from a brief survey of the case-law developed over the past twenty years, which forms a striking contrast with the series of cases already discussed from the previous century. In this survey we can trace the evolution of some new general principles developed by the courts as a guide to the incidence of strict liability. These cases also provide a further opportunity for examining the justification of strict liability, which can only be satisfactorily assessed in the context of the cases in which the doctrine may be relevant.

To start from the end of the war, the first important pronouncement of policy is to be found in a case reported in 1946, where the Divisional Court upheld the magistrates' acquittal of a defendant charged with a statutory offence involving an 'intent to deceive' on the ground that he had acted in good faith. Lord Goddard C J took the opportunity to remark that 'There are statutes . . . in which Parliament has seen fit to create offences and make people responsible before criminal courts although there is an absence of *mens rea*, but it is certainly not the court's duty to be acute to find that *mens rea* is not a constituent part of a crime.' He continued:[49]

'It is of the utmost importance for the protection of the liberty of the subject that the court should always bear in mind that, unless a statute either clearly or be necessary implication rules out *mens rea* as a constituent part of a crime, the court should not find a man guilty of an offence against the criminal law unless he has a guilty mind.'

These words were repeated by Lord Goddard in an important case reported in 1948[50]. The accused, the driver of a motor-lorry, had been convicted of an offence against section 22 (2) of the Road Traffic Act 1930, in that he had failed to report an accident whereby damage was caused to another vehicle. It was found that owing to the noise made by his lorry the defendant was unaware that the trailer, which was attached to his lorry, had collided with the other vehicle; but it was argued in support of the conviction that *mens rea* was not a constituent part of the offence. The argument was that in the corresponding section of the Motor Car Act 1903,[51] it was provided that if any person 'know ingly' acted in contravention of the section he should be guilty of an offence, while in the present section the word 'knowingly' had been omitted. The argument did not convince the court. Lord Goddard C J and Singleton J held that the effect of the change of wording was to shift the burden of proof (a view which had been advanced by Brett J as long before as *Prince* itself), while Humphreys J also re-echoed the earlier cases, by stating that, while the prohibition in the statute was absolute, nevertheless a person was entitled to be acquitted if, as in the present case, he was 'morally guiltless'. Yet it is significant that in this decision, at least, the principle of *mens rea* was reaffirmed.

Similarly, the following year, a Divisional Court of five judges held unanimously that, where a person is charged with 'wilfully and falsely' using the expression 'M D', he must be acquitted if he honestly believed that he was within his rights in so describing himself. Lord Goddard added:[52] 'He must, of course, have a reasonable ground for his belief.' Indeed, it was clear that there was considerable authority for the view that a mistaken belief must be reasonable if it is to be a good defence. But in a case which arose on similar facts two years later, Lord Goddard made it clear that, if the mistake was honestly made, it need not even be a reasonable one. The reasonableness of the mistake was usually good evidence of whether the mistake was honestly made, but it was no more than evidence; it was not a requirement laid down by law.[53]

The need to incorporate *mens rea* in the interpretation of statutes was again stressed by Lord Goddard in another case reported in 1951, where a coach proprietor was charged with an offence against section 72 (1) and (10) of the Road Traffic Act 1930. It was argued that the section imposed absolute liability on him for the actions of his customer; but Lord Goddard said:[54] 'Unless compelled by the words of the statute so to hold, no court should give effect to a proposition which is so repugnant to all the principles of criminal law in this Kingdom.' In the same case, Devlin J took the opportunity to consider the general justification of strict and vicarious liability, and one extract from his judgment must be quoted in full, since it clearly demonstrates how the development of the principles of criminal liability has been influenced by the judges' views as to the social purposes of the law. In a passage which has inspired a number of subsequent judgments, he said:[55]

'It may seem, on the face of it, hard that a man should be fined, and, indeed, made subject to imprisonment, for an offence which he did not know that he was committing. But there is no doubt that the legislature has for certain purposes found that hard measure to be necessary in the public interest. The moral justification behind such laws is admirably expressed in a sentence by Dean Roscoe Pound in his book *The Spirit of the Common Law*, at p.52: see The Law Quarterly Review, vol.64, p.176. "Such statutes", he says, "are not meant to punish the vicious will but to put pressure upon the thoughtless and inefficient to do their whole duty in the interest of public health or safety or morals,"

Thus a man may be made responsible for the acts of his servants, or even for defects in his business arrangements, because it can fairly be said that by such sanctions citizens are induced to keep themselves and their organisations up to the mark. Although, in one sense, the citizen is being punished for the sins of others, it can be said that, if he had been more alert to see that the law was observed, the sin might not have been committed. But if a man is punished because of an act done by another, whom he cannot reasonably be expected to influence or control, the law is engaged, not in punishing thoughtlessness or inefficiency, and thereby promoting the welfare of the community, but in pouncing on the most convenient victim. Without the authority of express words, I am not willing to conclude that Parliament can intend what would seem to the ordinary man (as plainly it seemed to the justices in this case) to be the useless and unjust infliction of a penalty . . . .'

Devlin J thus concluded that the imposition of strict liability in such cases was socially valueless and morally unjustifiable. He went on to propound a general principle which has since been developed into an important canon of construction of legislation of this type. He said:[56]

'I think it a safe general principle to follow . . . that where the punishment of an individual will not promote the observance of the law either by that individual or by others whose conduct he may reasonably be expected to influence then, in the absence of clear and express words, such punishment is not intended.'

The influence of this line of cases has been considerable, as many subsequent decisions have shown. To take a single example, in a case reported in 1952[57], the respondent was a butcher in whose shop were found parcels of meat bearing tickets showing the names of the purchasers and prices exceeding the maximum prices prescribed. The parcels had been prepared and the tickets attached during the respondent's absence from the shop and without his knowledge. Parker J quoted extracts cited above from two cases[58] and the Divisional Court held that the doctrine of vicarious liability could not be extended to include liability for an attempt.

The principle enunciated by Devlin J was expounded more fully in a decision of the Judicial Committee of the Privy Council in 1963[59], when he was himself a member of the Board. The relevant passage needs to be quoted in full if the exact scope of the principle is to be determined.[60]

'Where the subject matter of the statute is the regulation for the public welfare of a particular activity - statutes regulating the sale of food and drink are to be found among the earliest examples - it can be and frequently has been inferred that such activities should be carried out under conditions of strict liability. The presumption is that the statute or statutory instrument can be effectively enforced only if those in charge of the relevant activities are made responsible for seeing that they are complied with. When such a presumption is to be inferred, it displaces the ordinary presumption of *mens rea*. Thus sellers of meat may be made responsible for seeing that the meat is fit for human consumption and it is no answer for them to say that they were not aware that it was polluted. If that were a satisfactory answer, then as Kennedy L J pointed out in *Hobbs* v. *Winchester Corporation*, the distribution of bad meat (and its far-reaching consequences) would not be effectively prevented. So a publican may be made responsible for observing the condition of his customers: *Cundy* v. *Le Cocq*.

'But it is not enough in their Lordships' opinion merely to label the statute as one dealing with a grave social evil and from that to infer that strict liability was intended. It is pertinent also to inquire whether putting the defendant under strict liability will assist in the enforcement of the regulations. That means that there must be something he can do, directly or indirectly, by supervision or inspection, by improvement of his business methods or by exhorting those whom he may be expected to influence or control, which will promote the observance of the regulations. Unless this is so, there is no reason in penalising him, and it cannot be inferred that the legislature imposed strict liability merely in order to find a luckless victim. This principle has been expressed and applied in *Reynolds* v. *G H Austin & Sons Ltd.* and *James & Son Ltd.* v. *Smee.* Their Lordships prefer it to the alternative view that strict liability follows simply from the nature of the subject-matter and that persons whose conduct is beyond any sort of criticism can be dealt with by the imposition of a nominal penalty. This latter view can perhaps be supported to some extent by the dicta of Kennedy L J in *Hobbs* v. *Winchester Corporation* and Donovan J in *R* v. *St Margaret's Trust Ltd*. But though a nominal penalty may be appropriate in an individual case where exceptional lenience is called for, their Lordships cannot, with respect, suppose that it is envisaged by the legislature as a way of dealing with offenders generally. Where it can be shown that the imposition of strict liability would result in the prosecution and conviction of a class of persons whose conduct could not in any way affect the observance of the law, their Lordships consider that, even where the statute is dealing with a grave social evil strict liability is not likely to be intended.'

This pronouncement was clearly designed not only to restrict the operation of the doctrine of strict liability, but to do so in a more uniform and predictable manner than the previous expositions of the limits of strict liability. The criteria laid down are, it is true, not entirely free from their own difficulties. At first sight, the crucial test, 'there must be something he can do', appears somewhat vague. It does not make it clear what, if anything, a person is required to know if he is to be liable. Clearly a person may still be liable although he is ignorant of some of the material elements of the offence: since, if knowledge of all such elements were to become a condition of the imposition of liability in these cases, it could not be a condition of the imposition of strict liability. Again, the language of the critical passage seems to suggest that the test 'there must be something he can do' is the same criterion as the test 'whether putting the defendant under strict liability will assist in the enforcement of the regulations'. But the difference here is not merely one of the formulation of the test; for putting a defendant under strict liability, regardless of his innocence, may still assist in the indirect enforcement of the law, as seizing on a luckless victim always may, by serving to encourage the others. There is here a familiar ambiguity in the notion of enforcement. And apart from the difficulty that there is a wide variety of ways in which laws of different kinds can be directly or indirectly enforced, there is a sense in which any application of a law can be regarded as its enforcement.

One of the problems inherent in these particular criteria may be that the type of situation here envisaged was the rather special case where a person is held responsible for the actions of others working either under his direct supervision or at any rate within an organisation under his control. If this interpretation is correct then strict liability is to be considered as primarily appropriate within this class of cases to mismanagement in general and in particular to those who turn a blind eye to malpractices within an organisation under their control; but the effect of the judgment, and especially of the last two sentences of the quoted extract, was sufficiently wide in its implications to dispel the belief that strict liability was a principle of general application in the interpretation of penal legislation. In recent years the most important area in which the courts have been faced with the question of strict liability has been that of offences relating to drugs. But even in this area, in spite of the difficulties of proof and the grave social evils involved, the judges have been increasingly reluctant to impose absolute liability.

In *Yeandel* v. *Fisher* [61] an innkeeper and his wife were charged that they were persons concerned in the management of premises used for the purposes of smoking and of dealing in cannabis. The relevant section of the Dangerous Drugs Act 1964 read as follows: 'If a person (a) being the occupier of any premises, permits those premises to be used for the purpose of smoking cannabis or cannabis resin or of dealing in cannabis or cannabis resin (whether by sale or otherwise); or (b) is concerned in the management of any premises used for any such purpose as aforesaid, he shall be guilty of an offence against the principal Act.'[62] The defendants were convicted by the magistrates and appealed to the Divisional Court. The case stated found that on six days cannabis had been smoked or dealt in on the premises; the first defendant was not seen on the premises on any of those days, but his wife was in charge of the bar. The Divisional Court, in dismissing the appeal, used several dubious arguments to establish the conclusion that liability was intended

to be absolute. It attempted to draw a distinction between paragraphs
(a) and (b) of the sub-section, on the basis that the use of the word
'permit' implied knowledge, and because it could be implied that knowledge was required in paragraph (a), the incorporation of a requirement
of knowledge in that paragraph showed that no such requirement was
intended in paragraph (b)!

This highly artificial construction was supported by references to
the social importance of drugs and to the fact that the provision was
a regulation for the public welfare; considerations which, whatever (if
anything) they do prove, certainly do not justify any distinction between
the two paragraphs. Lord Parker C J concluded that 'the legislature
had in mind making those at any rate who were on the spot and concerned with the management of premises absolutely liable if those premises were used for these purposes, whereas they had in mind that in
the case of the occupier who might be an absent occupier and not on
the premises at all, that he would only be guilty if he wilfully and
knowingly permitted.' However realistic these hypotheses about the
intention of the legislature may be, they seem inconsistent with a subsequent decision[63] of the Divisional Court on an identically worded
offence against the Dangerous Drugs Act 1965[64]. The appellant in
this case, Stephanie Sweet, a teacher, lived in Oxford but had a sub-
lease of a farmhouse just outside the town in which she let rooms to
tenants. She retained the use of one room for herself and visited the
house occasionally, but the only form of control which she exercised
over her tenants was to complain if there was excessive noise late at
night on the infrequent occasions when she stayed overnight. The police
searched the house and garden in her absence and found receptacles
containing cannabis and LSD hidden in the garden and cigarette ends
containing cannabis in the kitchen. The magistrates found that 'she
had no knowledge whatever that the house was being used for the
purpose of smoking cannabis or cannabis resin.' They convicted her of
being concerned in the management of premises used for this purpose,
and she appealed to the Divisional Court. Her appeal was dismissed.
Although she was not present on the premises, the reasoning was that
she was concerned in their management, because she was in a position
to choose her tenants, she could put them under as long or as short a
tenancy as she chose, and she could make it a term of any letting that
the smoking of cannabis was not to take place. The argument was a
strange one and would have led to strange conclusions. If she had put
the desired term in the letting and it had not been observed, would
the court have held that she was not concerned in the management of
the premises? If the argument was valid, every occupier who let out

part of his house, or took lodgers or paying guests, would be liable. This time, however, the appellant pursued her appeal to the House of Lords, who allowed it[65]. Although they reached their conclusion on different grounds, all five judges introduced an important limitation on strict liability in drugs offences. Lords Reid, Wilberforce, and Diplock held that, for the offence to be committed, it must be shown that it was the appellant's purpose that the premises be used for smoking cannabis; that is, that she intended the premises to be so used. Lords Pearce and Morris of Borth-y-Gest held that she must be shown to have knowledge of the particular purpose to which the premises were being put.

The House of Lords was more divided on the question whether a person was to be regarded as in possession of a drug if he knew that he was in physical possession of the substance but was unaware of its true nature. In *Warner* v. *Metropolitan Police Commissioner*[66] the appellant was found with two boxes, and in the smaller box were twenty thousand tablets containing amphetamine sulphate, a drug prohibited under the Drugs (Prevention of Misuse) Act 1964. He denied any knowledge of the contents of the box, but the jury were directed that absence of this knowledge went only to mitigation. The House was divided on the question whether a person was to be regarded as in possession of a prohibited drug for the purposes of the Act if he knew that he was in possession of the package but was unaware of its contents. The only point on which unanimity was achieved was that although the jury had been misdirected or inadequately directed on the issue of possession, so that the appellant had been deprived of putting before the jury a defence which should have been open to him, nevertheless no reasonable jury would have believed his story and the conviction should therefore be upheld.

The principal significance for strict liability of the drugs cases is to show the fallacy of the argument that *mens rea* is not required where a 'grave social evil' is involved. If they are indeed serious offences, the case for *mens rea* is correspondingly greater. The maximum penalties are alone sufficient to demonstrate this. But apart from the formal penalty, the stigma of conviction of an offence of this type, and the extra-legal consequences which may follow it (exemplified by the case of Stephanie Sweet, who was fined a relatively modest £25 but lost her career as a teacher), demonstrates the iniquity of penalising by an arbitrary act of statutory interpretation conduct which by any other standards would be wholly innocent.

The particular significance of *Sweet* v. *Parsley* lies not only in the actual decision but in the recognition by Lords Reid, Pearce, and Diplock of the possibility of a defence in cases where proof of *mens rea* was not required, if the defendant could show that he had taken all reasonable care. They referred to a rule developed by the High Court of Australia

I

which considerably restricts the scope of strict liability. By this rule, even in cases where the prosecution does not have to prove *mens rea* for the defendant to be convicted, it is still open to the defendant to to secure his acquittal by proving that he did the act or omission charged owing to a reasonable mistake of fact of such a nature that, had the facts been as he believed, he would be innocent[67]. This rule has greatly reduced the incidence of strict liability; indeed, Professor Howard was able to say[68] in 1963 of the High Court of Australia that 'except on three occasions when the abnormal stresses of wartime conditions caused a departure from the usual rule, there is no case in which strict responsibility has been imposed in that court.'

Again, the influence of individual judges can be detected. The rule has been largely the creation of two Australian Chief Justices, Sir Samuel Griffith C J and Sir Owen Dixon C J. Australian courts have under their guidance moved away from strict liability, and Australian law has developed in the same direction as Anglo-American law but with more purpose and consistency. Professor Howard concluded[69] that: 'The nearer one approaches to the present day, the higher becomes the proportion and the wider the range of both High Court and State Supreme Court decisions and expressions of opinion in favour of the reasonable mistake rule and against strict responsibility.'

After this brief attempt to assess the current trends in relation to the extent of strict liability, we must try to examine the implications of the doctrine for the concept of criminal responsibility. It is necessary to ask, therefore, how far its adoption amounts to the elimination of responsibility from the criminal law. It is already clear that for a number of reasons the doctrine cannot automatically be equated with the complete elimination of responsibility. This must be true if only because the term strict liability cannot be given a single meaning but frequently has a different sense according to the context in which it is used. Often, for example, the term is used to mean that the prosecution is not required to allege or prove a particular intent; at other times, that a particular defence such as those of ignorance or mistake of fact is deemed irrelevant. Some writers regard the imposition of liability for negligence as tantamount to strict liability; one assumption here seems to be that 'strict liability' means 'liability without fault', and another assumption, a mistaken one, that because liability for negligence does not require a particular state of mind the notion of fault is necessarily excluded.

Whether or not the term should be extended to include liability for negligence may be thought to depend upon whether or not this form of liability requires fault, but it is clear that in general the use of the

term cannot be determined by any *a priori* analysis of the notion of
strict liability. It must be recognised that the term has been employed
to cover a number of different kinds of decision, and it is only by examining the decisions, not by an appeal to the concept of strict liability,
that we can see how far it eliminates responsibility.

The large majority of cases where the doctrine has been invoked have
been cases in which it precluded a defence of mistake of fact. A characteristic example is the American case[70] in which a banker was charged
with an offence against a statute prohibiting a director or officer of a
bank from borrowing excessively from its funds. He contended that he
had borrowed the money only after he had been assured by another
official of the bank that the money had come from a bank other than
his own. The court held that it was not open to him to adduce as a
defence even a reasonable mistake of fact. A decision of this type raises
a number of questions about the precise ambit of the doctrine of strict
liability. The first limitation on the doctrine is that it is not clear whether
no mistake of any kind, or no degree of ignorance, would serve to ex-
culpate a defendant. As an illustration of this argument, the hypothesis
might be entertained that the banker in a similar case had been mistaken
about the amount of his loan. Or to take the argument perhaps further,
it is not obvious what the decision might have been if the sum had
been credited to his account without his knowledge, or in error.

Secondly, even if the doctrine were interpreted in such a way as to
exclude altogether the requirement of *mens rea*, it could still be argued
that this still does not amount to a total elimination of responsibility.
For the question could still arise whether it excluded also those defences
which do not deny *mens rea* but deny that the defendant did the *actus
reus* in the sense defined by Professor Glanville Williams [71] as 'including
so much of the mental element as is contained in the definition of an
act'. For whether or not this division of the elements of an offence is
a defensible or even an intelligible one, there is undoubted authority for
the view that even when charged with an offence of supposedly strict
liability the defendant may still plead as a defence a complete loss of
control. Support for this view can be found in the cases of *Hill* v.
Baxter and *Burns* v. *Bidder* referred to above; and there seems no reason
why the same principle should not be applied to cases of coercion and
duress, and perhaps also to cases of automatism. In *Bratty's* case Lord
Denning said[72] that 'The requirement that it should be a voluntary act
is essential, not only in a murder case, but also in every criminal case.
No act is punishable if it is done involuntarily: and an involuntary act
in this context − some people nowadays prefer to speak of it as "automatism" − means an act which is done by the muscles without any

control by the mind, such as a spasm, a reflex action or a convulsion;
or an act done by a person who is not conscious of what he is doing,
such as an act done whilst suffering from concussion or whilst sleep-
walking.'

There remains the uncharted area of such general defences as infancy and insanity; here too there seems no reason why they should
be excluded by strict liability, though the subject is of little practical
importance.

In practice, therefore, a survey of recent case-law shows not only
that there is no evidence of a wholesale abandonment of the principle
of *mens rea*, and of any equation of strict liability with the elimination
of responsibility; it shows also that the fate of strict liability itself is
in the balance. In the criminal law, the courts have increasingly been
prepared to accept the defence of ignorance or mistake of fact, and
it is doubtful if the doctrine of strict liability ever did more than to
exclude certain forms of such defence. In the law of tort, the increase
in social welfare legislation and in all forms of insurance have lessened
rather than heightened the need for strict liability; for as extra-legal
techniques for meeting the hazards of an industrialised society have
developed, the law has been able to confine itself to basing liability
upon fault[73].

Chapter 5

Objective Liability

The present chapter is concerned with the doctrine of objective liability. It seeks to discover the part played by this doctrine in the development of the criminal law, its implications at the present time for the concept of criminal responsibility, and its rationale. As in the case of strict liability, it will be seen that the apparently simple doctrine conceals a number of difficult and complex ideas, but broadly stated, it can be said that what the doctrine involves is that where the law purports to make a particular state of mind, such as knowledge of certain facts, or foresight of certain consequences a condition of liability, that condition can be satisfied by showing, not that the accused himself had this knowledge or foresight, but that the so-called 'reasonable man' would have known, or would have foreseen the consequences. In effect, the law sets up a model, possessed of the characteristics considered necessary to serve the purposes of social control, and bases liability on the characteristics of the model rather than on those of the actual defendant.[1] If a person is neither an infant nor insane – and the criteria of insanity and infancy are themselves regarded as sufficiently objective – he is deemed to be a 'reasonable man': he is allowed to make mistakes but only reasonable ones; to respond to threats to his person or property, but only reasonably; and to retaliate if provoked, but only if the reasonable man would have been provoked, and then only within limits that the reasonable man would not have exceeded.

Most of the recent discussion of objective liability has arisen out of the decision of the House of Lords in *D.P.P.* v. *Smith*, which seemed in effect to make negligence the basis of liability in murder, and the modification of that decision by the Criminal Justice Act 1967; but it must be remembered that objective liability relates not only to the knowledge and foresight of the individual, but also to his capacities and temperament. It is proposed to confine discussion in the present chapter to what may be referred to as the generalised form of the rule in *Smith's* case, and its philosophical justification. Here too the rule is a creature of the common law; but the relative simplicity of the rule makes it unnecessary to consider the case-law at length. The principal case prior to *Smith* which adopted the objective approach was the highly controversial decision in *R. v. Ward.*[2]

The defendant in this case was a man of subnormal intelligence, suffering from gastric ulcers; he was cohabiting with a woman who had a backward child of eighteen months by another man. Returning home after work, he was so irritated by the child's continual crying that he picked her up and shook her with the result that she died. He said that his intention was only to make her quiet but he was convicted of murder. Pilcher J directed the jury that If, when he did the act which he did do, he must as a reasonable man have contemplated that death or grievious bodily harm was likely to result to the child as the result of what he did,ᵃthen . . . if you are satisfied about that, he is guilty of murder. If on the other hand he could not, as a reasonable man, have contemplated that death would result in consequence of what he did, then he is guilty of manslaughter.' The direction to the jury thus clearly laid down an objective test; and the argument for the appellant was rejected by the Court of Criminal Appeal. Lord Goddard C J described the summing-up as 'unimpeachable' and said: 'The objection is . . . that it brings in the test of a reasonable man, and you have to say what that particular man knew. Of course the test must be applied to all alike and the only measure that can be brought to bear in these matters is what a reasonable man would or would not contemplate. . . . If the jury come to the conclusion that any reasonable person, that is to say, a person who cannot set up a plea of insanity, must have known that what he was doing would cause at least grievious bodily harm, then that amounts to murder in law.'

Despite the criticisms of this decision the House of Lords adopted a similar approach in *D.P.P. .v. Smith.* The facts, however, were rather different, and there may have been less sympathy with the appellant. Smith was driving a car containing some stolen property when a policeman told him to draw into the kerb. Instead he accelerated and the constable clung on to the side of the car. The car followed an erratic course and the policeman fell off in front of another car and was killed. Smith drove on for 200 yards, dumped the stolen property, and then returned. He was charged with capital murder, and convicted; the Court of Criminal Appeal quashed the conviction for capital murder and substituted a verdict of manslaughter. The Crown appealed to the House of Lords, which restored the conviction for capital murder.

Although there were several grounds on which the summing-up of the trial judge was criticised by the Court of Criminal Appeal, 'the main complaint', in the terms of the House of Lords judgment,[3] 'is that the learned judge was . . . applying what is referred to as an objective test, namely, the test of what a reasonable man would contemplate as the probable result of his acts, and therefore would intend, whereas the question for the jury, it is said, was what the respondent himself intended. This, indeed, was the view of the Court of Criminal Appeal . . .'. The House of Lords rejected this view. Of the judgment of the lower court, it said:[4]

' . . . they were saying that it was for the jury to decide whether, having regard to the panic in which he said he was, the respondent in fact at the time contemplated that grievous bodily harm would result from his actions, or indeed, whether he contemplated anything at all. Unless the jury were satisfied that he in fact had such contemplation, the necessary intent to constitute malice would not, in their view, have been proved. This purely subjective approach involves this, that if an accused said that he did not in fact think of the consequences, and the jury considered that that might well be true, he would be entitled to be acquitted of murder.'

Relying on Holmes' lectures on *The Common Law*[5] as their first authority, the House of Lords ruled in favour of the objective approach. Taken at its face value, the case could be construed as undermining the basis of *mens rea*; but a number of attempts were subsequently made to qualify its less guarded pronouncements. Some of these, surprisingly, were made by judges themselves. Lord Justice Salmon attempted an extra-judicial exposition of the limits of the new doctrine;[6] still more unusual, Lord Denning, himself an undissenting member of the House in the case, devoted the larger part of a lecture entitled 'Responsibility before the Law' to an attempted justification of the decision.[7] Lord Denning argued, first of all, that the objective test was the correct one and indeed the only possible basis of liability; but he concluded by asserting that the test was really a subjective one, and that this alone was morally or legally defensible. Lord Denning was at any rate right to say that parts of the judge's direction to the jury were not incompatible with a subjective test; but he was more clearly wrong in claiming that it was this aspect of the ruling that was upheld by the House of Lords. In this context two sentences from Lord Kilmuir's speech are quite incontrovertible in their effect, At one point he said:

'Provided that the presumption is applied, once the accused's knowledge of the circumstances and the nature of his act has been ascertained, the only thing that could rebut the presumption would be proof of incapacity to form an intent, insanity, or diminished responsibility.' And further: 'Once however, the jury are satisfied as to that (i.e. that the accused was unlawfully and voluntarily doing something to someone), it matters not what the accused in fact contemplated as the probable result or whether he ever contemplated at all, provided he was in law responsible and accountable for his actions, that is, was a man capable of forming an intent, not insane within the M'Naghten Rules and not suffering from diminished responsibility.'[8]

The confusion apparent in Lord Denning's lecture, and perhaps reflected at some points in the judgment which bear the imprint of his style, can be traced back to the writings of Holmes himself with whom the doctrine of objective liability is especially associated.[9] Holmes at any rate does provide a reasoned and generally consistent defence of the doctrine of objective liability in the criminal law; and although his views have been subjected to a searching critique by Professor Jerome Hall,[10] it can perhaps be maintained that the most illuminating approach to the doctrine remains one based upon a detailed analysis of Holmes' position.

There are several reasons why Holmes' lectures on *The Common Law* can and should be singled out for special examination. Apart from the fact that they remain the *locus classicus* for the discussion of the doctrine of objective liability, they have a far more broadly based claim to fame; for they appear to constitute the first general attempt to provide a rationale for the basic principles of liability in the common law, and to supply the criminal law in particular with a coherent philosophy. As well as the reasoned argument which Holmes always provides his work is remarkable for its extraordinary influence throughout the common law world, and it is significant that Holmes, 'that persuasive authority', should be the first authority cited by the House of Lords in *Smith's* case.[11] Nor can the influence of Holmes on later writers be ignored; seen from this point of view, his arguments can also be regarded as illustrating characteristic features of the types of argument later advanced in support of similar doctrines. For all these reasons it may be suggested that an analysis of Holmes' lectures may be of particular value in assessing the doctrine of objective liability.[12]

First of all, however, it should be made clear that taken literally Holmes's doctrine is far-reaching in its application in a number of ways in which the rule in *Smith* was not. It can in fact be argued that Holmes's doctrine is wider than the rule in *Smith* in three principal respects. First, Holmes lays down a general doctrine of criminal responsibility the effect of which would be to remove altogether the subjective test of *mens rea* in relation to the consequences of an act. The precise scope of the rule in *Smith* has always been unclear. It will be discussed further below but at this stage it may be said that it specifically excluded cases of further intent; that it may have been intented only to apply to cases of murder and of wounding with intent under section 18 of the Offences against the Person Act 1861; and that it is arguable that it should be confined to murder alone.[13]

Secondly, Holmes's doctrine sets a higher standard than the rule in *Smith* because Holmes's 'reasonable man' is the man of average intelligence and prudence,[14] while the reasonable man in *Smith* was defined as 'an ordinary man capable of reasoning.[15] Third, Holmes's doctrine does not require that the act must be 'aimed at' somebody. The House of Lords explicitly stated that the requirement that the act must be aimed at somebody was necessary in order to exclude cases of dangerous driving.[16] The requirement would also exclude the type of case where for example a person causes an explosion resulting in death with the aim of releasing prisoners.[17] In all these respects Holmes's doctrine is of wider application than the decision in *Smith*.

Holmes differs from most advocates of objective liability in that he scorns the familiar argument from the difficulty of proving *mens rea*. We shall see that this argument does not really support the case for objective liability, since if carried to its logical conclusion it would lead straight to strict liability. Further objections to the argument are considered in the concluding chapter; but it is important to observe that in claiming to justify rather than apologise for the doctrine, Holmes rejects what is usually treated as the chief argument in its favour.

Apart for the arguments for and against the doctrine of objective liability, the question arises of the extent to which this doctrine represents an elimination of responsibility. As with the other developments which have already been examined, this question serves an additional purpose to that of eliciting current trends in the criminal law; for it may enable us also to clarify the concept of criminal responsibility, and to understand what might be involved in its elimination. The question can accordingly be divided into two parts; for, before we consider the present scope of the doctrine, we may ask how far it dispenses with *mens rea*. This question may conveniently be taken first, because it helps to make clear what the doctrine involves.

In one respect, objective liability does represent a greater encroachment on the doctrine of *mens rea* than strict liability itself. This apparent paradox is explained by the range of offences to which the respective principles of liability are applied. Although there are, as we have seen, some serious offences, notably bigamy, which are or have been subject to a partial form of strict liability, this type of liability is generally confined to minor offences. It is indeed the most common, if not the most convincing, of the arguments advanced in support of strict liability that the values sacrificed to convenience in the administration of the law are of a lesser importance in the case of minor statutory offences. This argument would itself prevent the extension of the principle to more serious cases; in addition, it can be argued, as is shown elsewhere[18], that the justification of administrative convenience cannot logically be generalised. It could for other reasons too be maintained, as is suggested in the concluding chapter, that it is not simply fortuitous that strict liability is found only in a restricted class of relatively minor offences.[19]

Objective liability, far from being confined to minor offences, is on the contrary more commonly associated with serious crimes, and *Smith's* case appeared to confirm its extension in England to the law of murder. Further, the objective test in the law of provocation, and the requiremen on a plea of self-defence, for example, that ignorance or mistake of fac must be reasonable, have their most important application in cases of homicide. In this respect, those who allege that the law is in the proce s of dispensing with responsibility might be able to adduce the extension of objective liability as evidence of this process. On the other hand, if we are considering the extent of the encroachment of objective liability on the doctrine of *mens rea*, it cannot be denied that, although perhaps more serious in its consequences when it is applied, it remains in principle for a number of reasons a lesser encroachment than strict liability

It is clear in the first place that, apart from a few exceptional cases where strict liability is partial, this doctrine generally operates in such a way as to preclude, within the limits already described, any defence of ignorance or mistake of fact; whereas objective liability, as we have seen, only precludes a person from claiming as a defence that he did not foresee the consequences of his action. Further, even where this defence is precluded, the defendant is presumed to foresee only the consequences foreseeable by the reasonable man, whereas under the operation of strict liability the law does not merely penalise negligence (however involuntary) but provides that even the most scrupulous precautions would not constitute a defence. Finally, while it is uncertain, in cases of strict liability, where the defences of ignorance and mistake are completely, or almost completely,[20] excluded, how far many of the general defences, such as insanity and automatism, would be allowed, there can be no doubt, in cases where the doctrine of objective liability is applied, that the general defences would operate. There could *ex hypothesi* be no argument that, because the statute defining the offence made no reference to *mens rea*, *mens rea* in the widest sense was excluded; for such an argument would necessarily make the offence one of strict, not objective liability. It can therefore be shown that in this respect too the effects of the doctrine are less far-reaching. All these qualifications must therefore be seen to restrict the equation of objective liability with the total elimination of responsibility.

Nevertheless, once the nature of the encroachment has been defined, there can be no denial that it exists. In order to assess its extent, it is necessary also to outline briefly the scope currently given to the doctrine by the law.

The first question to consider is the intended scope of the decision in *Smith* and it may be asked whether it was intended to apply beyond cases of murder. At one point the judgment states that the case is concerned with the proper direction of the jury as to intent in murder and in cases of wounding with intent under section 18 of the Offences against the Person Act of 1861.[1] Section 18 provided that a felony was committed by any one who 'shall unlawfully and maliciously by means whatsoever wound, or cause any grievous bodily harm to any person, or shoot at any person, or, by drawing a trigger, or in any other manner, attempt to discharge any kind of loaded arms at any person, with intent, in any of the cases aforesaid, to maim, disfigure, or disable any person, or to do some other grievous bodily harm to any person, or with intent to resist or prevent the lawful apprehension or detainer of any person.' It is possible to read this remark as referring to a later passage in the judgment dealing with the definition of grievous bodily harm[22], and this view appears to have been taken in the case of *Metharam* where the subjective test was clearly applied.[23] Further, the judgement in *Smith* subsequently distinguished[24] between crime where what it calls 'actual intent' or 'overall intent' is necessary, with regard to which the subjective view of intent was admitted to be correct, and other crimes where it would appear that an objectively determined intent would be enough. This would appear to exclude cases under section 18 from the scope of the rule.

The second question is how far the decision has been confined in subsequent cases. It should be observed that English courts,[25] the courts of the Commonwealth,[26] and the Judicial Committee of the Privy Council[27] have either refused to follow the case or have confined it as narrowly as possible. It was stated in subsequent English cases that the rule does not apply to attempted murder;[28] that it does not apply to section 7(2) of the Sexual Offences Act 1956;[29] and that it does not apply to unlawful and malicious wounding under section 20 of the Offences against the Person Act 1861.[30] Section 20 provided that a misdemeanour was committed by any one who 'shall unlawfully and maliciously wound or inflict any grievous bodily harm upon any other person, either with or without any weapon or instrument.' If the rule did apply here, then whenever the accused had inflicted grievous bodily harm and a reasonable man would have foreseen it, the distinction between section 20 and section 18 would altogether disappear. Even in cases of murder, a survey of subsequent trials has shown that trial courts have tended to put the issue of intent to the jury without apparent regard to the ruling in *Smith's* case, and in a way which generally suggests a subjective rather than an objective approach.[31]

The decision in Smith's case was heavily criticised, and the question was finally considered by the Law Commission, who came to the conclusion that a subjective and not an objective test should be applied in ascertaining the intent required in murder. They proposed two clauses, the first of which was incorporated in the Criminal Justice Act 1967. Section 8 of the Act provides:

'A court or jury in determining whether a person has committed an offence,

(a) shall not be bound in law to infer that he intended or foresaw a result of his actions by reason only of its being a natural and probable consequence of those actions; but

(b) shall decide whether he did intend or foresee that result by reference to all the evidence drawing such inferences from the evidence as appear proper in the circumstances.'

This provision is clearly of general application but its exact scope is still unclear. In their second clause the Law Commission defined the *mens rea* of murder as follows:

'(1) Where a person kills another, the killing shall not amount to murder unless done with an intent to kill.

(2) A person has an "intent to kill" if he means his actions to kill, or if he is willing for his actions, though meant for another purpose, to kill in accomplishing that purpose.

(3) It is immaterial whether the intent to kill is an intent to kill the person in fact killed or any particular person, so long as it is an intent to kill someone other than himself; and references to killing in subsection (2) above shall be construed accordingly.'

It is clear that this proposal would have abolished intention to cause grievous bodily harm as sufficient *mens rea* for murder, but the exact scope of the new criterion of 'willingness to kill' is less clear. This proposal, however, was not enacted; and the result is that the intention of the Law Commission to introduce a subjective test of intent in murder was not accomplished. For, as one textbook has expressed it,[32] section 8 of the Act relates to *how* intention and foresight must be proved, not *when* they must be proved. It is therefore still necessary to look at the substantive law to ascertain the *mens rea* of the particular offence; and if Smith's case is rightly regarded as laying down a substantive rule of law, rather than a rule of evidence, then it remains the leading authority on the *mens rea* of murder.

The major criticisms of the doctrine of objective liability fall into two classes. There are first the criticisms of some of the arguments advanced in support of the doctrine as misleading, or even confused. Much of the force of the classic exposition of the doctrine, Holmes' lectures on *The Common Law*, would be lost, as we shall see, if the necessary distinctions were to be drawn between tests and standards, between the purposes of criminal law and its principles of liability, between what is objective and what is external, distinctions which, if occasionally marked, are not consistently observed throughout the work.

Still more important are the substantive criticisms of the doctrine. It is argued convincingly that the imposition of objective liability of the type advocated by Holmes is unacceptable in any form or at any rate in a way which fails to reflect the moral distinction between intentional and negligent wrongdoing. Such criticisms are advanced by those who wish to see moral culpability as the basis of criminal liability, and in particular to posit the intentional commission of a moral wrong as the foundation of criminal guilt. This would seem to be the view of Professor Jerome Hall, one of the leading critics of objective liability.

Against this view it may be said that what is objectionable about the doctrine of objective liability is not that it penalises negligent conduct, since there are grounds for justifying liability for negligence; nor that it penalises those who may be morally innocent, since there is no necessary connexion between legal and moral guilt; but that it may penalise those who had no opportunity of conforming to the requirements of the law. On this view, the doctrine offends against the principle of legality, of which something has already been said. But one unsolved puzzle arising out of the doctrine still obstructs the proper evaluation of it and is in need of fuller discussion.

The conundrum can be stated shortly. What is the basis of the distinction implicit in the doctrine, and often explicitly stated in formulations of it, between the circumstances and the consequences of an action? Certainly according to Holmes himself, and perhaps on one interpretation of the decision in *Smith's* case, whereas the accused's foresight of the consequences of his action is tested by reference to what the reasonable man would have foreseen, this test is not applicable to the circumstances of his action, since actual knowledge on his part of the circumstances of his action is required as a condition of liability.

This is an exception to the doctrine of objective liability which greatly mitigates its effects. Holmes does not treat it as an exception or recognise that it is in fact inconsistent with his arguments yet it is clear that it must be an exception. If the 'actual condition of the defendant' is not and cannot be material, if liability is and must be 'objective and external' then it would not be possible let alone desirable to require that 'there must be actual present knowledge of the present facts which make an act dangerous.'[33] So much is clear. But what is the principle on which this distinction is based? For its justification, although by no means self-evident, is nowhere explained.

It does at first sight present a number of difficulties. There are, in the first place, no obvious criteria for deciding whether in a particular case a person's lack of awareness is to be described as ignorance of the circumstances, or as a failure to foresee the consequences, of his action. Such a decision will often depend upon the choice of a description for the action, which itself may be an arbitrary matter. In describing an action it may be a matter of indifference whether certain of the consequences of a person's movements are incorporated in the description, for example whether he is said to have pulled the trigger, or to have fired a gun, or to have shot pigeon; but the application of the distinction between circumstances and consequences seems to turn upon this arbitrary decision.

Even where the action has to be identified under a given description, as it may be for legal purposes under a particular rule of law, the application of the distinction is not always immediately apparent. Suppose, for instance, to take a classic example, that a person charged with, say, the offence of causing grievous bodily harm, is alleged to have thrown bricks from the roof of a house at people in the street below. If he claims that he was unaware that there were people in range of the bricks, the question is whether he is claiming ignorance of the circumstances, or failure to foresee the consequences, of his action. It can hardly be said that either is immediately evident as the more appropriate description. The application of the distinction to many cases of similar kinds must be equally obscure, and raises doubts about the utility of the distinction.

But even if it were possible to evolve consistent criteria for distinguishing between circumstances and consequences, the question would still remain whether there would be any justification for making the issue of liability turn upon this distinction. Why should a person be expected to foresee consequences which a reasonable man would foresee, but not to possess knowledge which a reasonable man would possess? If, in the case of consequences, it is argued: 'Perhaps he did not in fact realise; but he ought to have realised', why should the same argument not be of equal validity in the case of circumstances? If knowledge of circumstances is to be required as a condition of liability, why should foresight of consequences not be a condition too?

All these difficulties appear to cast doubt upon any rule which seeks to rely upon a distinction between the circumstances of an action and its consequences. The distinction appears both difficult in principle to draw consistently, and if it can be drawn anomalous in its practical application. Yet, although it lies at the root of the doctrine of objective liability, no satisfactory account of its rationale appears to have been offered by either the advocates or the critics of the doctrine.

In approaching this problem, we may perhaps seek a clue to the solution in the fact that there are two different applications of the test of the reasonable man, which the indiscriminate use of terms such as 'test' and 'standards' may have inadvertently confused. It may be a mistake to assume that the role of the reasonable man in the doctrine of objective liability is to set up standards to which men must conform at their peril. This interpretation leads naturally from a confusion of standards and tests; but it may be mistaken, not only because it is difficult, on this interpretation, to justify any distinction between circumstances and consequences, but also because there is, as we have seen, little evidence, apart from the special cases of manslaughter and murder, of the imposition of liability for negligence at common law, or indeed of any standard short of intentional wrongdoing.

But if the invocation of the reasonable man is treated as a rule of evidence and not as setting a standard of care, then it becomes possible not only to retain the theory that intentional wrongdoing is still required for liability but also to explain the otherwise puzzling distinction between circumstances and consequences. For while it would be verging on the absurd to suppose that a person actually knows in the particular circumstances of a case just those facts which a hypothetical person might be taken to know, it is at any rate not in principle absurd, although it may sometimes work injustice, to presume that a person has the foresight of a reasonable man.

Although the results may at times be unfair to a particular individual, the rule that we are taken to foresee the natural consequences of our actions is at least a more reasonable presumption than any rule crediting us with knowledge of all the circumstances of our actions. If, for example. I fire a gun at a person, it may or may not, according to the situation, be unreasonable to presume that I know it is loaded; but it is in any case less unreasonable to presume, if I am sane, that, if I do know it is loaded, then I foresee harmful consequences.

The explanation of this may be partly that, while we all frequently do make mistakes about our surroundings and the situations in which we finu ourselves, we all nevertheless understand the causal laws which govern the consequences of our movements. We know from experience that many of our errors are due to ignorance; but it is more than an empirical truth that a rational man is able to operate and apply well-known causal laws to his own activities. It may indeed be that in a particular case a person may fail to anticipate a consequence as the result of failing to apply causal laws with which he was generally familiar, that he may, so to speak, not actualise his knowledge. But this second presumption, the presumption of foresight of consequences, is at any rate less unjust than the first presumption, the presumption of knowledge of circumstances. For whereas to accept the first presumption would be to give up any attempt to individuate conditions of liability, to accept the second may only involve recognising that there is a limit beyond which these conditions cannot be individuated.

Whatever the other advantages or disadvantages of this explanation, it does at any rate have the merit that it does not make use of the argument employed by Holmes that factors other than knowledge cannot be conditions of liability because they are 'subjective' in a sense in which knowledge is not. Traces of this argument are to be found in Lady Wootton's assertion that by abandoning the cognitive approach of the M'Naghten Rules the law is left without any logical test of responsibility.[34] Both Holmes and Lady Wootton are surely wrong in attempting to different-iate knowledge on this ground from the other mental elements in criminal responsibility. Holmes in particular could hardly justify in these terms the exclusion of foresight, which can scarcely be a more subjective factor than knowledge.

The explanation that foresight of consequences can, as a matter of evidence, be more readily imputed to a person than knowledge of the circumstances of his action does have a *prima facie* credibility; it does not assume that there is a qualitative difference between knowledge and foresight; and it does not deny that responsibility may be affected by factors other than purely cognitive ones, such as a capacity to assess and respond to the situation in a normal way.

The distinction is of considerable practical importance for it must be generally more difficult to prove foresight than to prove knowledge. It can be shown that a person knew something if it can be shown that, for example, he looked to see; thus it can be shown that he knew a gun was loaded if he opened the breech. If the prosecution has the burden of proof it would have to prove foresight affirmatively when the accused was silent; and if the accused denied it the difficulty of proof would be greater. Thus the possibilities of proof provide one justification for distinguishing between knowledge and foresight.

A further difficulty in elucidating Holmes's arguments is that he does not always suceed in enabling the reader to avoid a natural con-fusion between the terms 'external' and 'objective'. He says, for example, that the desire for vengeance 'takes an internal standard, not an object-ive or external one,'[35] that 'while the law does still and always, in a certain sense, measure legal liability by moral standards, it nevertheless, by the very necessity of its nature, is continually transmuting those moral standards into external or objective ones, from which the actual guilt of the party concerned is wholly eliminated';[36] and that the con-duct of the average man, the man of ordinary intelligence and reason-able prudence, ' is an external or objective standard when applied to any given individual'.[37]

To leave aside for a moment the obscurity which surrounds this use of the term 'standard', it may be pointed out at this stage that there appear to be at least two different ideas underlying what Holmes calls the 'objective or external standard', which although sometimes separately stated are not always explicitly distinguished. One of these ideas is the obvious truth that any judgment of another's state of mind has a basis which must be in some sense of the word 'external'. We ordinarily base a judgment of another's state of mind on his behaviour. Even if it is based on his own statements, the evidence which these provide is still in a sense external. Holmes is clearly correct in contrasting the internal quality of a state of mind with the external character of the evidence for it. The second idea is one in which Holmes finds a distinguishing characteristic of the criminal law. It is, as Holmes says, the criminal law which is primarily concerned with imposing patterns of conduct. The idea can nevertheless be extended to the civil law; for here too, though in different ways, the law sets up a standard by which conduct is measured, a standard generally identified in the law of tort, for instance, with the degree of care which would be exercised by a reasonable man. But it will be seen that neither of the two ideas inextricably entwined in Holmes's account of 'external or objective standards' is sufficient, either in itself or in combination, to support his argument for objective liability.

The plausibility of the argument derives, it may be thought, from an occasional confusion of the two ideas. Thus Holmes uses the term 'external standard', which seems more appropriate to the second idea, in expressing the view that the law takes the reasonable man as the test of the state of mind of the individual.[38] To resolve this confusion is at once to invalidate the argument. For in the first place it does not follow from the fact that the law is concerned with the prevention or promotion of certain external patterns of conduct, that it should not, still less that it could not, take account of the actual state of mind of the individual. Even if it were true that the law could or should only concern itself with overt behaviour, this would require not objective liability but strict liability, of which Holmes is unable to express his approval.[39] Yet the objections of principle to strict liability apply with equal force, although over a narrower field, to objective liability.

Nor does it follow from the fact that the evidence is external that the law cannot take account of the state of mind of the individual. To carry this argument to its logical conclusion leads to the adoption of a behaviourist theory which precludes the possibility of evidence altogether. Holmes's argument here leads on to dangerous ground:

'Law only works within the sphere of the senses. If the external phenomena, the manifest acts and omissions, are such as it requires, it is wholly indifferent to the internal phenomena of conscience. . . . In other words, the standards of the law are external standards, and, however much it may take moral considerations into account, it does so only for the purpose of drawing a line between such bodily motions and rests as it permits, and such as it does not. What the law really forbids, and the only thing it forbids, is the act on the wrong side of the line, be that act blameworthy or otherwise.'[40]

K

Again the argument becomes one for strict liability. It is strange that Holmes is speaking here of the civil law, and it may be that the examples which he uses to illustrate his argument are inadequate to support his conclusions. But the principal difficulty here is a recurrent one, which appears to vitiate the foundation of his position, that he does not consistently distinguish between two quite separate concepts, between tests on the one hand and standards on the other, a distinction which is essential to any attempt to differentiate between substantive law and the law of evidence, or between the logical character of a proposition and the evidence for it. The confusion of tests and standards is a recurrent feature of the lectures on *The Common Law*, and it is necessary to examine it in further detail.

The crucial distinction which Holmes fails to mark is that between, on the one hand, setting up a standard of conduct which the idea of rules of law whatever their form necessarily involves, and on the other hand, providing a test of the individual's opportunity and capacity to conform to a standard so established. Such a test is contained in the rules regulating conditions of liability to the penalties or other consequences of failing to conform to the standards of conduct laid down; but it is necessary to distinguish between the standards themselves and the appropriate test of liability.

The distinction is clearly illustrated by the concept of negligence in the civil law, the analysis of which was previously confused by the ambiguity of the term. It is now generally recognised that there exists an independent tort of negligence which is constituted by the failure to take reasonable care to avoid injuring any person in a situation where the relationship between the parties is such that a duty of care may be said to exist. It is a quite separate question what the test of liability for such failure may be. The tort of negligence may be committed negligently, that is by failing to take due care, and this as we have seen is the commonest basis of tort liability in general; but it is alternatively possible to commit the tort intentionally by deliberately failing to take the required precautions. Negligence is thus both a mode of committing torts for which a general liability is established, and an independent tort, liability for which may be based either on negligence itself or on other principles.

So too in the criminal law, if this distinction between standards of conduct and tests of liability is preserved, it is immediately clear that to have a standard set by the capacities of the average man does not entail that the capacity of the individual to conform to the standard must be tested by the average man's capacities. Of course, if the test is taken not as a guide but as conclusive evidence, it must be conceded that the distinction between tests and standards is dissolved; but one cannot argue that tests must be conclusive by using the terms from the beginning of the argument as if they were in principle interchangeable.

A further objection to Holmes's arguments lies in the fact that, as the passage quoted already demonstrate, Holmes treats alike knowledge, intent, consciousness of right and wrong, conscience and other diverse mental states; yet it does not follow that, because a man's conscience, for example, cannot be of relevance to the law, his knowledge of the circumstances in which he acts is equally irrelevant. The vital distinction is between intention and motive. For a variety of reasons, which are discussed more fully in the final chapter, it seems to be a distinguishing feature of any system of law, as opposed to a possible code of ethics, that it must ignore the defence that a person did a prohibited act in good conscience, or with a good motive. But it can be shown quite simply that this does not entail the exclusion of *mens rea*, if that is interpreted in terms of the intention to do the prohibited act. For the exclusion of the defence of good motive does not offend, as the exclusion of *mens rea* would, against the principle that a person should not be liable to a conviction which he had no opportunity to avoid. A person who has a good motive necessarily acts intentionally, and therefore with full knowledge of its consequences he can reasonably be held responsible. A good motive may operate in mitigation of sentence but not to exclude liability. Much of Holmes's insistence on the non-moral quality of the principles of liability can be explained by his apparent confusion of intention and motive.

Similarly, it seems that he failed to distinguish between intelligence and prudence.[41] It is one thing to measure prudence by the test of the average man; it is another so to measure intelligence. Stupidity is a misfortune, not an offence, and if like Holmes we credit every offender with normal intelligence we fall into the mistake of Dr Johnson's schoolmaster, Mr. Hunter. 'He used,' so Johnson told Boswell, 'to beat us unmercifully; and he did not distinguish between ignorance and negligence; for he would beat a boy equally for not knowing a thing as for neglecting to know it . . . . Now, Sir, if a boy could answer every question, there would be no need of a master to teach him.'[42] Similarly it was said of the decision in *Ward's* case that the rule 'leads to the odd result that a man may be hanged for being stupid, and not because he intended to kill.'

It has already been remarked that it is essential to separate the exposition of a legal doctrine from its justification. There is here a further danger in confusing what the law is and what it ought to be. Both Holmes and Denning, although they do not go so far as to argue explicitly that objective liability is defensible because there are situations in which it is accepted by the law, do nevertheless appear to derive an illegitimate advantage in some of the arguments which they take from the law as it stands. For they do at times appear to suggest that certain other principles already recognised by the law, which an opponent of the doctrine of objective liability might wish to preserve, can only be defended on the basis of that doctrine. To refute this type of argument it becomes necessary for a critic of objective liability to show that the principles which he wishes to preserve are defensible on grounds independent of the doctrine which he criticises. One example is the principle that the law recognises self-defence as an excuse, so that 'even the deliberate taking of life will not be punished when it is the only way of saving one's own'; this principle is discussed further below, and it will be suggested that its implications are different from what Holmes would suggest.

A second example used in the course of Holmes's argument is taken from another rule basic to many systems of jurisprudence that ignorance of the law is no excuse for breaking it. Holmes argues as if this rule, which many opponents of objective liability might support, can only be defended on the basis of that doctrine. After rejecting two other possible justifications of the rule, he advances what he describes as 'the true explanation', which turns out to be a generalised version of the doctrine of objective liability.[43]

Even if Holmes's account is acceptable as a partial explanation of the rule, it is far from the whole of the story. There are, of course, the familiar arguments that point to the difficulties of proof mentioned by Austin[44] and to the abuse which would follow from any other rule. But, apart from the appeal to expediency, other arguments can be advanced which, if they do not of themselves wholly justify the rule, at least go some way towards removing its arbitrary character.[45]

Insofar as serious offences are concerned, it may be argued that it is not altogether unreasonable to assume a knowledge of legal rules which necessarily reflect to some extent the current conceptions of the prevailing social morality. In other cases, where there may be no exact correspondence between the prevailing morality and the law, it may be suggested that the duty of the citizen to acquaint himself with the provisions of the law is not always an illusion of the philosophy of democratic government. These arguments may not, of course, afford a complete justification of the rule that ignorance of the law is no excuse; but since they are entirely independent of the doctrine of objective liability they do at any rate show that this doctrine is not the only possible basis on which the rule can be supported.

Further, even if we deny the duty to know the law, it is arguable that
the rule that ignorance of the law is no defence is not open to the same
fundamental objection of principle as is the doctrine of objective liability.
For if the laws are duly promulgated then although a person may have no
duty to ascertain them he does at least have the opportunity to do so. On
this assumption, the citizen is not penalised for violating a law of whose
provisions he could not have been aware. By contrast where liability is
objective, it is not open to the defendant to show that he could not have
avoided the prohibited consequences. Thus the rule excluding ignorance
of the law as a defence does comply with the principle against which the
doctrine of objective liability offends, that the citizen should not be penalised for any infraction which he had no opportunity to avoid; though
it would be desirable to modify the rule to provide a defence to a person
who can show that he had no reasonable opportunity to discover the
law's provisions.

This is not the only case where dubious support is obtained from the
existing law. The third of Holmes's arguments is that the law 'takes no
account of incapacities unless . . . infancy or madness.' This shows, he
argues, that 'the tests of liability are external, and independent of the
degree of evil in the particular person's motives or intentions.'⁴⁶ The
immediate answer to this argument is that even the exceptions of infancy and insanity could not be justified on Holmes's premises.

The final example, which is used both by Holmes and Lord Denning,
is derived from the law relating to provocation. Here, the test of the
reasonable man is commonly applied before provocation is allowed,
whether as a defence or in mitigation of punishment. Provocation is generally not a defence but rather a mitigating circumstance to be taken into
consideration with the other circumstances of the case when the court
passes sentence after conviction. In a case of murder, however, where
the sentence is fixed by law, a successful plea of provocation will reduce
the offence to manslaughter, giving the court wide discretion over sentence. For the plea to succeed, the jury must be satisfied, not only that
the accused was actually himself provoked, but also that a reasonable
man would have been provoked to do what the accused did.

The effect of this rule is partially to eliminate subjective considerations
of the capacities of the accused; for the test of the reasonable man is
applied not simply as evidence of whether the accused was provoked; it
is a conclusive condition of the operation of the doctrine of provocation.
Yet the rule cannot for a number of reasons be legitimately used as an
argument for objective liability.

One preliminary objection to arguing from this rule is clearly that even

if there were no independent justification of it, the rule could hardly
be used as an argument for objective liability; for the rule is itself simply
an instance, though rather a special case, of objective liability. An
exemplification of a principle cannot be used as an argument for it;
and it is on this account difficult to see in what way the rule could
be counted, as Lord Denning maintains, as 'yet another reason why
the jury are entitled to test the position by an objective criterion.'[47]

It is clear that the law of provocation cannot be explained by the
doctrine of objective liability, any more than the doctrine itself can
be explained by the law of provocation. Still less can the one be used
to justify the other. But there in any case remain plausible justifications of the law of provocation which do not support a generalised
form of objective liability. Three possible arguments may be suggested.

In the first place it is possible to argue that the plea of provocation
is one which it is exceptionally difficult to disprove. On this argument,
it is true, the test of the reasonable man is applied as evidence, as it
is in the general doctrine; but the argument, since it relies on the
special difficulties of this particular plea, still does not support the
general doctrine.

A second justification is the argument from justice itself, which was
used in the classic case of *Lesbini*, in which the rule was laid down by
the Court of Criminal Appeal. In the course of argument in that case,
Mr Justice Avory said: 'It would seem to follow from your proposition
that a bad-tempered man would be entitled to a verdict of manslaughter
where a good-tempered one would be liable to be convicted of murder.'[48]

The argument was more fully stated in the Report of the Royal
Commission on Capital Punishment:

'It is a fundamental principle of the criminal law that it should be based on
a generally accepted standard of conduct applicable to all citizens alike, and it
is important that this principle should not be infringed. Any departure from it
might introduce a dangerous latitude into the law. Those idiosyncracies of individual temperament or mentality that may make a man more easily provoked
more violent in his response to provocation, ought not, therefore, to affect his
liability to conviction, although they may justify mitigation of sentence.'[49]

Accordingly, in amending the existing law as to provocation so as to
include words in addition to conduct as recognised forms of provocation, the Homicide Act 1957 expressly lays down in section 3 that the
jury shall decide 'whether the provocation was enough to make a
reasonable man do as he did'; and in determining this question 'the
jury shall take into account everything both done and said according
to the effect which, in their opinion, it would have on a reasonable
man.' The argument from the injustice which would follow from the

adoption of a purely subjective test, was emphasised by the Attorney-General in the debate on this provision in the House of Commons.[50] But while this argument has some plausibility as a defence of the particular rule, to generalise in into a justification of objective liability would amount to a *reductio ad absurdum.*

A third possible argument in favour of the rule, which is also clearly peculiar to that rule, might be found in the fact that those who are exceptionally easily provoked are also exceptionally dangerous. The law of provocation is designed primarily to meet the case of a person committing an assault who has been not unreasonably provoked, often by the conduct of his victim; it is not intended to protect those who resort to violence on relatively slight provocation.

It has so far been suggested that, whether or not the supporters of objective liability are concerned with the law as it is or with the law as it ought to be, they do often derive a surreptitious advantage in the arguments which they adduce from the law as it is, when they assume that the law as it stands can only be justified on the basis of the principles which they advocate. What is less clear from their arguments is what might be termed the social philosophy underlying the doctrine of objective liability, and it is this social philosophy which now requires to be revealed. It is far from obvious to the reader of Holmes's lectures on what principle he seeks to base his evaluation of the Law. He is primarily concerned to explain and to expound rather than to evaluate, and in so far as he is concerned to justify particular doctrines (for he rarely criticises) he does not make explicit the values on which any principle of legal criticism must be based. Indeed, it is difficult to find any principle of this type which would commend itself to Holmes. He does not hesitate to reject what might appear to be some of the more self-evident legal values or principles of legal criticism. He denies, for example, that the law should be humanitarian, and even that it should be consistent. But denial here is of course a form of assertion; and something can be learnt also from his attack on what he calls the 'dogma of equality', and from his refusing to see any objection to treating men as things.[51] Further many of his individual arguments illuminate, even where they do not explicitly state, the social philosophy underlying his work.

One such argument is used by Holmes in discussing the law of self-defence. 'The deliberate taking of life,' he says, 'will not be punished when it is the only way of saving one's own.' He argues that it is perfectly proper that the law should 'treat the individual as a means to an end' and use him 'as a tool to increase the general welfare at his own expense.'[52] Again Holmes displays an illuminating disregard of the possibility of other justifications of the law of self-defence. It could be said first of all that the principle enunciated by Holmes cannot stand, since a distinction must be drawn between the case of genuine self-defence (or defence of other lives) on the one hand and on the other taking an innocent life.[53] Holmes's failure to exclude the latter case is perhaps not without significance; indeed, his earlier illustration seems to symbolise his whole political outlook: 'If a man is on a plank in the deep sea which will only float one, and a stranger lays hold of it, he will thrust him off if he can. When the state finds itself in a similar position, it does the same thing.'[54]

In the former case, the case of genuine self-defence, the justification may be simply that, presented inevitably with a choice between two lines, the law has less difficulty in preferring the life of the victim of a murderous attack to the life of his assailant. Holmes does not take account of the possibility of alternative justifications. But the importance of these illustrations is less to reveal any fallacy in the argument than to expose the social philosophy underlying the theory of objective liability.

A different aspect of Holmes's social philosophy is illustrated by a comparison of the principles of criminal liability and the view which he advances of civil liability. The attitude to civil law, concerned with the safeguarding of economic rights over property, implicit in Holmes's writings, is very different from his views of the criminal law, where the principles of liability are of importance to the liberty of the individual rather than to his property rights. It is perhaps significant that he requires a chance to foresee as a condition of liability in tort but not in crime. This paradoxical view may follow from the differnt social classes affected by the two branches of law. Writing in a period of entrepreneurial values he regarded it as desirable to let losses lie where they fell even while imposing criminal liability in the absence of fault.

In his discussion of civil liability Holmes repeatedly emphasises that the defendant should not be responsible for consequences of his actions which he did not have a chance to foresee;[55] but there is no corresponding stipulation in his discussion of criminal liability. It is true that he begins this discussion by remarking that 'the choice must be made with a chance of contemplating the consequences complained of, or else it has no bearing on responsibility for that consequence.'[56] But it appears that this provision is thought to be necessary to remove difficulties about causation and remoteness of damage: 'If this were not true, a man might be held answerable for everything which would not have happened but for his choice at some past time.'

The important thesis of Holmes's lectures, that criminal liability is and should be objective, is in clear and paradoxical contrast to his view of civil liability. Although 'the general principles of criminal and civil liability are the same,'[57] when we are dealing with the criminal law 'we should expect there more than elsewhere to find that the tests of liability are external.'[58]

Holmes argues that 'so far from its being true, as is often assumed, that the condition of a man's heart or conscience ought to be more considered in determining criminal than civil liability, it might almost be said that it is the very opposite of the truth.'[59] Yet this is hardly the natural inference from the proposition that 'the chief and only universal purpose of punishment is prevention'[60] while 'civil liability, in its immediate working, is simply a redistribution of an existing loss between two individuals.'[61]

Holmes's position is in fact doubly paradoxical. Although in his day the criminal law was witnessing the origins of the doctrine of strict liability, the general trend of both criminal and civil law was, as is seen elsewhere in the present argument, precisely the reverse of the tendency which he depicted. The nineteenth century was, as has been seen, the era above all in which the concept of *mens rea* was continually refined and adapted to the criteria of moral responsibility. And on the question what ought to be the conditions of liability, sufficient arguments have already been adduced to show that it is in the civil law that objective liability is more readily justifiable.

It has been suggested above that Holmes's doctrines may be partly explicable by a concern for the protection of the rights of property. It may be objected that such a concern might lead equally to the adoption of a principle of liability independent of fault. Granted that liability based upon fault serves to protect the rights of the person causing harm, it may be argued that liability independent of fault protects the rights of person injured. This objection is for several reasons unconvincing. In the first place, since an award of damages for a civil injury is in itself a deprivation of property, those concerned with the preservation of property rights will attempt to reduce as far as possible the incidence of liability, and to let the loss lie where it falls. Secondly, any law of civil injuries tends to work in two ways against the interests of property owners; it is they who in the course of commercial life are prone to cause injuries, and it is they alone who can compensate those they injure. An employee is more likely to bring an action against his employer than the reverse. Finally, it is perhaps self-evident that the 'entrepreneur morality' will be concerned to extend as far as possible the freedom of action of the entrepreneur. From this point of view the desire to reduce the incidence of delictual liability in the spirit of nineteenth century *laisser-faire* may be compared with the reverence attached in the same period to the concept of freedom of contract.

The political doctrine behind Holmes's legal analysis may therefore be described as a form of economic liberalism; but it is a liberalism which, although it recognises the values of independence and competition in commercial life, attaches little importance to the comparable values of personal liberty protected by the criminal law. The great merit of his analysis is the frank, almost blatant profession of the policy choices and social values which determine his formulation of the principles of legal liability. His argument compares favourably in this respect with those of more recent critics who purport to have dispensed with such considerations and to advance supposedly value-free theories. In so doing, these critics have unconsciously repeated, in a different form, the error of the earlier jurists who confined themselves to the analysis of legal concepts, but failed to ask what their function was. It was Holmes, here as elsewhere, who exposed the error, and showed that the concept of criminal responsibility raises more fundamental questions. These are the subject of the concluding chapter.

Chapter 6

Premises and Conclusions

In the preceding chapters we have examined in detail some recent developments in the law, and have tried to discern their implications for the concept of responsibility. We have seen that these developments do not appear to indicate any general departure from the principle of *mens rea*; and we have been able to consider the justification of this principle in the context of the individual doctrines examined.

In the present chapter we may try to go beyond these individual doctrines and consider the concept of responsibility in its wider aspects. In doing so we may hope to discover the philosophical presuppositions underlying the theories we have previously examined in isolation. We shall try to show that at a number of points much of the traditional debate about the concept of responsibility and the function of the criminal law has been misconceived; for it will be suggested that both the advocates of *mens rea* and their opponents have used arguments which fail to establish their case. In criticising the arguments on both sides we shall attempt to supply the principle of *mens rea* with a valid foundation in terms of the social purposes of the modern law.

One example of such misplaced arguments has already been discussed. We have seen that many of the supporters of *mens rea* have tried to justify it on the basis of equating legal and moral guilt. These include such leading criminal lawyers as Professor Jerome Hall in the U S A, Professor Brett in Australia, and Lord Devlin in England. Their critics, on the other hand, have argued that *mens rea* is superfluous once the distinction between legal and moral guilt has been drawn. Thus Holmes and Lady Wootton both deny that the principles of criminal liability require any ethical justification. But it has been suggested that both kinds of argument are misconceived; for there is still a moral justification of *mens rea* whatever the moral content of the criminal law. This justification is to be found in the principle that no one should be liable to the law's sanctions if he did not knowingly fail to comply with its requirements, or at the very least if he had no reasonable opportunity of compliance.

Later in the chapter it will be necessary to examine some arguments which would have the effect of refuting even this minimal moral basis of the concept of criminal responsibility. But it will be suggested that these arguments too are misconceived; and that they, like the other arguments, only conceal the true issue, which is whether the social cost of retaining *mens rea* is so heavy that the price paid for the valuable principle which it embodies is too high for a modern society to be able to afford it.

First, however, it should be observed that many of these arguments would exclude altogether the question whether or not it was desirable on principle or on grounds of policy to retain the requirement of *mens rea*. On one view, the questions which must be asked, if *mens rea* is required, are incapable of any rational answer. On this view, the very notion of *mens rea* is suspect, and insofar as we pretend to make use of it we only delude ourselves. On another view, it is not the retention, but the abolition of *mens rea* which is regarded as impossible; here it is said that *mens rea* is a necessary feature of the law. On either view, no question would arise of whether *mens rea* was for any reason desirable.

Let us consider first the view that *mens rea* is a necessary rather than a desirable feature of any legal system. This view is exemplified by the argument that *mens rea* is not a moral requirement, but a logical necessity. It is said that the requirement of a particular state of mind often serves not only to mark a moral distinction, but also to delimit certain basic legal categories in a way which is fundamental to our thinking both within and outside the law. But the conceptual argument here again is fallacious. The concept of possession is an instructive case. Can a person be said to possess something if he does not know that it is 'in his possession'? The discussion of strict liability above shows that ultimately this is a question of policy, not to be solved by an appeal to ordinary language. The words may, if the legislature so intends or the courts so construe, exclude all implication of knowledge or belief.

A stronger case may be based on offences requiring some further intention, such as burglary which consists *inter alia* of entering a building as a trespasser with intent to steal anything in the building.[1]

But apart from these substantive offences, there must also be considered every offence of attempting to commit a crime, as well as other auxiliary offences, where it may seem impossible to remove all reference to the intentions with which the acts are done. This argument is well illustrated by the remarks of Parker J in *Gardner* v. *Akeroyd*, on the question whether *mens rea* is necessary for a preparatory act. Regulation 90 (1) of the Defence (General) Regulations, 1939, provided that: 'Any person who attempts to commit, conspires with any other person to commit, or does any act preparatory to the commission of, an offence against any of these regulations, shall be guilty of an offence against that regulation punishable in like manner as the said offence.' The Queen's Bench Divisional Court held that whereas on a charge of a completed offence liability would be vicarious, because the relevant provisions made the prohibition an absolute one, liability for a preparatory act under this Regulation requires *mens rea.* One of the arguments advanced by Parker J in support of this conclusion was that if *mens rea* was necessary for a conviction of an attempt to commit an offence, it was all the more necessary in the case of doing an act merely preparatory to the commission of an offence. He continued: 'Further, whether or not such an act is an act preparatory to the commission of an offence must, it seems to me, depend on intent. The purchase of a box of matches might or might not be an act preparatory to the commission of an offence of arson according to the circumstances and the intent.'[2] He thus suggests that *mens rea* may be necessary, not merely to determine liability, but on the prior question of how the acts in issue are to be categorised within or outside the law.

A similar argument could be used in the case of many substantive offences. Can a course of conduct be characterised as stealing, for example, if no reference is allowed to the person's intent? It seems that we must be able to require that he intended to deprive the owner, at any rate for a period of time, of his property, and also to require that he should have believed it to be the property of another.

The argument that it is only the intention which gives the act significance was stated in similar terms by Bracton: 'For take away the will, and every act will be indifferent, for your meaning imposes a name upon your act, and a crime is not committed unless a guilty intention intercede . . . .'[3]

Thus, it could be argued that it is not simply the legal definitions of crimes such as burglary, robbery, and fraud which require the ingredient of intent; but rather that the concept of intention is built in, so to speak, to the vocabulary which we use every day to describe human actions. The idea of stealing, for example, seems necessarily to involve a belief on the part of the thief that the thing stolen is the property of another; so that to take another's property believing it to be one's own could not count as stealing at all.

The objection to this argument is that even in some of these cases the issue is still a moral one in conceptual form. Certainly our use of language does seem to require that a person who took an umbrella believing it to be his own would not ordinarily be said to have stolen it; but the objection is that this use of language simply reflects a conventional moral distinction. For we customarily tend to attach less blame to those who take things under a genuine misapprehension; but there is no reason to suppose that a distinction based upon these tendencies is inherent in the nature of the world. It might be added (although this is not essential to the argument) that the real issue, from the point of view of social cost, turns on whether the threat to the institution of property is the same whatever the beliefs with which it is appropriated. On this basis, it could be said, we can justify our accepted habits of thought; for the person who takes another's umbrella by mistake may be more likely to return it when he discovers his error, and less likely to re-peat his offence. But to say this is not to suggest that his intention is a necessary ingredient of any description of human action.

Similar objections can be raised in the case of attempted crimes. Here too it can be said that the intention is not a necessary part of any definition of an attempt; for here too an alternative definition could be adopted which did not refer to the agent's state of mind. Such a definition might be framed in terms of general patterns of behaviour, and their typical tendencies, rather than in terms of the agent's knowledge, and his intention to produce certain consequences. It could be argued that developments of this kind are not unknown to the existing law. The law already recognises, for example, that con-duct may be criminal if it is intended 'or likely' to occasion a breach of the peace. Furthermore, in a case which was the foundation of the modern law of criminal attempts, the wide proposition was laid down that 'all offences of a public nature, that is, such acts or attempts as tend to the prejudice of the community' are indictable.[4] And there is a familiar ambiguity in the law's constant references to acts 'cal-culated' to lead to certain consequences.[5] We have seen that even in cases where the law ostensibly requires a specific intent as a condition of liability, proof of the probable tendencies of the accused's conduct may be accepted as conclusive evidence of that intent; while the maxim that he is deemed to intend the natural or probable consequences of his acts has had wide repercussions in many departments of the crim-inal law.[6]

A parallel suggests itself at this point with recent developments in the law of divorce. The parallel is appropriate because this branch of the law is traditionally based on the doctrine of the matrimonial offence, such as desertion or cruelty. Recent cases suggest, however, that in the law of divorce the courts are turning away from the trad-itional doctrine of the matrimonial offence requiring evidence of in-tention and are moving towards the principle of breakdown of mar-riage, or as it has been described 'divorce without fault'.

A move in this direction was taken in the law of constructive desertion in the case of *Lang* v. *Lang*.[7] Previously, as Denning L J had said in an earlier case,[8] two conflicting views could be extracted

from the English authorities: first, that a husband is not to be found
guilty of constructive desertion, however bad his conduct, unless he
had in fact an intention to bring the married life to an end; secondly,
that if his conduct is so bad or unreasonable that his wife is forced
to leave him, he must be presumed to intend her to leave however
much he may in fact have desired her to remain.

The conflict was resolved by the Judicial Committee of the Privy
Council in *Lang* v.*Lang*. In this case it was held that where a husband's
conduct towards his wife was such that a reasonable man would know
— that the husband must have known — that in all probability it would
result in the departure of the wife from the matrimonial home, then
that in the absence of rebutting evidence was sufficient proof of an
intention on his part to disrupt the home and even though in fact he
desired her to stay he was guilty of constructive desertion.

Perhaps the most dramatic illustration of the new approach, however,
is found in its application to the concept of cruelty, another form of
matrimonial offence, in two cases decided at the same time by the House
of Lords in 1963. Briefly, it held in *Gollins* v. *Gollins*[9] that an intention
to injure the spouse is not an essential ingredient of cruelty; and in
Williams v. *Williams*[10] it went on to hold that insanity was not neces
sarily a defence to a charge of cruelty. The majority of the Court of
Appeal had taken the view that cruelty required a particular state of
mind, and, as a corollary, that a person who did not know what he was
doing could not be guilty of cruelty. This view was shared by Lords
Morris and Hodson in the House of Lords; but the majority, Lords
Reid, Evershed, and Pearce, having adopted the view in *Gollins* that an
intention to injure is not a necessary element of cruelty, proceeded in
Williams to the conclusion that insanity did not itself constitute a defence to a suit for divorce on the ground of cruelty. They recognised
that the intention may be relevant in various way: thus, in the words
of Lord Reid, 'Often the conduct must take its colour from the state
of mind which lay behind it.'[11] But although a desire to hurt, for
example, might be a relevant factor in assessing whether the conduct complained of was sufficiently grave and weighty to amount to cruelty, no
particular state of mind was necessary. The new approach was summarised by Lord Reid at the end of his judgment: 'If the conduct complained
of and its consequences are so bad that the petitioner must have a remedy,
then it does not matter what was the state of the respondent's mind.'[12]

These cases show that cruelty and constructive desertion are becoming
what could be described in criminal terms as offences of strict liability
for which a guilty mind is no longer required. There seems no reason
why parallel developments could not occur in the criminal law. There
are at any rate very many crimes where the definition could exclude any

refence to the offender's state of mind, and where the question is one
not of practicability but of policy.

We must now turn to another argument designed to show that strict
liability cannot be generalised. This argument is advanced in an original
and perplexing form by Professor Fuller in his book *The Morality of Law.*
Professor Fuller argues that:

'If strict liability were to attend, not certain specified forms of activity, but
all activities, the conception of a causal connexion between the act and the resulting injury would be lost. A poet writes a sad poem. A rejected lover reads
it and is so depressed that he commits suicide. Who "caused" the loss of his
life? Was it the poet, or the lady who jilted the deceased, or perhaps the
teacher who aroused his interest in poetry? A man in a drunken rage shoots
his wife. Who among those concerned with this event share the responsibility
for its occurrence – the killer himself, the man who lent the gun to him, the
liquor dealer who provided the gin, or was it perhaps the friend who dissuaded
him from securing a divorce that would have ended an unhappy alliance?'[13]

It is not always easy to see the point of Professor Fuller's illustrations,
picturesque though they often are. The difficulties which he raises
are difficulties for the most part about causation and it is not obvious
how these would be affected by the introduction of strict liability.
The trouble may perhaps be either that he believes that questions of
causation cannot be answered independently of questions of intention,
or that he believes simply that causal responsibility is too wide. He
continues:

'Some inkling of the nature of this sort of problem we can get from the
difficulties encountered in administering those forms of strict liability we already
have. One such liability is that imposed by the Workmen's Compensation Laws.
Obviously some causal connexion must be established between the employee's
job and the illness or injury to be compensated. The phrase used in the statutes
is that the injury or illness must "arise out of and in the course of the employment". The interpretation of this clause has given rise to a most unsatisfactory
and often bizarre body of law. To see what a universal application of strict
liability would involve we need only ask how we would apply a rule that required
only that the plaintiff's loss or injury should "arise out of" the defendent's
conduct.'

This argument is puzzling for several reasons. In the first place it is
difficult to see why questions of intention should in principle be
easier to answer than questions of causation. And unless it is assumed
that the concept of causation in some ways presupposes the concept
of intention, it is difficult even to detect its relevance. To base liability
upon intention does not remove the difficulties about causation, it
only makes necessary a further set of questions; so that there is no
reason to think that to cease to base liability upon intention would

increase the problems of causation. The example of the poet, if it presents difficulties, certainly does not do so because of strict liability, since the questions of causation which it raises have nothing to do with strict liability.

Although Professor Fuller present the argument in an original form, the idea that problems of causation would be insuperably complex if strict liability were universalised is not a new one. Traces of the same idea are to be found in the lectures of O W Holmes, some other aspects of which have already been discussed. Holmes starts his discussion of criminal liability with an important concession, which is perhaps not fully realised in the development of his doctrine. He says that 'the choice must be made with a chance of contemplating the consequence complained of, or else it has no bearing on responsibility for that consequence.'[14] Yet the motive behind this concession is not as might be thought a desire to construct a just theory of responsibility; it is apparently the need to solve possible difficulties about causation; for Holmes continues: 'If this were not true, a man might be held answerable for everything which would not have happened but for his choice at some past time.' Yet it seems obvious that we have and apply to situations where human action is not involved criteria of causation sufficiently tight to exclude the infinite nexus which Holmes fears and at the same time independent of the notion of intention; and that our desire to make human responsibility dependent not only upon a causal connexion but also upon the agent's state of mind derives not from a desire to avoid difficulties about causation (since it would only replace them with other difficulties) but rather from a belief in the central importance of intention in our attitudes to human behaviour.

It may therefore be concluded that the generalisation of strict liability cannot be ruled out on *a priori* grounds. As a further confirmation of these arguments, reference might be made to the evidence provided by a primitive system of law of the type earlier discussed. Although the more extreme hypotheses about the extent of absolute liability in this type of system cannot for various reasons be fully substantiated, it cannot be denied that there is at any rate a possibility that this doctrine operated both in the written rule and in practice to a far wider extent than would nowadays be generally acceptable.

While advocates of *mens rea* may assume that it could not be eliminated, their opponents have tended to suggest that it cannot be retained. Here it is essential to draw at the outset a distinction between the arguments merely designed to show that it is very difficult in practice to make judgments necessary to support attributions of responsibility, and those designed to show that it is simply not possible in principle to make these judgments. Arguments of the former kind are more easily debated, since

L

they often do not depend on any philosophical presuppositions but depend rather upon a tacit assessment of the relative importance of the different interests protected by the criminal law. It can be argued, for example, that in the case of offences of relatively minor importance the effort required to prove *mens rea* might be disproportionate to the results, and might even seriously impair in certain cases the enforceability of the law.

So far as this argument is concerned, it is necessary at this stage only to point out that there are two reasons why it cannot support a more general elimination of responsibility. First, the explicit premises of the argument specifically confine its scope to minor offences. One proposal commonly made is to meet the difficulty by transferring the onus of proof in these cases from the prosecution to the defence; this proposal would meet the objection by removing the difficulties of proof without discarding the principle of *mens rea*. But whatever proposal is adopted it then becomes a matter of evidence, and cannot be considered in isolation from the rest of the legal process, which must be examined as a whole if the correct balance is to be achieved between the interests of the individual defendant and the interests of society at large. The aim here as elsewhere will be to secure that the innocent are fully protected so far as is reasonably compatible with the effective enforcement of the law.

A second reason why this particular argument cannot be used to support a general elimination of responsibility is to be found in the implicit premises of the argument. The argument rests fundamentally upon the principle of administrative convenience; and the objection to it most generally heard is that administrative convenience should not be an important consideration in the administration of justice. But it is worth pointing out another objection, not generally acknowledged, which meets this argument on its own ground. This objection is that the general abandonment of *mens rea* might lead not to administrative convenience but to administrative chaos, if every case of causing death, or causing injury,or misappropriation of property, had to be investigated by the courts or at any rate by the prosecuting authorities. The argument from the difficulty of proving *mens rea* thus raises wider issues of social policy which are discussed further at the end of the chapter.

The views of those who contend that it is not merely difficult, but impossible to make the judgments required by the doctrine of *mens rea* appear to have less connexion with the every-day administration of the law. It can hardly be said that the whole doctrine is a practical impossibility, since it is operated daily by courts everywhere. Just as the suggestion that the law cannot dispense with *mens rea* is contradicted by the evidence of early law, so the suggestion that the law cannot operate with *mens rea* is contradicted by the experience of a modern legal system. Instead the contention must rest upon philosophical premisses, open or covert. The argument must be that the law cannot logically retain *mens rea*. A medical writer expresses a view shared by many when he says that ' the whole concept of criminal responsibility is fictional and logically untenable',[15] and others who have not criticised the whole doctrine of *mens rea*, have criticised in similar terms specific aspects of it. The doctrine of diminished responsibility, in particular, has been subject to a great deal of controversy, and objections have been made to the theory behind it not only by writers in the mental and social sciences but even by judges. Many of these objections have not been confined to the operation of the doctrine in the everyday practice of the courts, but have suggested that it is illogical as well as unworkable.

It is proposed to examine three different forms of philosophical argument which seem to lie beneath the assertion that it is not possible in principle to make the judgments necessary to support attributions of responsibility. The first is a general form of scepticism which denies the possibility of making any true statements about other minds. The second is a dualist theory descended from Descartes which draws a fundamental line of demarcation between a public world of overt acts and a private mental world. The third theory suggests that there is a logical flaw in the concept of responsibility itself.

The argument that it is not possible to make judgments about another's state of mind has been used by many writers of differing philosophical persuasions from Thomas Aquinas to Barbara Wootton. Aquinas sees its significance for his distinction between the law of man and the law of God: 'Now man, the framer of human law, is competent to judge only of outward acts; because *man seeth those things that appear,* according to I Kings XVI 7: while God alone, the framer of the divine law, is competent to judge of the inward movement of wills . . . .'[16] Lady Wootton suggests in plainer terms that 'it is not possible to get inside another man's skin'[17] and elsewhere argues that the answer to questions of a person's responsibility, or of his capacity to resist temptation, are beyond mere mortals; they lie 'buried in his consciousness into which no human being can enter.'[18] This claim too has a medieval ring which recalls the saying of Brian C J in 1477 that 'it is common learning that the intent of a man shall not be tried; for the Devil has no knowledge of the intent of man.'[19]

A second theory underlying the belief that it is not possible to make the judgments necessary to support attributions of responsibility is a dualist theory of which traces can be found in Austin and later in Holmes, and which is perhaps derived from Descartes via John Locke[20] and Jeremy Bentham.[21] Neither Austin nor Holmes, being experienced lawyers, denied the possibility of proving *mens rea*; but they both distinguished two separate processes in human actions, one mental and one physical. According to Austin's account, a voluntary action consisted on the one hand of a set of 'volitions', or acts of will, and on the other hand of certain bodily movements.[22] Holmes similarly conceived of human actions in terms of mental acts of volition producing appropriate muscular contractions. To constitute an act, such contractions had to be willed. An act, Holmes said, 'is a muscular contraction, and something more. A spasm is not an act. The contraction of the muscles must be willed.'[23] The connexion between this analysis of an act and the 'external' approach of the law is evident from a passage already cited where Holmes argues that 'the standards of the law are external standards, and, however much it may take moral considerations into account, it does so only for the purpose of drawing a line between such bodily motions and rests as it permits, and such as it does not.'[24]

Although he appears to have accepted a version of Cartesian dualism, it is clear that Holmes did not rely on the general sceptical argument. His general theory of objective liability admitted of certain exceptional cases where he recognised that the law did require proof of an actual intent,[25] and he conceded of course that 'the question of knowledge is a question of the actual condition of the defendant's consciousness.'[26]

In opposition to the dualist philosophies mention must also be made of the monist theories which led from opposite premises to identical conclusions. Hobbes for example seems to have argued that all phenomena mental or otherwise could be explained in terms of a series of material processes governed by mechanical laws;[27] and the influence of these views on the law culminated in the writings of the great French jurist Saleilles at the end of the nineteenth century, who argued that it was necessary to 'materialise' the civil law *(matérialiser le droit civil)* and proposed to throw out the psychological aspect of law *(jeter pardessus bord le cote psychologique du droit).* But although some critics of *mens rea* have appeared to rely on psychological or philosophical theories of this kind, they do not yet seem to have produced any arguments going beyond mere assertion. And since the foundations of this position, insofar as they can be coherently formulated, have been effectively attacked in a variety of ways by modern philosophers, notably Gilbert Ryle[28] and P F Strawson[29], it is not proposed at this point to consider further the theories based upon them.

The third theory, which has received far wider currency and requires more detailed attention, suggests that there is a philosophical insecurity in the concept of responsibility, a logical flaw in the concept itself which necessarily vitiates all attempts to ascribe responsibility. Lady Wootton's work, *Social Science and Social Pathology*, may from this point of view be regarded as the most important single contribution to the sociology of deviant behaviour, and she may for our purposes be considered as a representative of the critics of the logical basis of the concept of criminal responsibility. Lady Wootton is concerned to discover the conceptual foundations of competing criminological theories as well as to test them empirically; and on the question of criminal responsibility itself she develops the view that there is no logically adequate criterion for distinguishing between those who are and those who are not responsible on the ground of what is conventionally recognised as mental abnormality.[30] After surveying a number of different possibilities, she summarises her conclusions in the following remarkable passage:

'Once we allow any movement away from a rigid intellectual test of responsibility on M'Naghten lines, our feet are set upon a slippery slope which offers no real resting place short of the total abandonment of the whole concept of responsibility. All the intermediate positions, described in the foregoing pages, have shown themselves to be logically quite insecure. Already in many countries, amongst which England must now be included, the first steps down this slope have been taken and the possibility cannot be dismissed that the relaxation of definitions of responsibility which is already in progress is the beginning of a process which, in the remoter future, is destined to result in the total destruction of the concept itself.'[31]

We are not at present concerned with the wider social aspects of Lady Wootton's thesis, or with her philosophy as a whole, although some of the more important sociological implications will be discussed below. We are at the moment concerned only with the suggestion, often hinted at by many criminologists but never fully developed even by Lady Wootton herself, that there exists some kind of logical deficiency, a sort of conceptual muddle, in the very notion of criminal responsibility.

Central to this idea seems to be the belief that all arguments designed to show that a person is not responsible are somehow circular. The importance which Lady Wootton attaches to the notion of circularity is evident from the fact that it is used consistently to evaluate the various 'criteria of responsibility' which are in turn examined and rejected. Speaking of the M'Naghten rules, for example, she says:

'Since his insanity is thus inferred from aspects of his behaviour other than his actual offence, there is comparatively little risk of becoming involved in the circular argument that the offender "must have been mad to do such a thing." '[32]

Again, discussing the concept of motiveless behaviour, or of eccentrically motivated behaviour, she finds a similar negative characteristic to recommend it:

> 'It does at least provide a criterion for distinguishing normal from abnormal deviants which avoids circular argument; since the abnormality is inferred from the peculiarity of the motive, not from the fact of the deviant behaviour itself.'[33]

Her approach to the criterion of 'abnormality' is similar:

> 'This criterion has many virtues. Chief of these is its strength as a defence against the circular argument which explains antisocial behaviour by ill-health, while inferring the ill-health from the behaviour.'[34]

These are three quotations from nine of similar purport. Those who, like Lady Wootton rely on the notion of circularity nowhere say what it is for an argument to be circular, and it is not easy to see why they should think that such arguments as these are circular. There are occasions when they use the notion of circularity which could be accounted for if they held some general philosophical position which they do not declare; for example, if they held a behaviourist view, or if they believed that the meaning of a proposition was identical with the means of its verification. But, on the assumption that they hold neither of these positions, there is still an explanation of their use of the notion of a circular argument which would make their criticism intelligible though invalid. This is that the criticism rests upon two underlying ambiguities; on the one hand, an ambiguity between criteria and evidence; on the other hand an ambiguity between two senses of 'responsible'. Once these two ambiguities are resolved, the criticism can be re-stated in such a way that it does not any longer depend on the notion of circularity, but is then demonstrably invalid.

In the first place, it seems that these critics are not sufficiently discriminating in their use of such terms as 'definition', 'meaning', 'criteria', and 'evidence'. In the previous chapter of her book, for example, Lady Wootton investigated the concept of mental health and mental illness.[35] Much of this chapter resembles in its method the Socrativ hunt for a definition. She quotes no fewer than twenty-five definitions of mental health and several attempts to define forms of mental disorder. The unavailing search for a definition is combined with the use of some arguments advanced in 1938 by another critic, Professor Kingsley Davis.[36] Professor Davis declared, after following the same method of collecting definitions, that the American concept of mental health was strongly tinctured with the 'Protestant open-class ethic' or the ideals of the American 'free enterprise' society. He argued, that is, that the criteria which are used in deciding whether a person is mentally ill are not objective criteria of universal validity, but incorporate moral and social values. Lady Wootton applies this criticism to several accounts of mental health and concludes: 'Value-soaked definitions and explanations thus leave the scientific, objective status of the concept of mental health in a decidedly shaky condition.'[37]

But it has frequently been observed that difficulties in defining a general concept do not in any way invalidate our use of the concept. Even though we correctly use such a concept every day, we may be at a loss to define it. St Augustine used the notion of time to illustrate his point: 'What then is time? If no one asks me I know: if I wish to explain it to one that asks I know not.'[38] Professor Jerome Hall has pointed out in the present context that difficulties in defining mental disease do not invalidate the findings of psychiatrists.[39]

Even if it is worthwhile to look for a definition of mental health, it is necessary to distinguish the question of definition from the question whether the criteria of mental health are to be described in a derogatory way as subjective. Lady Wootton appears to hold that these two questions are connected with, if not the same as, the question whether mental health 'exists':

'If mental health and mental illness are not objective realities, definable otherwise than in terms of social misbehaviour, then plainly, there can be no criterion by which to divide those who indulge in such behaviour into the sick and the healthy.'[40]

We shall see shortly that the notion of objectivity requires further analysis and scarcely supports this conclusion. But Lady Wootton's principal concern seems to be that our criteria of mental health are not 'independent'. Independent of what? it may be asked. Sometimes it is the behaviour which mental disorder is adduced to explain; sometimes it is moral values; sometimes social norms.

To see the difficulty here, it is important to clarify the notion of criteria, a term which may easily lead to confusion. It appears that she does not always distinguish criteria from evidence, and that there is a crucial ambiguity in the notion of a test.

For instance, in a passage already referred to she speaks of the M'Naghten rules as providing an intellectual test of responsibility, and says that the 'criteria' are external.[41] Now 'test' here might mean either criteria or evidence. If it meant criteria, then we should be saying, if we adopted the M'Naghten rules, that the only questions to be asked, in deciding whether a person was responsible, would be questions about his knowledge. It would not be a further stage to ask whether, given this state of mind, he was responsible. If 'test' meant evidence, on the other hand, we should be saying that, once we knew about the person's state of mind, we could then go on to ask about his responsibility.

The difference between criteria and evidence can best be explained by an example. Suppose a man is drawing up a road map of Oxfordshire. He has to classify all roads as either *A* roads, which are to be marked on the map in red, or *B* roads, to be marked in green. A *B* road is one which motorists are recommended not to use if there is an *A* road available. Now the person drawing up the map, before he starts to look for evidence, will want to decide on his criteria. These may be the width or the gradients of the roads, the frequency with which they are repaired, or the availability of facilities such as petrol stations. The decision about criteria logically precedes the search for evidence. Admittedly, he may be influenced in his choice of criteria by the accessibility of the evidence. But he cannot tell what kind of evidence to look for until he has considered his criteria. Suppose that he decides that width is to be the criterion: every road over twenty feet wide will count as an *A* road and be marked in red. He can now replace the question 'Which roads are to be marked in red?' with the question 'Which roads are over twenty feet wide?' The fact that on a particular road his own car was forced off by another can will be evidence, but not a criterion, of *B* status.

One important difference between evidence and criteria is that evidence is the same for everyone, while criteria may differ. For example, the cartographer's criterion of an *A* road may be that it is over twenty feet wide, or that it has no gradient steeper than one in eight. But whatever the cartographer's criterion may be, the motorist's criterion will be different; for the motorist's criterion of an *A* road is that it is marked in red on his map. Of course the evidence will be different for different people if they are employing different criteria; but the evidence of a given fact, such as that a road is twenty feet wide, is the same for everybody. People may use criteria in order to know what criteria to use; but they do not use criteria to know what counts as evidence.

Even when criteria differ, the meaning may be unchanged. Wherever a rule for acting is prescribed, the criteria must be distinguished, not only from evidence, but also from meaning. The definition of the term 'B road' already given may be the same for both cartographer and motorist although the criteria they use are different. Indeed, no sense could be attached to the idea of the criteria being different, unless the meaning was the same.

What is then an intellectual test of responsibility? It might mean that such questions as 'Did he know what he was doing?' were the criteria of responsibility. It might mean that the answers to such questions were merely evidence. But whether these questions were the criteria of responsibility, or merely requests for evidence, would they be part of the meaning of responsibility? Would the asking of different questions, not about his knowledge, necessarily be a 'relaxation of definitions of responsibility' as Lady Wootton says? Clearly not, if they were simply requests for further evidence. Nor even, as we see once we distinguish criteria from evidence and meaning, if they introduced fresh criteria.

There is a further distinction which helps to elucidate the arguments of the critics. It has been pointed out that the concept of responsibility has two different functions which can be described by saying that the word 'responsible' may be used either in a descriptive or in an ascriptive way. Where it is used in an ascriptive way to say that a person is not responsible is to refuse to ascribe responsibility to him, or, in a legal context, to refuse to hold him liable. An illustration of the descriptive use is provided by the Homicide Act of 1957, which speaks of a person's 'mental responsibility'; to say that a person is not responsible in this sense may be a reason for refusing to ascribe responsibility to him.

We can now detect the flaw in the critics' arguments. If the question is asked, 'Why should a person who is not responsible be excused?', then the answer is that if 'responsible' is used in an ascriptive way, it is necessarily true that a person who is not responsible should be excused; while if it is used in a descriptive way, for example to describe his mental capacity, then he should be excused if his mental incapacity was such that it was not reasonably in his power to act otherwise. This would be an example of our criteria of responsibility; a person is not responsible if his mental incapacity was such that it was not reasonably in his power to act otherwise. We may of course have difficulty in establishing this, and these difficulties are referred to elsewhere in this chapter; but it is important to observe that these difficulties are difficulties of proof, and have nothing to do with definitions or criteria but only with evidence.

We can now distinguish, among the critics' arguments, two different claims. The first is the claim that our criteria of responsibility are not independent of moral and social values; the second is that our evidence for saying that a person is not responsible for his behaviour is not independent of that behaviour. These two claims are of course quite separate and must be treated separately; and we can now see that when we consider criteria of responsibility we are using the word 'responsible' in an ascriptive way, while when we consider evidence of responsibility we are using the term in a descriptive way.

About the first claim, that our criteria are not independent of moral and social values, there is little to be said, since, as we have seen, in the relevant sense of 'responsible' it is necessarily true that a person who is not responsible ought not to be punished; so that it is difficult to see how moral and social values could be left out. Lady Wootton infers that there is an important difference between mental health and the more 'objective' and 'scientific' status of physical health:

> 'In a less sophisticated age we should have said that one of the merits of full employment was that it made it easier for mental defectives to obtain employment. Now apparently we have to say that it actually reduces the number of suc defectives. To appreciate the full significance of this distinction we may imagine what would happen if similar reasoning were applied to the analogous case of some incontestable physical disability, such as the loss of a limb. Full employment certainly makes it easier for legless persons to get jobs, but no one in his senses would take this to mean that under full employment there are fewer persons without legs.'[42]

The analogy between mental and physical health may be more complete than Lady Wootton allows, as one of her critics has demonstrated. He says that 'it is perhaps true that the concept of physical defect is not altered by the state of employment', but argues that whether a person is incapacitated will necessarily be affected by the kind of job he is required to do; higher standards of health will be required by civil servants who are to work in the jungle.[43]

Indeed, it is not clear that it is necessary to concede that the concept of physical defect is not altered by the state of employment. It is well known that in the nineteen thirties, for example, men who were out of work found doctors less reluctant to give them a medical certificate, and such elastic categories as that of bronchitis were considerably extended. In any case, the term 'unfit', at least, is one which cannot be applied until we know what kind of job is available; and, apart from the question of full employment there is no doubt that by the standards of an earlier age many of the sedentary executives (or philosophers) of today would be pronounced unfit. It could be argued that the concept of physical health was no less culture-relative than the concept of mental health. But even if the concept of mental health were not culture-relative, the demand that we should supply criteria of responsibility independent of moral and social values is a demand which could still not be satisfied.

The demand that we should have evidence, other than his behaviour, that a person is not responsible for his behaviour, is one that is also not possible to satisfy. We cannot have evidence of another person's mental state which is in some way 'independent' of his behaviour. But of course the behaviour which furnishes us with the evidence that he is not responsible may not be the same behaviour as that for which he is said not to be responsible. He may be said not to be res-

ponsible for some action, and the evidence that he is not responsible
may be some other actions.

Many of the arguments used in this context are indeed open to a more
general criticism. It may be said that many of them, although ostensibly
directed to the specific issue of the responsibility in law of the mentally
abnormal, would if valid have far wider implications not only throughout the law but in all current ways of thinking about human conduct.
Not simply the concept of *mens rea*, it could be argued, but our whole
set of attitudes to our own and other people's behaviour, would necessarily undergo revolutionary changes if the general thesis implicit in
these arguments could be sustained. Such implications are beyond the
immediate scope at this point although some aspects of them must be
discussed later on. For our present purposes it is sufficient to concen-
trate attention on what Lady Wootton describes as 'anti-social behaviour'
It will be observed that, while the social sciences have enabled us to
identify and classify some of the diverse forms of anti-social behaviour,
Lady Wootton sometimes speaks as if this notion represented a single
entity which was being offered as an explanation of itself. She says:

'It is the anti-social behaviour which is the precipitating factor that leads to
mental treatment. But at the same time the fact of the illness is itself inferred
from this behaviour: indeed it is almost true to say that the illness *is* the behaviour for which it is also the excuse.'[44]

We are presented with the following dilemma. If the evidence for
saying that a person is not responsible is his 'anti-social behaviour',
then no one who engages in anti-social behaviour is responsible. If the
evidence for saying that a person is not responsible is not his anti-social
behaviour, then we are compelled to say that the psychopath is responsible, 'the persistent offender who shows no symptoms other than his
complete resistance to the influence of social norms.'[45] The fact that
he shows no other symptoms 'logically . . . must leave the psychopath
with full responsibility for his actions.'[46] A similar approach to the
psychopath is familiar from other sources. The Royal Commission on
Capital Punishment came to the conclusion that:

'For the present we must accept the view that there is no qualitative distinction,
but only a quantitative one, between the normal average individual and the psychopath, and the law must therefore continue to regard the psychopath as criminally
responsible.'[47]

The drafters of the American Law Institute's Model Penal Code reached
a similar conclusion, and the following provision was designed to give
effect to it: 'The terms "mental disease or defect" do not include an abnormality manifested only by repeated criminal or otherwise anti-social
conduct.'[48] The implication appears to be the same as that contained in
Lady Wootton's argument, that it is somehow unsafe to rely on a person's

behaviour as evidence of his lack of responsibility for his actions. Lady Wootton returns to this argument in a later climactic passage:

'The psychopath is a critical case for those who would retain a distinction between the responsible and the irresponsible. For . . . the psychopath makes nonsense of every attempt to distinguish the sick from the healthy delinquent by the presence or absence of a psychiatric syndrome, or by symptoms of mental disorder which are independent of his objectionable behaviour. In his case no such symptoms can be diagnosed because it is just the absence of them which causes him to be classified as psychopathic. He is, in fact, *par excellence*, and without shame or qualification, the model of the circular process by which mental abnormality is inferred from anti-social behaviour while anti-social behaviour is explained by mental abnormality.'[49]

The reasoning is not convincing. The fact that one thing is evidence of a second thing does not make it illegitimate to explain it in terms of the second thing. To take one of her own examples, the fact that a person's behaviour is evidence of his bad temper does not make it illegitimate to say: 'He is behaving like that because he is in a bad temper.' This explanation is an informative one, if only because another explanation might have been given of his behaviour, such as that he was pretending to be in a bad temper. Whether bad temper not only explains, but also excuses, his behaviour, is quite a separate question; it may do so, for example, if his bad temper is the result of illness.

The fact that bad temper explains certain kinds of behaviour does not make it difficult to recognise bad temper or to tell whether a person is bad-tempered. It may be difficult to tell whether a person is a psychopath; although it might be thought that, without any specialised training, one could tell whether a person consistently sacrificed his long-term interests to the satisfaction of an impulse without recognising that he or others were losing by his so doing. The descriptions of psychopathic personality encourage the belief that it is readily recognisable; according to one authority 'They are persons who indulge in vice with such persistence, at a cost of punishment so heavy, so certain and so prompt, and who incur their punishment for the sake of pleasure so trifling and so transient that they are by common consent considered insane although they exhibit no other indications of insanity.'[50] Another vivid description was given in evidence before the Royal Commission on the Law relating to Mental Illness and Mental Deficiency, where psychopaths were said to be mentally abnormal patients 'whose daily behaviour shows a want of social responsibility and of consideration for others, of prudence and foresight and of, ability to act in their own best interests. Their persistent anti-social mode of conduct may include inefficiency and lack of interest in any form of occupation; pathological lying, swindling and slandering; alcoholism and drug addiction; sexual offences, and violent actions with little motivation and an entire absence of self-restraint, which may go as far as homicide. Punishment or the the threat of punishment influences their behaviour only momentarily, and its more lasting effect is to intensify their vindictiveness and anti-social attitude.' [51]

The Royal Commission's Report makes it very clear that too much significance should not be attached to the lack of an agreed definition of the psychopath's personality.

'The difficulty of describing them is a difficulty of language rather than of diagnosis . . . . Such a description would probably have to mention the particular aspects of the personality which may be affected, and possibly also try to give some guide as to the cause of the disorder. But there are too many different types of psychopathic personality, and too little is at present known about their essential nature and causes for a description of this kind to be easily agreed . . . . Lack of knowledge about the nature and causes of particular forms of disorder does not mean that they cannot be recognised and successfully treated in individual patients. There was no difficulty in diagnosing "unsoundness of mind" when even less was known than is known today about the causes and nature of mental illness.'[52]

In any case, difficulty in diagnosing and classifying psychopaths is one thing, logical impossibility another. Even if it were hard to establish that a person was suffering from this condition, or to establish that this condition did not excuse his anti-social behaviour, the difficulty is not one of logic.

Discussion in some detail of these arguments is justified by their influence. Although they had meanwhile been effectively criticised, for example by Professor Fitzgerald,[53] they were repeated by Lady Wootton in her Hamlyn Lectures of 1963 on *Crime and the Criminal Law.*[54] A similar argument is used by Professor Glanville Williams in the context of diminished responsibility. He says:

'The very crime with which the accused stands charged, if the facts are proved against him, shows that he failed in the circumstances to exercise self-control to avoid committing the crime. Thus an approach in terms of self-control creates the possibility of finding diminished responsibility in every charge of crime.'[55]

Here there is an ambiguity exactly parallel to those detected in the previous arguments. Proof that a person committed a particular crime does not show that he was incapable of exercising self-control on the occasion; it shows only that he did not in fact exercise self-control. The ambiguity here lies in the notion of failure. To say that Cambridge failed to win the Boat Race may imply that they could not win it; to say that a person failed to report for duty implies only that he did not appear, not that he was unavoidably prevented. Similarly, to say that a person failed to exercise self-control may imply that he could not exercise it, or may only imply that he did not do so; it has yet to be shown that an irresistible impluse is one which is not resisted.

The Scientific Argument

Apart from these philosophical arguments, the appeal to 'science' is frequently used to discredit the concept of responsibility and its application in the law. Here again it is essential at the outset to distinguish two quite different forms of argument which may be conflated in the literature. There are first the comparatively innocuous arguments that rely upon the undisputed contention that the mental and behavioural sciences are as yet less developed than, say, the physical sciences, and are correspondingly less competent to classify their subject-matter:

'It is unlikely that toxicologists would be tolerated in courts of law if one would assert that he found a large quantity of arsenic in the body fluids of a deceased person, and another would state that he found, by the allegedly same operations none. Yet this sorry spectacle is commonplace in regard to psychiatric findings.'[56]

Secondly and more significant are the assertions that the whole process of making judgments about the state of mind of a person is in some way scientifically unsound. It is this belief which appears to form the implicit premise, and occasionally the explicit foundation, of many of the arguments advanced by those who profess a scientific approach. The underlying assumption may be that behaviour patterns are more readily reducible to scientific generalisations and explicable in terms of scientific laws than are mental processes, although few social psychologists may be prepared openly to adopt an undiluted behaviourism.

The legal doctrine which more than any other has evoked criticisms based upon this type of argument is the doctrine of diminished responsibility. Lady Wootton has said that an examination of the cases in which this doctrine had been invoked reinforced her belief that judgments about responsibility are 'impossible':

'But the crux of the whole matter lies in the inherent impossibility of making valid decisions about other people's responsibility, in the sense of their capacity to have acted otherwise than as they have in fact acted; in the inherent impossibility of maintaining a reliable distinction between the wicked and the weak-minded. Three years ago, after reviewing some seventy-odd cases in which a defence of diminished responsibility had been raised, I wrote that "I have never found, either in the records of court proceedings or in literature, any convincing demonstration that an intelligible distinction between psychopathy and wickedness can be drawn in terms of any meaningful concept of moral or criminal responsibility,"[57] and a similar analysis, since that date, of a further 126 cases has served only to fortify this opinion.'[58]

Not only laymen, but lawyers also, have expressed criticisms of the doctrine of diminished responsibility in similar terms. It is notorious that judges have had difficulty in explaining the terms of section 2 of the Homicide Act of 1957 to juries, and have indeed resorted to quite desperate expedients in attempting to do so. But the courts have also made the separate point that, as Lord Parker said in one case, the questions raised are 'incapable of scientific proof'.[59] In accordance with this criticism, Lady Wootton argued that section 2 requires juries to 'answer questions which are not only beyond the competence of experts, but are by their very nature unanswerable by anybody.'[60]

The first observation which these criticisms must provoke is the importance of distinguishing, as the courts have done but Lady Wootton has not, between the question whether these problems are open to a solution based upon the operations of science and the question whether they are open to any form of proof. It is significant that in the case mentioned Lord Parker said: 'These problems which in the present state of medical knowledge are scientifically insoluble the jury can only approach in a broad, common-sense way.'[61] This common-sense approach combined with a refusal to treat 'mental' facts as more arcane than 'physical' facts may recall the observation of Bowen L J in a civil action of the nineteenth century that 'the state of a man's mind is as much a fact as the state of his digestion.'[62]   The answers to these questions may not be susceptible to scientific demonstration, yet answers may still be possible. This is true not only of the doctrine of diminished responsibility but of all the various defences which may be raised under the name of *mens rea*. The defendant's ignorance or lack of foresight, his subjection to coercion or duress, even his susceptibility to provocation, are equally incapable of scientific proof, without thereby losing any significance. Nor is it easy to see why the M'Naghten rules are scientifically more reliable than other criteria of non-responsibility. The whole doctrine of *mens rea*, in short, necessarily rests upon judgements about mental processes or states of mind, which may lack many of the characteristics of experimentally controlled hypotheses.

To say that juries cannot answer questions of this kind is readily controverted by the every-day experience of the criminal courts. Questions of *mens rea* are generally the most important which the jury must answer: did he intend to keep the property for himself? Did he know that the cheque was forged? Did he believe that the statement in the prospectus was correct? In another civil case Lord Justice Bowen said: 'So far from saying that you cannot look into a man's mind, you must look into it, if you are going to find fraud against him; and unless you think you see what must have been in his mind, you cannot find him guilty of fraud.'[63] The same is of course true of questions of *mens rea* in criminal cases. These questions are not only answerable by a jury in ordinary experience; their answers are susceptible to reasoned appraisal, and can be set aside on appeal if unreasonable on the evidence. Sometimes, indeed, a question of *mens rea* may be the only question for the jury to decide. A man accused of stabbing to death his fiancee pleads guilty to wounding with intent to cause grievous bodily harm, contrary to section 18 of the Offences against the Person Act 1861, but not guilty to the graver charge of wounding with intent to murder, which requires an intention to kill. The only question for the jury is whether his state of mind at the time was sufficient to support the charge of attempted murder. Evidence is not lacking on these questions; in this case, it will consist of the events leading up to the affair, both on his own account and those of other witnesses; of his actions, and his statements, afterwards, of his motives, avowed and unavowed. In the case of most crimes, the accused's own attitudes, his statements and his demeanour, his gain, intended or actual, are often the most eloquent evidence of his mental processes; they do not amount to the type of evidence with which the scientist customarily deals, but they are evidence nonetheless. It would not be necessary to emphasise this truism if it were not apparently overlooked.

Closely connected with the argument from science are those arguments designed to show that the law cannot securely rest upon specific principles of morality. These principles are said to conflict with the need to place the regulation of behaviour by the law on a scientific basis. But here too a number of different arguments about the significance and status of moral judgments can be distinguished. Reference must be made first to the view that they are simply meaningless or absurd. Secondly there is the belief that moral judgments are essentially subjective, and therefore inadequate when compared with the apparently objective propositions of science. Finally it is suggested that moral judgments are incompatible with some form of determinism which is regarded as a necessary postulate of the human sciences. The most basic attack on the introduction of the concept of responsibility appears to question the significance of value judgments in any form. In this context the word 'metaphysical' is a favourite pejorative epithet apparently contrasted with the verifiable propositions of science. Thus one writer has referred to 'the public policy issue as to what extent a system of criminal justice based on metaphysical concepts of moral responsibility is to be or can be replaced – in whole or in part – by a system based upon the operational philosophy of contemporary science;'[64] while another describes the 'concepts of responsibility and punishment popular in legal and psychiatric practice' as 'theological and metaphysical anachronisms' best relegated to the 'amusement of the religious and others of that kidney.'[65] Even Professor Glanville Williams in his textbook on *Criminal Law* permits himself a reference to 'the mystical theory of moral responsibility'.[66] Again there seems to be implied a false dichotomy, based perhaps on an extreme form of logical positivism, between empirically verifiable propositions which alone are significant, and all other non-analytic propositions which are described indifferently as metaphysical or meaningless. The short answer to criticisms of this type is to point out that if they are intended to deny the significance of all forms of value judgment, they appear to preclude the possibility of any rational, critique whatever of social and political institutions.

A more qualified criticism derives from the belief that moral judgments are essentially subjective and therefore compare unfavourably with the apparently objective status of scientific propositions. The acceptance of moral relativism was regarded on both sides as a serious obstacle to the notion of *mens rea*, and has been particularly emphasised by modern writers who wish to apply to the criminal law a 'value-free' scientific approach of the kind advocated by Weber.

Here again it can be shown that the controversy has been conducted on a fallacious assumption. In 1880 one writer suggested that the principles of criminal liability were demonstrable in the same way as mathematical truths;[67] while Stephen reacted to the opposite extreme by an unqualified adherence to moral relativism:

'General theories as to what ought to be the conditions of criminal responsibility may not be useless, but they must depend on the tastes of those who form them and they cannot, so far as I can see, be said in any distinct sense to be either true or false.'[68]

We have seen too that both Holmes and Lady Wootton have been influenced by the lack of objectivity in ethical standards and have concluded that they should have no place in the criminal law. But it is now clear that the doctrine of *mens rea* is independent of any form of 'moralism' in that it does not entail any specific view as to the moral content of the law; and it is clear that the value judgments which are used to justify *mens rea*, although they differ both from the analytical propositions of mathematics and from the empirically verifiable statements of the experimental sciences, are not therefore necessarily incapable of being true or false.

M

Mens rea and free will

A final and more fundamental criticism of the introduction into the law of moral criteria of responsibility is based on the belief that they are incompatible with some type of determinism which is a necessary postulate of the scientific explanation of human behaviour. Thus the central issue is stated by Dr Sheldon Glueck in terms of a dispute between 'those who stress the prime social need of blameworthiness and retributive punishment as the core-concept in crime and justice and those who, under the impact of psychiatric, psycho-analytic, sociological and anthropological views insist that man's choices are the product of forces largely beyond his conscious control.'[69] It may be argued that if it is in principle possible to formulate laws coordinating observed regularities in all froms of human behaviour, then it is impossible to allocate a place among the causes of human action to the exercise of a free choice which is a condition of the concept of responsibility. The wider issues raised by this argument cannot be considered within the present terms of reference; but it may be permissible to sketch the outline of a possibly reply. The first question to be asked would be whether this criticism, like the earlier one, also precluded the possibility of evaluating human actions and social institutions altogether. The answer to this question would presumably depend upon the form of determinism postulated by the criticism. But if this were not precluded, then it could perhaps be argued that the principles of responsibility had an importance which was independent of the determinist hypothesis. For it could be argued in the first place that the infringement of liberty involved in the abandonment of *mens rea* is of a different order altogether from the denial of freedom involved in any form of determinism. It is of course true that the doctrine of *mens rea* was traditionally based on the assumption of free will. This is evident from the classic justifications of the doctrine. In what is perhaps the first attempt to construct a general rationale of *mens rea* in English law, Hale makes this very clear: 'Man is naturally endowed with these two great faculties, understanding and liberty of will, and therefore is a subject properly capable of a law properly so called, and consequently obnoxious to guilt and punishment for the violation of that law, which in respect of these two great faculties he hath a capacity to obey . . . . And because the liberty or choice of the will presupposeth an act of the understanding to know the thing or action chosen by the will, it follows that, where there is a total defect of the understanding, there is no free act of the will in the choice of things or actions.'[70]

But even if the assumption of free will is challenged, there is still an undisputed value in the preservation of a different form of freedom, the freedom from unpredictable coercion. It is hard to see why any kind of determinist should be led to deny the supreme importance of predictability in the criminal law; on the contrary, the work of some philosophers would suggest the reverse. For it can be seen that many of those thinkers who have gone furthest in recognising the limitations upon human freedom have at the same time, and without inconsistency, been most emphatic in their insistence upon the need for men to understand and to anticipate the nature of these limitations. Indeed, it could be said that one of the most conspicuous developments of recent thought has been the development of the idea that the greatest restriction of human freedom lies in the fact that men are ignorant of the implications of their own actions. Influential writers otherwise as divergent in their philosohies, and as critical of the canons of conventional morality, as Karl Marx, Sigmund Freud, and Jean-Paul Sartre, while emphasising that the restrictions on human freedom were far greater than was generally imagined, have all advanced independent arguments to show that, given a greater understanding of themselves and of their situation, men can attain a greater freedom by recognising the forces which determine their actions. They have thus given original interpretations of the old teaching, associated especially with Spinoza, that freedom consists in the knowledge of necessity. It could be argued that the law, by its assumption that men are capable of choosing the consequences of their actions, has enabled people to predict the extent to which it will impinge upon their activities; and that by enabling men to identify its restraints in advance, and to act in the knowledge of them, it has kept those restraints to a minimum.

Lady Wootton at any rate accepts that the issue does not turn on the question of free will; and she criticises the approach of Dr Sheldon Glueck exemplified in the passage quoted above. She objects to this type of approach on the ground that it leads to the conflict between psychiatry and the law being fought, as she expresses it, on the wrong ground.

'Indeed Dr Glueck's discussion of the relation of psychiatry to law is chiefly devoted to an analysis of the exculpatory effect of psychiatric knowledge, and to the changes that have been, or should be, made in the assessment of guilt as the result of the growth of this knowledge. In consequence much intellectual ingenuity is wasted in refining the criteria by which the wicked may be distinguished from the weak-minded. For surely to argue thus is to argue from the wrong premises: the real difference between the psychiatric and the legal approach has nothing to do with free will and determinism. It has to do with their conceptions of the objectives of the criminal process, with the question whether the aim of that process is punitive or preventive, whether what matters is to punish the wrongdoer or to set him on the road to virtue; and in order to take a stand on that issue, neither party need be a determinist.'[71]

Although Lady Wootton does not distinguish between the claim of the psychiatrist that some apparently free actions can be causally explained, which might lend point to an attempt to refine the criteria of responsibility, and a comprehensive determinism which might make such attempts futile, she is clearly right to doubt the relevance of this issue to the question whether responsibility should be altogether bypassed.

The changing functions of the criminal law
Nevertheless, it seems that, to use her own metaphor, she also seeks to fight the battle on the wrong ground. Her use, in particular, of the term 'wicked', and her frequent references to a 'punitive' or 'retributive' view of the function of the criminal law, suggest that she can see no *via media* between this position at one extreme and her own Utopia in which responsibility is altogether disregarded. Similarly, Dr Glueck has argued that 'the question of responsibility would not have to be raised, if the concept of management of the anti-social individual were changed from that of punishment . . . to a concept of the anti-social individual as a sick person, in need of treatment rather than punishment.'[72]

We have seen, however, that the antithesis between treatment and punishment cannot be so readily made, and we have remarked, in examining the law relating to children and young persons, on the difficulties to which the distinction gives rise in practice. Since the same measures may in one case be described as a punishment, but in another case as a form of treatment, it is clear that the question may be in danger of becoming purely terminological. The only alternative is to suggest that the appropriate description depends upon the intention with which the measures are imposed, or on the attitudes to them of the offender and of society generally. Here too, however, no clear demarcation is possible; since, as we have seen, measures normally used as a punishment may in a particular case be imposed as a form of treatment; while it could be argued that any form of treatment, if compulsory, will be generally regarded as a punishment.

Treatment may and does carry its own stigma; and notoriously offenders have preferred a specific penalty to an indeterminate form of treatment. Although punishment is overtly condemnatory, treatment as well carries the implication that the behaviour in question is socially undesirable.

Nor can the requirement of deterrence be satisfactorily accommodated within this narrow conceptual framework. If we were to adopt it consistently, we should be reduced to the absurd conclusion that the element of individual deterrence in a particualr sentence could be classed as treatment, because it was intended to affect the offender's behaviour alone, while any element of general deterrence would have to be described as punishment.

In practice little attempt is made to preserve this distinction. Thus for some time psychiatric treatment has been available in prison, and more recently in England a 'psychiatric prison' has been introduced;[73] while it is well known that some psychopathic patients respond to measures which would ordinarily be regarded as punishment.[74]

No single description of the functions of the criminal law is likely to be adequate to the social changes of the past century. Clearly the emphasis on forward-looking measures together with the great proliferation of regulatory offences must not be minimised. But enough has been said to show that nothing in the transformation of the law has justified the elimination of responsibility. In the treatment of offenders, a number of varying and often conflicting considerations have to be taken into account; the need to provide facilities for rehabilitation and constructive training, to protect the public, to deter potential offenders, and to satisfy public opinion that justice is being done. But it can be argued that so long as coercive measures are required, under whatever name, the concept of responsibility must be retained.

Nor can it be argued that it is unnecessary when there is no longer a close correspondence between the criminal law and the moral law. For we have seen that no equation between legal and moral guilt is necessary to support the principle of *mens rea*; it can be given a moral justification on different grounds.

The social cost and benefits of *mens rea*
It has been suggested that the controversy over *mens rea* has been based on false assumptions, and has therefore served only to conceal the true question. The conclusion must be that the value of the principle of *mens rea* should be recognised, and that the important issue is that of its social cost. It will appear that against the cost of retaining it there must be off-set the cost of abolishing it; yet strangely the question seems never to have been investigated by either the supporters of *mens rea* or their opponents.

Perhaps the closest approach to this question has been taken by those who have debated the difficulty of proving *mens rea*; but even here the question has not been pursued far enough. The argument from the difficulty of proof can be found in the law reports as a justification of strict liability as far back as 1824. A carrier was charged with a statutory offence of having game in his possession. His defence was based on the

ground that his agent was unaware that any game had been placed in
the carrier's waggon, and he argued that he could not be convicted
because the information did not allege that he was knowingly in possession of the game. This argument was rejected by Abbott C J who
said: 'If it were necessary to aver that the defendant had actual knowledge it would cast on the prosecutor a burden of proof which could
not easily be satisfied.'[75] We have already seen that the argument from
administrative convenience cannot be generalised. It can be shown too
that serious consequences would follow from a wider acceptance of
strict liability, and that given the limited resources available for the
enforcement of the law, the social cost of eliminating *mens rea* would
be extremely high.

First of course there is the direct cost of the detection and disposal
of the cases concerned. But there is also the indirect cost in terms of
law enforcement generally, once it is recognised that the limited resources, both of an offical kind, whether of police, judges, social
workers and so forth, and of society generally in its capacity to understand and conform to the law and in its willingness to respect the law,
should not be diluted over a multiplicity of offences and offenders.
This is an argument of general importance, independent of considerations of individual liberty, for restricting the ambit of the criminal
law.

In any case it can be seen that any disadvantages which may attend
the requirement of *mens rea* may be overcome by transferring the
burden of proof, in minor offences, from the prosecution to the defence, without resorting to the more drastic expedient of strict liability.

One argument from social cost which is often advanced against
mens rea is that so long as this requirement is retained there can be
no incentive for the factory owner, for example, to improve his system
of work. So long as his liability depends upon proof of knowledge, he
has no incentive to introduce new safety methods to prevent future
accidents. Again, however it is not strict liability, but rather a modification of the traditional conditions of responsibility, which is required
to overcome this problem. Indeed it could be said that the social cost
of strict liability would be higher in this field than that of *mens rea*;
first, because under a regime of strict liability evidence of the system
actually operated by the factory owner might be disregarded by prosecuting authorities satisfied to obtain a bare conviction; secondly,
because the minimal penalty often imposed in strict liability cases
would have little deterrent effect compared with the substantial penalty which might follow proof of *mens rea* . Perhaps what is required i
these cases is provision for a substantial penalty without proof of know-

ledge, but subject to a defence, not of reasonable ignorance or mistake, but that the defendant took all reasonable precautions. The court would then be not merely empowered but required to investigate the system of work, and to fix the penalty accordingly. Proof by the prosecution of the *actus reus*, which would be simple enough in the case of selling adulterated food, or a factory accident, would be sufficient to justify imposing on the defendant the onus of proving a safe system; and failure by the defendant to adduce the defence would in itself constitute evidence of a defective system. The objection in terms of social effectiveness to the use of strict liability in these cases is that it serves to exclude precisely that evidence which it is most important to have before the court.

So far as objective liability is concerned, we have seen that there is even less force here in the argument based on the difficulty of proving *mens rea;* for objective liability requires a finding that the reasonable man would have foreseen the prohibited consequences in the light of the facts as they were actually known to the defendant.

Nevertheless the argument can be advanced that the imposition of liability for negligence, at any rate, is necessary under modern social conditions. It may be asked whether we can afford to exempt the accident-prone. It is possible that so long as *mens rea* is retained, a person who by the damage he does represents a considerable social danger may never be convicted by a court, if the harm which he causes, however frequent and however serious, is always the result of inadvertence. People who are clumsy, for example, or very careless, may do more damage in an industrialised environment than those who act on premeditation. From the point of view of social control, such a person may be more dangerous than one who commits a calculated murder which he is unlikely to repeat.

This is a stronger argument, but even here it may be though that there would still be a price to pay for the removal of *mens rea*. It is arguable that, while there is assumed to be no social value in deliberate law-breaking, there may well be considerable social value in activities where an offence would be simply an unintended and unforeseen by-product. The effect of removing *mens rea* in such cases is really to penalise activities which may be of considerable social utility.

Further, it may be suggested that there are more general grounds for believing that there may be considerable social benefit in retaining *mens rea*. Here again it is necessary to consider the indirect as well as the direct consequences. Ultimately it could be said, for instance, that a general abandonment of the principle that a person is responsible only for those consequences of his actions which he could reasonably foresee might encourage a general indifference to the consequences of our actions; for it may well be true that only if we believe that we have a genuine choice of conforming to the law are we likely to try to do so. It may therefore be at any rate expedient for the law to provide this opportunity, since it is a truism that the effectiveness of any legal system depends largely on voluntary compliance.

This raises the wider question as to what social attitudes to the criminal law would be likely to follow a complete elimination of responsibility. It is already clear that no system of rules could operate unless men were in general capable of understanding and conforming to them. In this sense it may be regarded as a necessary condition of the efficacy of any system for the regulation of human behaviour by means of rule. It may be said that although this does not entail that the rules must incorporate as a condition of liability the capacity to understand and comply with them, it does show how fundamental such capacity is to any form of social control.

If the effectiveness of a legal system depends upon voluntary compliance, there must be some conformity between the principles upon which it operates and what may be described as the social mores. The clearest evidence of this is provided by those legal systems such as international law where the mechanisms of enforcement are least developed; but it is true also of every system, and perhaps more true as the system becomes more complex. These considerations may suggest that the indirect cost of eliminating responsibility may be extremely high.

Notes

Chapter 1

1   *Harding* v.*Price*, [1948] 1 K.B. 695, 700.
2   *Lambert* v. *Bassey*, T Ray, 421 [1681].
3   Stephen, *A General View of the Criminal Law of England* [1863], 1–2.
4   Salmond, *Law of Torts* (6th ed. 1924), 11–13.
5   Holmes, *The Common Law* [1881], 96.
6   Holmes, *op. cit.*, Lectures III and IV.
7   Holdsworth, *History of English Law*, VIII [1925], 446, 464–5, 489.
8   Wigmore, 'Responsibility for Tortious Acts': Its History', *Select Essays in Anglo-American Legal History*, III [1909], 475
9   Ames, 'Law and Morals', *Lectures on Legal History* [1930], 437.
10   *Read* v. *Lyons & Co. Ltd.*, [1947] A.C. 156 at 170–171.
11   *Rylands* v. *Fletcher*, [1866] L.R. 1 Ex. 265; [1868] L.R. 3 H.L. 330.
12   *Read* v. *Lyons & Co. Ltd.*, [1947] A.C. 156 at 170–171.
13   Winfield, 'The Myth of Absolute Liability', 42 L.Q.R. [1926], 37.
14   Fifoot, *History and Sources of the Common Law* [1949].
15. Fifoot, *Judge and Jurist in the Reign of Victoria*[1959], 31–56.
16   *Fowler* v. *Lanning*, [1959] 1 Q.B. 426; cf. *Stanley* v. *Powell*, [1891] 1 Q.B. 86; *National Coal Board* v. *Evans*, [1951] 2 K.B. 861.
17   Law Reform (Contributory Negligence) Act 1945, s. 1.
18   Cf. *Davie* v. *New Merton Board Mills Ltd.*, [1959] A.C. 604.
19   But cf. *ICI Ltd.* v. *Shatwell* [1965] A.C. 656.
20   E.g. *Lloyd* v. *Grace, Smith & Co.*, [1912] A.C. 716
21   E.g. *Smith* v. *Leech Brain & Co.*, [1962] 2 Q.B. 405
      Hughes v. *Lord Advocate*, [1963] A.C. 837.
22   Kant, *Metaphysik der Sitten* [1785];
      F H Bradley, *Ethical Studies.*
23   Plato, *Protagoras* 324.
24   Paley, *The Principles of Moral and Political Philosophy* [1785], VI, Chapter 9; cf. Blackstone, cited in Heath, *Eighteenth Century Penal Theory* [1963], 185.
25   Bentham, *An Introduction to the Principles of Morals and Legislation* [1789].
26   Hart, *Punishment and Responsibility* [1968], 244.
27   Kant, *op. cit.*, cited in Ewing, *The Morality of Punishment* [1929], 15.
28   Wharton, *Treatise on Criminal Law* (8th ed. 1880), I, 8.
29   Holmes, *The Common Law* [1881], 44.
30   Holmes, *op. cit.*, 48.
31   Hart, *op. cit.*, 211f.
32   *R.* v. *Larsonneur* [1933], 149 L.T. 542.
33   Bentham, *op. cit.*, Ch. XIII.

N

34 Bracton, *De Legibus et Consuetudinibus Angliae,* ed. Woodbine [1915].
35 *Leges Henrici Primi,* c. 90, 11.
36 *Leges Henrici Primi,* c. 88, 6.
37 Walter, Corpus Juris Germanici, I, 668, cited in Wigmore, 7 *Harvard Law Review* [1893–4], 315, 321.
38 Cf. Selden Society, *Select Pleas of the Crown,* No. 70 [1203].
39 Sayre, *'Mens Rea'* 45 *Harvard Law Review* [1931–2], 974, 979–80.
40 Road Traffic Act 1960, ss. 1, 2.
41 Austin, 'A Plea for Excuses', *Philosophical Papers* [1961], 142.
42 Blackstone, *Commentaries,* LV 186.
43 Sayre, *op. cit.,* 985f.
44 Bodenstein, 'Phases in the Development of Criminal *Mens Rea*', [1919] *South African Law Journal* 323, 335f.
45 *D P P* v. *Smith,* [1961] A.C. 290.
46 Coke, *Third Institute* [1644] 32f.
47 *R* v. *Keate,* [1697] Comb. 406; *R* v. *Plummer* [1700] Kel. 109.
48 Royal Commission on Capital Punishment, 1949–53, *Report* Cmd 8932 [1953] 30; Appendix 7 (b).
49 *R* v. *Jarmain,* [1946] K.B 74
50 *R* v. *Creamer,* [1966] 1 Q.B. 72;
51 *R* v. *Church,* [1966] 1Q.B. 59.
52 *R* v. *Tolson,* [1889], 23 Q.B.D. 168.
53 See e.g. Wootton, *Crime and the Criminal Law* [1963].

Chapter 2

1   See Walker, *Crime and Insanity in England* [1968].
2   Bracton, *De Legibus et Consuetudinibus Angliae,* ed. Woodbine [1915].
3   Modestinus 821. 11.
4   Digest 1. 18. 14.
5   Beverley's case [1603], 2 Coke's Rep. 571.
6   Hale, P C I [1736]. Ch. IV.
7   *Ibid.*
8   *R* v. *Arnold* [1724] 16 St Tr 695.
9   Hawkins, *A Treatise of Pleas of the Crown* [1716] I, 1
10 *R* v. *Ferrers,* [1760] 19 St Tr 886.
11 *R* v. *Hadfield,* [1800] 27 St Tr 1281.
12 *R* v. *M'Naghten,* [1843] 10 Cl & F 200.
13 *The Times,* 6 March 1843, cited by Walker, *op. cit.,* 95.
14 Hansard, Third Series, LXVII, 714.
15 For the questions and answers see [1843] 10 Cl & F 200 at 209–12
16 *R* v. *Codere* [1916] 12 Cr App R 21.

17 *R* v. *Windle*, [1952] 36 Cr App R 85.
18 B P P 1846, Vol 24.
19 Hale, *op. cit.*,Ch. III.
20 Walker, *op. cit.*, 81.
21 Walker, '1883 and all that,' [1966] Crim L R 17;
     Crime and Insanity in England [1968] 190.
22 *R* v. *Ireland* [1910] 4 Cr App R 74, 87.
23 *R* v. *Machardy* [1911] 6 Cr App R 256, 272.
24 *Felstead* v. *R*, [1914] A C 554.
25 *R* v. *Kemp* [1957] 1 Q B 399, 403.
26 Stephen, H C L [1883] Vol II 151.
27 Cmd 2005, p 12.
28 Criminal Statistics 1967.
29 Stephen, *op. cit.*, 171.
30 Queensland Criminal Code, s.27.
31 Tasmanian Code, s.16 (1).
32 Criminal Justice Act (Northern Ireland) 1966.
33 American Law Institute, Model Penal Code, Proposed Official Draft
     [1962], 4.01.
34 *A–G for South Australia* v. *Brown,* [1960] A.C. 432
35 *R* v. *True* [1922] 16 Cr App R 164.
36 Report of the Committee on Insanity and Crime [1923] Cmd 2005.
37 See the report of the debate on the second reading of the Bill,
     Hansard, Fifth Series, LVII, col 443 f.
38 *R* v. *Kopsch* [1925] 19 Cr App R 50, 51.
39 Cmnd 8932, para 317.
40 B P P 1846, Vol 24.
41 Devlin, 'Mental Abnormality and the Criminal Law', in *Changing Legal
     Objectives* (ed R St J MacDondald, 1963), 71, 85.
42 Wootton, *Social Science and Social Pathology* [1959], Ch VIII.
43 Cmd 2005, p 4.
44 Weihofen, *Insanity as a Defense in Criminal Law* [1933], 16
45 Stephen, *op. cit.*, 183
46. *Durham* v. *U S* 214 F 2d 862 [1954]
47 Wechsler, 'The criteria of criminal responsibility', 22 U Chi L Rev 367
     [1955].
48 Cmnd 8932, para 333.
49 Cd 4202 [1908].
50 Mental Deficiency Act 1913, s. 1.
51 Cmnd 8932, para 212.
52 Cmnd 8932, para 344.
53 Mental Deficiency Act 1913, s.8 (1)
54 Mental Deficiency Act 1927, s.1 (2)
55 Walker, *op. cit.*, 129 f.
56 Walker, *op. cit.*, 133, table 4 and appendix C.
57 Criminal Statistics 1967

58   Wootton, *Crime and Criminal Law* [1963], 64–5
59   Sparks, 'Diminished responsibility in theory and practice', 27 M L R [1964]
      9; see Table A below.
60   *R v. James* [1961] Crim L R 842; cf *R* v. *Morris* [1961] 2 Q B 237.
61   Williams, *Criminal Law: The General Part* (2nd ed 1961), 557;
      Wootton, *op. cit.,* 72.
62   Criminal Statistics 1967.
63   Hansard, Fifth Series CCLXXXV, col 1813 (H L).
64   *R v. Byrne* [1960] 44 Cr App R 246
65   *Rose* v. *R* [1961] 45 Cr App R 102 (P C).
66   Wootton, 'Diminished responsibility: a layman's view', 76 L Q R [1960],
      224.
67   Sparks, *op. cit.*
68   p 16.
69   p 14.
70   Walker, *op.cit.,* 238
71   Criminal Appeal Act 1968, s.15.
72   Criminal Statistics 1967.
73   Walker, op. cit., 161–2.
74   Blom-Cooper, *The Times,* 26 April 1961; Wootton, *op.cit.,* 225;
      Williams, *op. cit.,* 553.
75   *Chandler* v. *Webster* [1904] 1 K B 493; The *Fibrosa Case* [1943]
      A C 32; Law Reform (Frustrated Contracts) Act 1943, s 1 (2).
76   Law Reform (Contributory Negligence) Act 1945.
77   Mental Health Act 1959, s.4 (2).
78   s. 4 (3).
79   s. 4 (4).
80   s. 4 (5).
81   *R v. Hall* [1962] Crim L R 647.
82   Criminal Procedure (Insanity) Act 1964, s.1.
83   Mental Deficiency Act 1913, s.3.
84   s.8 (1).
85   National Health Service Act 1946, s.50, Sched IX, Part 1.
86   *R* v. *Morris* [1961] 2 Q B 237, 243.
87   Wootton, *Crime and the Criminal Law* [1963], 61–2
88   p 76–7.
89   Cmnd 8932, para 281.

Chapter 3

1   *Chappie* v. *Cooper*, [1844] 13 M & W 252; *Clements* v. *London and North-Western Railway Company*, [1894] 2 Q B 482; Infants' Relief Act 1874, ss.1,2.

2   *Burnard* v.*Haggis*, [1863] 14 C B N S 45; *Jennings* v. *Rundall*, [1799] 8 Term Rep 335; *Ballett* v. *Mingay*, [1943] K B 281.

3   Tappan, *Juvenile Delinquency* [1949], 170

4   Departmental Committee on the Treatment of Young Offenders, *Report*, Cmd 2831 [1927], 8.

5   Departmental Committee on the Treatment of Young Offenders, *Report*, Cmd 2831 [1927], 7.

6   Wilkinson, *Leges Anglo-Saxonicae* 65 f.

7   Kean, 'The History of the Criminal Liability of Children', 53 L Q R [1937], 364.

8   Children and Young Persons Act 1933, s.50.

9   Committee on Children and Young Persons, Report, Cmnd 1191 [1960].

10 Fitzgerald, *Criminal Law and Punishment* [1962]. 262–3.

11 Children and Young Persons Act 1963, ss.2 (1) (a), 2 (2) (a).

12 Children and Young Persons Act 1963, s.2 (1) (b).

13 Watson, *The Child and the Magistrate* [1965], 305.

14 Departmental Committee on the Treatment of Young Offenders, *Report*, Cmd 2831 [1927], 6; cf Home Office Children's Department, *Sixth Report* [1951], 70.

15 Children and Young Persons Act 1933, s.44 (1).

16 Children and Young Persons Act 1963, s.6 (1).

17 Clarke Hall and Morrison, *The Law relating to Children and Young Persons* (6th ed 1960), 71.

18 Children and Young Persons Act 1933, s.54.

19 Care of Children Committee, *Report*, Cmd 6922 [1946], 172.

20 Criminal Justice Act, 1948, s.18.

21 Williams, *Criminal Law*, (2nd ed 1961), 842 n 14.

22 'Penal Practice in a Changing Society', Cmnd 645 [1959], para 33.

23 Criminal Justice Act 1948, s.19.

24 Criminal Justice Act 1961, s.10.

25 Attendance Centre Rules, S I 1958, No. 1990, r 2 (1).

26 Watson, *op.cit.*, 204–5

27 *R* v. *Evans*, [1958] 3 All E R 673.

28 Criminal Justice Act 1961, s.13.

29 Criminal Justice Act 1961. s.1.

30 The Borstal (No. 2) Rules, S I 1949. No. 1283 r 4 (1); cf. Prison Commission, *The Principles of the Borstal System* [1932].

31 'Penal Practice in a Changing Society', Cmnd 645 [1959], para 37.

32 'The treatment of young offenders': Advisory Council on the Treatment of Offenders, *Report* [1959], para 47.

33   Clarke Hall, *Children's Courts* [1926], Chapter III, cited in Watson, *op. cit.*, 49–50.
34   Departmental Committee on the Treatment of Young Offenders, *Report,* Cmd 2831 [1927], 17–20.
35   'Children and Young Persons, Scotland', Cmnd 2306 [1964].
36   'Children and Young Persons, Scotland', Cmnd 2306 [1964], para 197.
37   'Social Work in the Community', Cmnd 3065 [1966].
38   'The Child, the Family and the Young Offender', Cmnd 2742 [1965].
39   Criminal Statistics 1965, Cmnd 3037 [1966].
40   Wootton, *Social Science and Social Pathology* [1959], Chapter VI.
41   Wootton, *op. cit.*, Chapter V.
42   Mannheim and Wilkins, *Prediction Methods in Relation to Borstal Training* [1955], 145
43   Radzinowicz and Turner, (ed), *Detention in Remand Homes*[1952], 43.
44   Watson, *op. cit., 291.*
45   Cmnd 3601.
46   Cmnd 3601, p 5.
47   Children and Young Persons Act 1969, s.1 (2).
48   S.4
49   S.3 (3)
50   S.5
51   S.1 (3)
52   S.11
53   S.7(2)
54   S.7 (5)
55   S.7 (6)
56   *Ibid.*
57   S.7 (7)
58   S.7 (5)
59   S.7 (1)
60   S.20 (3)

Chapter 4

1   Theft Act 1968, s.1.
2   Theft Act 1968, s.2 (1) (b).
3   See *Korten* v. *West Sussex C C* [1903], 72 L J K B 514.
4   See *Goldsmith* v. *Deakin* [1934] 150 L T Rep 157.
5   Cited in *Margate Pier Co.* v. *Hannam,* [1819] 3 B & Ald 266 at 270
6   *Cundy* v. *Le Cocq* [1884] 13 Q B D 207.
7   *Sherras* v. *De Rutzen*, [1895] 1 Q B 918.
8   *Hobbs* v. *Winchester Corporation*, [1910] 2 K B 471 at 483; cf.
     Stallybrass, 'The Eclipse of *Mens Rea*', 52 L Q R [1936], 60.

9   *Reynolds* v. *G H Austin & Sons Ltd.*, [1951] 2 K B 135 at 148

10 *R* v. *Prince*, [1875] L R 2 C C R 154.

11 *R* v. *Hibbert* [1869] 1 C C R 184.

12 Holmes, The Common Law [1881], 49.

13 *R* v. *Tolson* [1889] 23 Q B D 168.

14 *R* v. *Wheat and Stocks*, [1921] 2 K B 119.

15 *R* v. *Gould* [1968] 1 All E R 849.

16 Williams, *Criminal Law* (2nd ed 1961) 259–60.

17 Fuller, *The Morality of Law* [1964], 76.

18 *Newstead* v. *London Express Newspaper Ltd.*, [1940] 1 K B 377.

19 *In re Polemis and Furness Withy & Co.*, [1921] 3 K B 560; *Overseas
    Tankship (U K) Ltd* v. *Morts Dock & Engineering Co Ltd (The
    Wagon Mound)*, [1961] A C 388.

20 *Donoghue* v. *Stevenson* [1932] A C 562.

21 *Hedley Byrne & Co* v. *Heller & Partners*, [1964] A C 465.

22 Griffith, ' "Fault" Triumphant', 28 *New York University Law Review*
    [1953], 1069; Street, 'The Twentieth Century Development and
    Function of the Law of Tort in England', 14 *International and
    Comparative Law Quarterly* [1965], 862, 870–2.

23 *James & Son Ltd* v. *Smee*, [1955] 1 Q B 78.

24 *R* v. *Spurge* [1961] 2 Q B 205.

25 Road Traffic Act 1930, s.11 (1), as amended by Road Traffic Act
    1956, s.51 and para 12 (1) of Schedule 8 thereto, repealed and
    re-enacted by Road Traffic Act 1960, s.2 (1)

26 *R* v. *Evans*, [1963] 1 Q B 412, 418.

27 *Hill* v. *Baxter*, [1958] 1 Q B 277; cf. *Watmore* v. *Jenkins*, [1962]
    2 Q B 572.

28 *Burns* v. *Bidder*, [1966] 3 All E R 29, 36.

29 *Sherras* v. *De Rutzen*, [1895] 1 Q B 918.

30 *Sherras* v. *De Rutzen*, [1895] 1 Q B 918 at 922.

31 *Pearks, Gunston & Tee Ltd* v. *Ward* and *Hennen* v. *Southern Counties
    Dairies Ltd*, [1902] 2 K B 1 at 11.

32 Howard, *Strict Responsibility* [1963], 19.

33 *Shaw* v. *D P P* [1962] A C 220 at 267.

34 *R* v. *Prince*, [1875] L R 2 C C R 154; *Fletcher* v. *Rylands*, [1866] L R
    1 Ex 265; *R* v. *Stephens*, [1866] L R 1 Q B 702; *Fitzpatrick* v.
    Kelly, [1873] 8 Q B D 337; cf. *Hollins* v. *Fowler*, [1875] L R
    7 H L 757.

35 *R* v. *Prince*, [1875] L R 2 C C R 154 at 174, 175.

36 *R* v. *Middleton*, [1873] L R 2 C C R 38

37 *R* v. *Prince*, [1875] L R 2 C C R 154 at 170

38 *Hearne* v. *Gorton*, [1859] 2 E & E 66.

39 *R* v. *Ashwell*, [1885] 16 Q B D 190.

40 *R* v. *Tolson*, [1889] 23 Q B D 168 at 172.

41 Holmes, *The Common Law* [1881], 51–2.

42 Stephen, *History of Criminal Law* [1883], II, 112.

43 *R* v. *Bishop*, [1880] 5 Q B D 259.

44   *R* v. *Tolson*, [1889] 23 Q B D 168, 188, 191.
45   Sayre, 'Public Welfare Offences', 33 *Columbia Law Review* [1933], 55.
46   Stallybrass, 'The Eclipse of *Mens Rea*', 52 L Q R [1936], 60.
47   Cf Brett, *An Inquiry into Criminal Guilt* [1963], 103, 111 f.; Howard, *Strict Responsibility* [1963], 189–190.
48   Cf. Williams *op. cit.*, 255–61; Hall, *General Principles of Criminal Law* (2nd ed 1960), 342–51; Howard, *op. cit.*, Ch 1.
49   *Brend* v. *Wood*, [1946] 62 T L R 462 at 463.
50   *Harding* v. *Price* [1948] 1 K B 695 at 700.
51   Motor Car Act 1903, s.6;
52   *Younghusband* v. *Luftig*, [1949] s K B 354 at 369
53   *Wilson* v. *Inyang* [1951] 2 K B 799 at 803
54   *Reynolds* v. *G H Austin & Sons Ltd* [1951] 2 K B 135 at 144.
55   *Reynolds* v. *G H Austin & Sons Ltd* [1951] 2 K B 135 at 149.
56   *Reynolds* v. *G H Austin & Sons Ltd* [1951] 2 K B 135 at 150.
57   *Gardner* v. *Akeroyd*, [1952] 2 Q B 743.
58   N 43 and n 48, above: *Gardner* v. *Akeroyd*, [1952] 2 Q B 743 at 746–8
59   *Lim Chin Aik* v. *The Queen*, [1963] A C 160.
60   *Lim Chin Aik* v. *The Queen*, [1963] A C 160 at 174–5.
61   *Yeandel* v. *Fisher*, [1965] 3 All E R 158.
62   Dangerous Drugs Act 1964, s.9 (1).
63   *Sweet* v. *Parsley*, [1968] 2 All E R 337.
64   Dangerous Drugs Act 1965, s.5.
65   *Sweet* v. *Parsley*, [1969] 3 All E R 347.
66   *Warner* v. *Metropolitan Police Commissioner* [1968] 2 All E R 356.
67   Cf. *Proudman* v. *Dayman*, [1941] 67 C L R 536 at 540–1.
68   Howard, *op. cit.*, 85.
69   Howard, *op. cit.*, 86.
70   *State* v. *Lindberg*, 125 Wash 51, 215 Pac 41 [1923].
71   Williams, *Criminal Law* (2nd ed 1961), 22.
72   *Bratty* v. *Attorney-General for Northern Ireland*, [1963] A C 386 at 409.
73   Cf. Friedmann, *Law in a Changing Society* (Pelican ed 1964), Chapter V.

Chapter 5

1   Goldstein, *The Insanity Defence* [1967], 16
2   *R* v. *Ward*, [1956] 1 Q B 351.
3   *D P P* v. *Smith* [1961] A C 290 at 326.
4   *D P P* v. *Smith* [1961] A C 290 at 326–7
5   Holmes, *The Common Law* [1881].
6   Salmon, 'The Criminal Law Relating to Intent', 14 *Current Legal Problems* [1961], 1.

7 Denning, *Responsibility before the Law* [1961].

8 *D P P* v. *Smith*, [1961] A C 290 at 331, 327.

9 Holmes, *op. cit.*, Lectures I–IV.

10 Hall, *General Principles of Criminal Law* (2nd ed 1960), Ch V.

11 *D P P* v. *Smith*, [1961] A C 290 at 327.

\12 For criticisms of Holmes' "infectious fallacy" see H.L.A. Hart
  Punishment and Responsibility [1962], 242–4.

13 Williams,'Constructive Malice Revived', 23 *Modern Law Review* [1962],
  605.

14 Holmes, *op. cit.*, 51.

15 *D P P* v. *Smith*, [1961] A C 290 at 331.

16 *D P P* v. *Smith*, [1961] A C 290 at 327

17 *R* v. *Barrett*, [1868], cited in *R* v. *Serne*, [1887] 16 Cox 311 at 314.

18 Below, p 149 f.

19 Below, p 150 f.

20 Subject to the limitations suggested above, p 119

21 *D P P* v. *Smith*, [1961] A C 290 at 324.

22 *D P P* v. *Smith*, [1961] A C 290 at 334.

23 *R* v. *Metharam*, [1961] 3 All E R 200 at 202.

24 *D P P* v. *Smith*, [1961] A C 290 at 331–2.

25 Below, n 31.

26 *Parker* v. *The Queen*, [1963] 111 C L R 610 at 632–3.

27 *R* v. *Sharmpal Singh*, [1962] A C 188.

28 *R* v. *Grimwood*, [1962] 2 Q B 621.

29 *R* v. *Hudson*, [1965] 1 All E R 721; by the Sexual Offences Act 1956,
  s.7 (2), it is a defence to the charge of unlawfully having sexual
  intercourse with a defective if the accused 'does not know and has
  no reason to suspect her to be a defective'.

30 *Wilkins* v. *An Infant*, [1965] *The Times*, 21 October; cf. *R* v. *Church*
  [1965] 2 All E R 72.

31 Buxton, 'The Retreat from Smith', [1966] *Criminal Law Review, 195.*

32 Smith and Hogan, *Criminal Law* (2nd ed 1969), 198.

33 Holmes, *op. cit.*, 54.

34 Wootton, *Social Science and Social Pathology* [1959], 249.

35 Holmes, *op. cit.* 40.

36 Holmes, *op. cit.* 38.

37 Holmes, *op. cit.* 51; cf. 136.

38 Holmes, *op. cit.* 161–2.

39 Holmes, *op. cit.* 59, 153.

40 Holmes, *op. cit.* 110.

41 Holmes, *op.cit.*, 51.

42 Cited in Radbruch, 'Jurisprudence in the Criminal Law', 18 *Journal of
  Comparative Legislation* [1936], 212, 224; cf. Williams, 72 L Q R
  [1956], 167.

43 Holmes, *op. cit.*, 47–9.

44 Austin, *Lectures on Jurisprudence* (4th ed 1879), I, 498.

45 Cf. Allen, *Law in the Making* (4th ed 1946), 390–1; Hall, *General
  Principles of Criminal Law* (2nd ed 1960), 376 f.

46   Holmes, *op, cit.*, 50.
47   Denning, *Responsibility before the law* [1961], 23–4.
48   *R* v. *Lesbini*, [1914] 3 K B 1114 at 1118.
49   Royal Commission on Capital Punishment, 1949–53, *Report*, Cmd 8932
        [1953], 53.
50   561 H C Deb, col 504 (Nov. 28, 1956).
51   Holmes, *op.cit.*, 43–4; 46–7; 63.
52   Holmes, *op.cit.* 46–7.
53   *R* v. *Dudley*, [1884] 14 Q B D 273; Fuller, 'The Speluncean Explorers',
        62 *Harvard Law Review* [1948–9], 616.
54   Holmes, *op. cit.*, 44.
55   Holmes, *op. cit.*, 144, 145, 149, 163.
56   Holmes, *op. cit.*, 54–5.
57   Holmes, *op. cit.*, 44.
58   Holmes, *op. cit.*, 50.
59   Holmes, *op. cit.*, 49–50.
60   Holmes, *op. cit.*, 46.
61   Holmes, *op. cit.*, 50.

Chapter 6

1   Theft Act 1968, s.9.
2   *Gardner* v. *Akeroyd*, [1952] 2 Q B 743 at 747.
3   Bracton, *Legibus* II f 101 b, ed Twiss [1879], 127.
4   *R* v. *Higgins*, [1801] 2 East 4 at 21.
5   *Concentrated Foods Ltd* v. *Champ*, [1944] K B 342 at 349–51;
        McDowell v. *Standard Oil Co.*, [1927] A C 632; cf Burrows,
        Words and Phrases Judicially Defined [1943], I, 374, s v 'Calculated
        to deceive'.
6   Williams, *Criminal Law* (2nd ed 1961), 89–99.
7   *Lang* v. *Lang*, [1955] A C 402.
8   *Hosegood* v. *Hosegood*, [1950] 66 T L R (Pt 1) 735 at 738.
9   *Gollins* v. *Gollins*, [1964] A C 644.
10   *Williams* v. *Williams*, [1964] A C 698.
11   *Gollins* v. *Gollins*, [1964] A C 644 at 660.
12   *Gollins* v. *Gollins*, [1964] A C 644 at 666–7.
13   Fuller, *The Morality of Law* [1964], 76.
14   Holmes, *op. cit.*, 54–5.
15   Hobson, 'Psychiatric Evidence in Murder Trials', 9 *Howard Journal* [1955],
        109.
16   Aquinas, *Summa Theologica*, II–I, Q 100, Art 9.
17   Wootton, *Crime and the Criminal Law* [1963], 74.

18   Wootton, 'Diminished Responsibility: A Layman's View', 76 L Q R [1960], 224, 232.
19   Y B Pasch Ed IV fi pl 2.
20   Locke, *An Essay concerning Human Understanding* [1690] ; cf. Gibson, *Locke's Theory of Knowledge* [1917], 207.
21   Bentham, *An Introduction to the Principles of Morals and Legislation* [1789], Chapters VII and VIII.
22   Austin, *Lectures on Jurisprudence* (5th ed 1885), Lecture XVIII, 411–5.
23   Holmes, *op. cit.*, 54.
24   Holmes, *op. cit.*, 110.
25   Holmes, *op. cit.*, 67, 70.
26   Holmes, *op. cit.*, 56; cf 62.
27   Hobbes, *Leviathan* [1651], Pt 1; *De Corpore* [1655].
28   Ryle, *The Concept of Mind* [1949].
29   Strawson, *Individuals* [1959].
30   Wootton, *Social Science and Social Pathology*, [1959] Chapter VIII.
31   Wootton, *op. cit.*, 249.
32   Wootton, *op. cit.*, 231.
33   Wootton, *op. cit.*, 235.
34   Wootton, *op. cit.*, 238.
35   Wootton, *op. cit.*, Chapter VII.
36   Davis, 'Mental Hygiene and the Class Structure', *Psychiatry* [1938], cited in Wootton, *op. cit.*, 214, 216–7.
37   Wootton, *op. cit.* 220.
38   Augustine, *Confessiones*, xiv 17.
39   Hall, *The Purposes of a System for the Administration of Criminal Justice*, [1963], 7–13.
40   Wootton, *op. cit.*, 207.
41   Wootton, *op. cit.*, 231.
42   Wootton, *op. cit.*, 258.
43   Haksar, 'The Responsibility of Mental Defectives', 38 *Philosophy* [1963], 61, 67.
44   Wootton, *op. cit.*, 225.
45   Wootton, *op. cit.*, 238.
46   *Ibid.*
47   Royal Commission on Capital Punishment, 1949–53, *Report*, Cmd 8932 [1953], 139.
48   American Law Institute, *Model Penal Code* (Fourth Tentative Draft 1955), s.4.01 (2).
49   Wootton, *op. cit.*, 250.
50.   Mercier, cited in Haksar, 'The Responsibility of Psychopaths', 15 *Philosophical Quarterly* [1965], 135, 137.
51   Royal Commission on the Law relating to Mental Illness and Mental Deficiency, 1954–7, *Minutes of Evidence*, 8th day, 287; cf. Royal Commission on Capital Punishment, 1949–53, *Minutes of Evidence*, Q 3753 and 462 (17); Cleckley, *The Mask of Sanity* [1955], 292.

52   Royal Commission on the Law relating to Mental Illness and Mental
      Deficiency, 1954–7, *Report,* Cmd 169 [1957], paras 166, 357.
53   Fitzgerald, *Criminal Law and Punishment* [1962], 135 f, 140 f.
54   Wootton, *Crime and the Criminal Law* [1963], 49, 73.
55   Williams, *Criminal Law* (2nd ed 1961), 548.
56   Szasz, 'Psychiatric Expert Testimony – Its Covert Meaning and Social
      Function', 20 *Psychiatry* [1957], 313, 314.
57   Wootton, 'Diminished Responsibility: A Layman's View',   76 L Q R
      [1960], 224.
58   Wootton, 'The Law, the Doctor and the Deviant', *British Medical Journal*
      (27 July 1963), 197–8.
59   *R* v. *Byrne,* [1960] 2 Q B 396 at 404.
60   Wootton, 'Diminished Responsibility: A Layman's View', 76 L Q R
      [1960], 224, 236–7.
61   *R* v. *Byrne,* [1960] 2 Q B 396 at 404.
62   *Edgington* v. *Fitzmaurice* [1889] 29 Ch D 459 at 483.
63   *Angus* v. *Clifford,* [1891] 2 Ch 449 at 471.
64   Roche, *The Criminal Mind* [1958], 248–9.
65   Macdonald, 'The Concept of Responsibility', 101 *Journal of Mental
      Science* [1955], 704, 715–6.
66   Williams, *Criminal Law* (2nd ed 1961), 816.
67   Clark, *Analysis of Criminal Liability* [1880].
68   Stephen, *History of the Criminal Law of England* [1883], II, 96
69   Glueck, *Law and Psychiatry* [1962], 6.
70   Hale, *Pleas of the Crown* (Emlyn ed 1736), I, 14–5.
71   Wootton, *Crime and the Criminal Law* [1963], 78.
72   Glueck, 'Changing Concepts in Forensic Psychiatry', 45 *Journal of Criminal
      Law, Criminology and Police Science* [1954], 123, 127;
73   'Penal Practice in a Changing Society', Cmnd 645 [1959], para 75;
      Snell, 'The Prison Medical Service', 10 *Howard Journal* [1959], 75.
74   Royal Commission on the Law relating to Mental Illness and Mental
      Deficiency, 1954–7, *Report,* Cmnd 169 [1957], paras 344, 345.
75   *R* v. *Marsh*, [1824] 2 B & C 717 at 721.

Index